BETWEEN FRAGMENTATION
AND DEMOCRACY

Between Fragmentation and Democracy explores the phenomenon of the fragmentation of international law and the proliferation of international institutions with overlapping jurisdictions and ambiguous boundaries. The authors argue that this problem has the potential to sabotage the evolution of a more democratic and egalitarian system and identify the structural reasons for the failure of global institutions to protect the interests of politically weaker constituencies. This book offers a comprehensive understanding of how new global sources of democratic deficits increasingly deprive individuals and collectives of the capacity to protect their interests and shape their opportunities. It also considers the role of the courts in mitigating the effects of globalization and the struggle to define and redefine institutions and entitlements. The book is an important resource for scholars of international law and international politics, as well as public lawyers, political scientists, and those interested in judicial reform.

EYAL BENVENISTI is Whewell Professor of International Law at the University of Cambridge and the Director of the Lauterpacht Centre for International Law. He is also Professor of Law at Tel Aviv University and Global Visiting Professor at New York University School of Law.

GEORGE W. DOWNS (1946–2015), a member of the American Academy of Arts and Sciences, was a leading scholar of international relations, international security, human rights, international law, and public policy. He was a Professor of Politics at New York University from 1998 to 2015 and also served there as Chair of his department (1998–2000) and Dean for Social Sciences (2000–2009). Prior to that, he was a Professor in the Department of Politics and in the Woodrow Wilson School of Public and International Affairs at Princeton University (1987–1998).

T0370818

BETWEEN FRAGMENTATION AND DEMOCRACY

The Role of National and International Courts

EYAL BENVENISTI

University of Cambridge

GEORGE W. DOWNS

New York University

CAMBRIDGE
UNIVERSITY PRESS

CAMBRIDGE
UNIVERSITY PRESS

University Printing House, Cambridge CB2 8BS, United Kingdom

One Liberty Plaza, 20th Floor, New York, NY 10006, USA

477 Williamstown Road, Port Melbourne, VIC 3207, Australia

314-321, 3rd Floor, Plot 3, Splendor Forum, Jasola District Centre, New Delhi - 110025, India

79 Anson Road, #06-04/06, Singapore 079906

Cambridge University Press is part of the University of Cambridge.

It furthers the University's mission by disseminating knowledge in the pursuit of education, learning and research at the highest international levels of excellence.

www.cambridge.org
Information on this title: www.cambridge.org/9781108403399
DOI: 10.1017/9781108236607

© Eyal Benvenisti 2017

First published 2017
First paperback edition 2018

A catalogue record for this publication is available from the British Library

Library of Congress Cataloging in Publication data
Names: Benvenisti, Eyal, author. | Downs, George W., author.
Title: Between fragmentation and democracy : the role of national and international courts / Eyal Benvenisti, George W. Downs.
Description: Cambridge [UK] ; New York : Cambridge University Press, 2017. | Includes bibliographical references and index.
Identifiers: LCCN 2017032448 | ISBN 9781108416870 (hardback)
Subjects: LCSH: Courts. | International courts. | International law. | Globalization. | Democratization. | BISAC: LAW / International.
Classification: LCC K2110 .B46 2017 | DDC 341.5/5—dc23
LC record available at https://lccn.loc.gov/2017032448

ISBN 978-1-108-41687-0 Hardback
ISBN 978-1-108-40339-9 Paperback

CONTENTS

ACKNOWLEDGMENTS

The chapters of this book are adapted from articles and book chapters (or parts thereof) that we have published previously, and we acknowledge permission to incorporate parts of them into this book. By Eyal Benvenisti and George W. Downs: *The Empire's New Clothes: Political Economy and the Fragmentation of International Law*, 60 STANFORD L. REV. 595 (2007); *Court Cooperation, Executive Accountability and Global Governance*, 41 N.Y.U. J. INT'L L. & POL. 931 (2009); *National Courts, Domestic Democracy, and the Evolution of International Law*, 20 EUROP. J. INT'L L. 59 (2009); *Prospects for the Increased Independence of International Tribunals*, in LAWMAKING BY INTERNATIONAL TRIBUNALS 99 (Armin von Bogdandy and Ingo Venzke eds., 2012); *The Premises, Assumptions, and Implications of Van Gend en Loos: Viewed from the Perspectives of Democracy and Legitimacy of International Institutions*, 25 EUROP. J. INT'L L. 85 (2014); *Democratizing Courts: How National and International Courts Promote Democracy in an Era of Global Governance*, 46 N.Y.U. J. INT'L L. & POL. 741 (2014); *National Courts and Transnational Private Regulation, in* ENFORCEMENT OF TRANSNATIONAL REGULATION: ENSURING COMPLIANCE IN A GLOBAL WORLD 131 (Fabrizio Cafaggi ed., 2012); *The Democratizing Effects of Transjudicial Coordination*, 8 UTRECHT LAW REVIEW 158 (2012); *Toward Global Checks and Balances*, 20 CONSTITUTIONAL POLITICAL ECONOMY 366 (2009). By Eyal Benvenisti: *Exit and Voice in the Age of Globalization* 98 MICHIGAN L. REV. 167 (1999); *Reclaiming Democracy: The Strategic Uses of Foreign and International Law by National Courts*, 102 AMERICAN J. INT'L L. 241 (2008).

We are indebted to our many colleagues, friends, and students for their comments and critique of our work over the years. We are grateful to New York University School of Law and the New York University Wilf Family Department of Politics and our many friends there for providing us with an intellectually stimulating and supportive academic home. We thank Ilene Cohen and Shai Dothan for commenting on the entire manuscript, as well as Gershon Hasin, Jamie Savren, and Yuval Spitzer for their research assistance in preparing the manuscript for publication.

***

We had been working on this book for more than a year and were set to complete it, when, in the summer of 2014, George became ill. He died on January 21, 2015. In doing the final work to ready the book for publication, I have attempted to remain true to George's thinking.

Eyal Benvenisti
2016

TABLE OF CASES

International Tribunals

International Court of Justice (ICJ)

Court of Justice of the European Union (CJEU)

European Court of Human Rights (ECtHR)

National Courts

Australia

A v. Minister for Immigration & Ethnic Affairs, (1997) 190 CLR 225
Al-Kateb v. Godwin, (2004) 219 CLR 562
Applicant S v. Minister for Immigration & Multicultural Affairs, (2001)
  FCA 1411 (Fed. Ct. Austl.)
Minister for Immigration & Multicultural Affairs v. Applicant Z, (2001)
  116 FCR 36 (Fed. Ct. Austl.)
Minister for Immigration & Multicultural Affairs v. Khawar, (2002) 210
  CLR 1
S v. Minister for Immigration & Multicultural Affairs, (2004) 217 CLR 387

Bangladesh

Farooque v. Bangladesh, 48 D.L.R. (1996) 438
Farooque v. Gov't of Bangladesh, 17 B.L.D. (A.D.) 1 (1997) (App. Div.
  1996)
Islam v. Bangladesh, 52 D.L.R. (2000)
Islam v. Bangladesh, ILDC 477 (BD 2000)

Belgium

Minister for Economic Affairs v. Fromagerie Franco-Suisse "Le Ski"
[1972] C.M.L.R. 330

Canada

Abdelrazik v. Minister of Foreign Affairs & Attorney General of Canada,
  [2009] F.C. 580
Canada (Attorney Gen.) v. Ward, [1993] 2 S.C.R. 689
Canadian Council for Refugees v. The Queen, [2007] F.C. 1262
Charkaoui v. Canada (Citizenship & Immigration), [2007] S.C.C. 9, 2007
  Can. Sup. Ct. LEXIS 9
Re Jaballah, [2006] F.C. 1230, Fed. C.C. LEXIS 1441
Soc'y of Composers, Authors & Music Publishers of Canada v. Canadian
  Ass'n of Internet Providers, [2004] 2 S.C.R. 427
Suresh v. Canada (Minister of Citizenship & Immigration), [2002] 1
  S.C.R. 3, [2002] S.C.C. 1

Czech Republic

Treaty of Lisbon II, 03.11.2009 [Decision of the Constitutional Court of Nov. 3, 2009], Pl. ÚS 29/09

France

Conseil constitutionnel, [CC] [Constitutional Court] decision No. 96–377 DC, Jul. 16, 1996, *translated at* http://www.conseil-constitutionnel.fr/conseil-constitutionnel/root/bank/download/96377DCa96377dc.pdf

Iraqi State v. Corporation Dumez GTM (SA), Appeal (cassation) judgment, Cour d'appel [CA] [regional court of appeal] Paris, 1e civ, Apr. 25, 2006, ILDC 771

La Province de la Hollande septentrionale contre Etat Ministre de l'Environnement, Tribunal Administratife de Strasbourg, Jul. 27, 1983, *rep. in* (1983) 4 Rev. Jur. Envn't 343, overturned (Conseil d'Etat), Apr. 18, 1986, *rep. in* (1986) 2–3. Rev. Jur. Envn't 296.

Germany

Brunner v. The European Union Treaty, German Federal Constitutional Court Judgment of Oct. 12, 1993 (trans. in [1994] 57 Common Mkt. L. Rep.)

Bundesgerichtshof [BGH] [Federal Court of Justice], Jun. 26, 2003, III ZR 245/98 (*Distomo Massacre* case), *translated in* 42 Int'l Legal Materials 1030 (2003)

Bundesverfassungsgericht (Federal Constitutional Court) [BVerfG], 2 BvR 2236/04, Jul. 18, 2005

BVerfG, 2 BvR 260/98, Aug. 10, 2000

BVerfG, Feb. 15, 2006, 115 Entscheidungen des Bundesverfassungsgerichts 118

BVerfG, EuGRZ 1986, 18, Jul. 17, 1985

Bundesverwaltungsgericht (BVerwG) (Federal Administrative Court), 104 BVerwGE 254, Apr. 15, 1997

BVerwG, 95 Entscheidungen des Bundesverwaltungsgerichts, Jan. 18, 1994

BVerwG, 105 BVerwGE 187, Sept. 2, 1997

Lisbon Treaty Judgment of the German Constitutional Court, Bundesverfassungsgericht [BVerfG], 2 BvE 2/08, Jun. 30, 2009

United States

Zimbabwe

1

Introduction

1.1   Global Governance and the Challenges to Democracy

Theorizing about democracy and its meaning has traditionally been the province of political philosophers and political scientists who envisioned a country whose politics were largely insulated from outside pressures and reflected the inputs and preferences of mainly domestic actors, such as voters, parties, and interest groups. As a result, the sources of potential democratic market failures that concerned them were primarily domestic ones: discrimination against discrete and insular minorities or capture by indigenous interest groups. But since the end of the Cold War, as the process of globalization continued to accelerate, increasing the dependency of most states on foreign actors, there arose additional reasons for concern about the deterioration of the individual's capacity for agency. Popular resentment toward neoliberal globalization served by multilateral institutions finally erupted in 2016, as anti-globalism swept both the left and the right, prompting angry voters in Britain to opt for leaving the European Union and to support anti-globalization candidates in the Democratic and Republican parties in the United States.

In the past few decades it has become increasingly apparent that a substantial number of the international institutions operating as global venues for policy-making are poorly designed to address the democratic deficits that increasingly plague politics at the national level. This is either because the global venues are controlled by the same domestic forces that dominate national politics or because the global bodies are effectively dependent on one or more of the powerful states. As a consequence, many international institutions have functioned to further disempower diffuse domestic electorates by expanding the executive power of powerful states and increasing the leverage of multinational corporations. The net result is that all too often the move to international institutions has to varying degrees led to an erosion of the traditional constitutional checks and balances found in many democracies, as well as of other domestic oversight and monitoring mechanisms intended to check executive discretion. At the same time, too few new checks and balances have been created to compensate for the loss.

The new global sources of democratic deficits increasingly jeopardize the long-held assumption that domestic democratic processes reliably provide individuals and collectivities with the opportunity and capacity to shape their life opportunities. Addressing these deficits necessitates fresh thinking. Clearly, we must provide opportunities for individuals and communities to exert effective influence on the policy-making that affects them, even if the decision-maker creating that policy is a foreign government. The key question is whether we can continue to rely on global institutions to remedy these deficits, or whether doing so is likely to exacerbate the democratic losses even further.

This book explores the structural reasons for the failure of global institutions to protect the interests of the diffuse, politically weaker constituencies that were led to trust distant bureaucrats who actually served narrow interests. We explain why and how the new global sources of democratic deficits, whether by design or not, increasingly deprive individuals and collectives of the opportunity and capacity to protect their interests and shape their life opportunities. But we also describe the surprising role of courts in mitigating at least somewhat the brute forces of globalization. The various democratic deficits associated with the vigorous scramble for new markets, the creation of global supply chains, and the establishment of transnational economic and regulatory institutions at the end of the Cold War have been met, with varying degrees of success, by the calls of national and international courts for accountability and inclusion. These courts have proved themselves the unlikely heroes in the perennial struggle to define and redefine economic and political institutions and entitlements. While for most democracies these entitlements were traditionally determined by domestic laws and institutions, globalization has reshaped the struggle by opening up various supranational and international arenas where entitlements have been shaped through formal and informal, public or private agreements. These new global venues promised not only new business opportunities for movable capital but also freedom from domestic democratic constraints. Given entrenched synergies between economic and political institutions,[1] the novel opportunities in the new global markets also signal new challenges for those who sought to ensure that economic

---

[1] Daron Acemoglu & James A. Robinson, WHY NATIONS FAIL (2012).

and political power remains widely distributed. Surprisingly, these were courts–institutions relatively insulated from economic and political influence–that have risen to the occasion. Motivated at least partly by their own concern to protect their turf, they proved to be the most decisive set of actors that insisted on maintaining at least some market discipline. They thereby acted against the usurpation of power by the few. In this book, we seek to explain the ways in which in the post–Cold War era the few sought to shape domestic and global institutions to augment and solidify their own power and then to assess the unexpected judicial responses that to some extent proved effective in curbing global capital and ensuring the vitality of inclusive decision-making processes.

With the exponential proliferation of various forms of global regulation–from formal international organizations to informal private standard-setting bodies–and the massive transfer of regulatory functions to them in almost all aspects of life,[2] a set of fundamental questions came to the fore, such as the concern over fair and inclusive decision-making within international organizations and the anxiety within democracies regarding the loss of their autonomy to supranational regulatory bodies led by powerful nations. While global governance bodies are indispensable for resolving coordination and cooperation problems and for promoting global welfare, they also, at the same time, cast a shadow over the achievements of our constitutional democracies. Although some international regimes were designed with the explicit goal of enhancing domestic democratic processes (for example, the Aarhus Convention on access to domestic environmental decision-making)[3] and international tribunals have the capacity to guarantee voice to weak stakeholders at the domestic level (for example, in the areas of human rights or trade),[4] most international organizations were not intended to address democratic deficits at the national level; to the contrary, they were actually designed to exploit such deficits. As will be shown in Chapter 2, many international organizations have functioned to further disempower diffuse domestic electorates by expanding the executive power of powerful states and increasing the leverage of

---

[2] Sabino Cassese, THE GLOBAL POLITY: GLOBAL DIMENSIONS OF DEMOCRACY AND THE RULE OF LAW (2012).

[3] Convention on Access to Information, Public Participation in Decision-Making and Access to Justice in Environmental Matters, Jun. 25, 1998, 38 I.L.M 517, 2161 U.N.T.S 447, *available at* www.unece.org/fileadmin/DAM/env/pp/documents/cep43e.pdf.

[4] Robert O. Keohane, Stephen Macedo & Andrew Moravcsik, *Democracy-Enhancing Multilateralism*, 63 INT'L ORG. 1 (2009).

multinational corporations. The net result was that all too often the move to global regulation has to varying degrees eroded the traditional constitutional checks and balances that defined many democracies, as well as other domestic oversight and monitoring mechanisms intended to check executive discretion.[5] The transfer of regulatory authority from the domestic to the international realm has enabled a handful of powerful public and private actors to escape the entrenched domestic checks and balances, such as public lawmaking, separation of powers, court independence, and limited government, that have played an important role in safeguarding democratic deliberation and individual rights within states.

What characterizes the new global institutions is their fragmented nature: a large number of functionally specialized international organizations and international tribunals determine policy in almost all aspects of life. But their distinct, clearly defined competences ensure that there will be little or no institutional cooperation among them, despite their potentially related interests. Such fragmentation essentially operates as a "divide and rule" strategy that prevents relatively weaker actors from aggregating their voices to resist the fewer but stronger actors. This, in turn, has hampered the emergence of political competition at the global level by isolating policy-making within narrow, functional venues that are effectively monitored and controlled by the executive branches of a small group of powerful states (or, rather, by elites within those states).[6] These states have long played a disproportionately large role in selecting key personnel to steer international organizations and tribunals, and their bureaucracies are among the few with the variety and depth of regulatory expertise to effectively monitor the varied activities of international organizations and prevent goal displacement. Although there are numerous international judicial bodies whose overlapping spheres of activity provide them with abundant opportunities to pass judgment on

---

[5] Richard B. Stewart, *Remedying Disregard in Global Regulatory Governance: Accountability, Participation, and Responsiveness*, 108 Am. J. Int'l L. 211 (2014) (discussing strategies to address the evolving gaps in the efficacy of domestic political and legal mechanisms of participation and accountability resulting from shifts of regulatory authority from domestic to global regulatory bodies). *See also* Chapter 2. There may be additional reasons for the concentration of power in the executive and the decline of domestic checks. *See* Bruce Ackerman, The Decline and Fall of the American Republic (2010) (discussing what he sees are the (domestic) factors that lead to the rise of an unchecked US presidency).

[6] According to Stewart, fragmentation of regulatory decision-making at the domestic level can have similar consequences, see Richard B. Stewart, *Madison's Nightmare*, 57 U. Chi. L. Rev. 335 (1990).

each other's policies, there have been far fewer cases of robust review than lawyers might have expected.[7] As a result, the large and heterogeneous global public residing outside the small group of powerful state elites could never be confident that their interests were being adequately protected from the exercise of arbitrary power. These newly created judicial bodies were accountable, but only to certain specific actors who controlled and funded them, but not necessarily to those they affect.[8] Developing countries, in particular, often lacked the administrative capacity to meet new regulatory standards,[9] much less possessed the expertise and political clout necessary to influence the character of those standards or ensure that agencies reliably fulfilled their mandates.[10] Diffuse constituencies in developed countries were disadvantaged by international organizations' opaque decision-making processes, which limited their opportunities to participate in and shape outcomes.

This book seeks to explain these developments. It also explores the prospects for achieving the basic prerequisites of a rule-of-law-based global system of regulatory governance that strives to ensure distribution of political power and responds to the standards that we have come to expect in well-functioning democracies. To explore how best to achieve this goal, we begin by analyzing the political and economic factors that have shaped the evolution of the existing system. Chapter 2 examines the

---

[7] Abigail C. Deshman, *Horizontal Review between International Organizations: Why, How, and Who Cares about Corporate Regulatory Capture*, 22 Eur. J. Int'l L. 1089 (2011), see infra Chapter 6.

[8] Stewart, *supra* note 6, at 26–27 (noting that international organizations "are often subject to powerful but in many cases informal mechanisms of supervisory and fiscal accountability to the most powerful states that create, fund, and support these global institutions"); Nico Krisch, *The Pluralism of Global Administrative Law*, 17 Eur. J. Int'l L. 247, 250 (2006) (noting that the problem with international organizations is:

> "[N]ot an absolute accountability 'deficit' . . . [r]ather . . . [they are] accountable to the wrong constituencies. The World Bank, it is often claimed, should respond to the people affected by its decisions, rather than primarily to the (mostly developed) countries that fund it. The FATF should be accountable to those states subject to its measures, not just to its members. Or the Security Council should have to answer to the individuals it targets directly with its sanctions, not only to its member governments or the broader membership of the UN").

[9] Benedict Kingsbury & Kevin Davis, *Obligations Overload: Adjusting the Obligations of Fragile or Failed States*, (Nov. 22, 2010) (Preliminary Draft), *available at* www.iilj.org/courses/documents/HC2010Dec01.DavisKingsbury.pdf.

[10] Krisch, *supra* note 8, at 275–76. In fact, many of these countries face difficulties complying with their obligations under the various treaties, see Kingsbury & Davis, *supra* note 9.

phenomenon of fragmentation and how it has institutionalized the role of powerful states while simultaneously undermining the ability of weaker states to coordinate effectively. Chapter 3 looks behind the veil of "the state" and analyzes the interplay between the key domestic actors–the executive, legislature, courts, interest groups, and civil society–as they vie to realize their goals in a fragmented system of global institutions.

This description of the political economy background of global governance enables us to assess the potential role of courts in promoting a global rule of law. Chapters 4 and 5 address the role of courts as the key defragmenting institutions in the emerging system of global governance. Chapter 4 discusses the promise and limits of international tribunals for reining in global regulatory institutions. Chapter 5 does the same for national courts. Chapter 6 assesses the interplay between national and international courts and explores the potential effect of their cooperation on the realization of a global rule of law. The chapter closes with an assessment of the extent to which court cooperation can increase the effectiveness of the international regulatory system by decreasing the discretionary powers of state executives.

Chapter 7 moves from the descriptive to the normative. It begins by addressing the prevalent concern that judicial involvement in global governance is fundamentally undemocratic. While acknowledging that this is always a danger, we argue that coordination between national and international courts holds out the promise of being able to maintain a proper distribution of political power at both the domestic and the international levels by helping to ensure that the interests of a greater share of relevant stakeholders are taken into account by decision-makers, with the goal of reaching better informed, more balanced outcomes.

The rest of this introduction provides a bird's-eye view of the course of this book.

1.2   Background: The Fragmentation of International Law

The decades following the end of the Cold War have witnessed the growing proliferation of international regulatory institutions with overlapping jurisdictions and ambiguous boundaries. Although practicing jurists have voiced concern about the effect of this increased fragmentation of international law, international legal theorists have tended for the most part to dismiss these concerns. Indeed, many regard the resulting competition for influence among institutions as a generative, market-like pluralism that has led to greater progress toward integration and democratization than could ever have been achieved through more formal means.

In Chapter 2, we argue that the problem of fragmentation is more serious than is commonly assumed, because it has the potential to sabotage the evolution of a more democratic and egalitarian international regulatory system. It opts for rule by law rather than abiding by the rule of law standards, and it thereby undermines the reputation of international law for integrity. It is also more resistant to reform than is generally assumed. Powerful state executives labor to maintain and even actively promote fragmentation because it enables them both to preserve their dominance in an era in which hierarchy is increasingly viewed as illegitimate and to break the rules opportunistically without seriously jeopardizing the system they have created.

Fragmentation accomplishes this in three ways. First, by creating institutions along narrow, functionalist lines and restricting the scope of multilateral agreements, it limits the opportunities for weaker actors to build the cross-issue coalitions that could potentially increase their bargaining power and influence. Second, the ambiguous boundaries and overlapping authority created by fragmentation dramatically increase the transaction costs that international legal bodies must incur in trying to reintegrate or rationalize the resulting legal order. Third, by suggesting the absence of design and obscuring the role of intentionality, fragmentation frees powerful states from having to assume responsibility for the shortcomings of a global legal system that they themselves have been instrumental in creating. The result is a global regulatory space that reflects the interests of the powerful, a regulatory space that only they can alter. To make matters worse, an additional type of fragmentation has recently emerged in the wake of the growing practice of private standard-setting by producers, consumers, and other private actors without the input of governments.

1.3   The Domestic Sources of Global Fragmentation

In Chapter 3, we focus on the role of sub-national actors in global governance bodies. We argue that the fragmentation of international law at the global level has been promoted by certain domestic actors who sought global standard-setters and regulators that were relatively insulated from public scrutiny. Political economists long ago demonstrated that state institutions often provide the means by which organized interest groups can exploit less organized domestic groups in the competitive market for political goods (such as taxes, subsidies, and favorable market regulation). In this market, more organized groups composed of a relatively small number of individuals can outbid larger groups because the former realize higher per capita benefits from cooperation with fellow group members and pay lower costs for monitoring and sanctioning free riders. Hence, other things being equal, smaller groups, such as producers and employers, will often be able to obtain collective goods more efficiently than can larger groups of consumers or employees. Over time this enables them to secure a disproportionate share of the aggregate social welfare while passing on a significant part of their production costs to the larger, more diffuse groups.

For the smaller groups, globalization has meant the ability to exploit new markets for political goods with fewer constraints. For them, therefore, the turn to international markets and international law has always been an effective way of overcoming domestic legal limitations. The most effective domestic constraints they faced were imposed not by politicians, relatively easy prey, but–in states where political power was more evenly distributed–by bureaucrats and judges who were relatively more insulated from the political system. But bureaucrats and judges were more hesitant to interfere in the executive's management of the state's foreign affairs. Domestic courts, traditionally the bastions of individual rights vis-à-vis domestic actors, tended to defer to the politicians and bureaucrats on matters concerning the external affairs of their state. Not only did they refrain from attaching any strings to the extraterritorial activity of the executive or domestic firms; they also found myriad ways to rebuff challenges to such activities, despite seemingly clear language in domestic or international law that prohibits them. Courts in all jurisdictions have developed an array of doctrines–such as the political question doctrine, justiciability, and act of state–to minimize their role as effective keepers of the rule of law in the international arena.

This strong judicial deference opened the door for small groups to shield themselves from the vagaries of the democratic electoral process and rigorous judicial review. For them, the emerging global regulatory space operated like a vast field in which to play hide-and-seek with the ubiquitous review mechanisms. Even better, recourse to permissive international treaties preempted domestic legislation against them. Whereas no constitution was beyond legislative interpretation or immune to popular amendment, which often operates to the detriment of small groups, international law and the courts' deference to the executive in the international arena offered small groups the ultimate protection for their interests. The fragmented, consent-based nature of international law continued to enable smaller groups to evade national regulations and exploit the global commons. In fact, these smaller groups have had an even greater influence on the development of international law than on domestic law, primarily because information gathering and assessment costs are much higher in the international arena, and relatively smaller and better organized groups are more effective than larger, diffuse constituencies in meeting these costs. The edge enjoyed by small groups can be traced by following the development of international norms.

1.4   The Failed Hope for Cohesion Ensured by International Tribunals

One could have anticipated that the reaction to the evasive efforts of the designers of fragmentation would come from international tribunals and other global review bodies. After all, the story of the taming of domestic administrative agencies is the story of the rise of domestic judicial review of administrative action through law developed primarily by the courts. Unfortunately, the same domestic forces that promoted the rise of global regulatory bodies and the fragmentation of global legal space were the ones to establish and oversee the operation of international tribunals. It should therefore come as no surprise that international tribunals have been less effective than their domestic counterparts in checking their respective regulators. In this chapter, we draw upon the theoretical and empirical literatures on the evolution of court independence in modern democratic states to identify aspects of their political environments that have fostered judicial independence at the domestic level. We then extend that analysis to examine the role that these or similar factors are likely to play in facilitating the independence and legitimacy of international tribunals at the global level.

To date, most of the literature on the independence of international tribunals, like most of the literature dealing with judicial independence at the domestic level, has focused on the rules connected with the ways that judges are nominated, selected, and tenured. While it is true that these formal structural features have an important role to play in determining judicial independence, they are not sufficient in and of themselves to ensure credibility. The effectiveness of international tribunals and their freedom to interpret and develop the law in whatever way they deem appropriate are also functions or attributes of the broader political context in which they are embedded.

In Chapter 4, we focus on two such broad aspects of the global environment not normally associated with the independence of international tribunals: the extent of political division between states that are parties to an international tribunal (interstate competition) and the extent of political division within states between state executives and national courts (interbranch division). We suggest further that the conditions that facilitate such independence have increased in recent years and are likely to continue to do so. But we also conclude that the best hope for a more independent international judiciary is the potential for symbiotic relations with increasingly assertive national courts.

1.5   The Emergence of Interjudicial Cooperation at the National Level

Chapter 5 describes the potential for the resilience of national courts in the face of pressures from global actors. It argues that these very pressures are the catalyst for the growing assertiveness of national courts in responding to global regulations. The chapter also suggests that this newfound judicial courage is the key to promote coordination with international tribunals and to the empowerment of the latter.

It was not so long ago that the overwhelming majority of courts in democratic countries shared a reluctance to refer to foreign and international law. This reflected a policy of avoiding any application of foreign sources of law that would clash with the position of their domestic governments. However, since the early 2000s, courts in several democracies (aside from the US Supreme Court) have begun to adopt a different approach, often engaging quite seriously in the interpretation and application of international law and heeding the constitutional jurisprudence of other national courts. National courts have gradually abandoned their traditional policy of deference to their executive branches in the field of foreign policy and are beginning to engage more aggressively in the interpretation and application of international law. This change has been precipitated by the recognition by courts in democratic states that continued passivity in the face of a rapidly expanding international regulatory apparatus raises constitutionally related concerns about excessive executive power and risks further erosion in the effective scope of judicial review.

Reacting to the forces of globalization that were placing increasing pressure on governments, legislatures, and courts to conform to global standards, national courts have begun to exploit the expanding scope and fragmented character of international regulation. Their goal was to create opportunities to act collectively by engaging in a loose form of inter-judicial coordination, that is, by forging coalitions with their peers in other countries. They seemed to have realized that in an era of growing global interdependency, rapid growth, and increased intergovernmental cooperation, judicial involvement–to be effective–required courts to forge cooperative coalitions across national boundaries so that they can coordinate their stances vis-à-vis each other and also vis-à-vis international bodies. Such collective action increases their ability to resist external pressures on their respective governments and reduces the likelihood that any particular court or country that a court represents will be singled out and punished as an outlier by either domestic or foreign actors. The courts increasingly sought to expand the space for domestic deliberation and strengthen the ability of national governments to withstand the pressure brought to bear by interest groups and powerful foreign governments. For this strategy to succeed, courts had to forge a united judicial front. This entailed using the common language of international law and comparative constitutional law to coordinate their policies with similarly positioned courts in other countries. Such cooperation enabled national courts to ensure that litigants will face similar outcomes in various jurisdictions, thereby limiting the opportunities to shop for a more amenable jurisdiction. Courts could facilitate cooperation by adopting similar interpretations of domestic or international law and by various means of informal communication.

1.6   Inter-Court Cooperation as the Unlikely Driver of an Emerging Global Rule of Law

While initially the operation of national courts helped domestic actors to resist external pressures on the respective domestic arenas of deliberation and policy-making, their resistance has indirectly spilled over to the global sphere. International bodies had to consider the real possibility that national courts would refuse to respect their immunity from judicial scrutiny. For example, national courts may adjudicate claims of employees of international organizations against their employers or refuse to adopt resolutions of international organizations that fail to protect the constitutional rights of individuals. This possibility has emboldened international tribunals to make their own demands of international bodies. In turn, international courts can bolster the independence of national courts by insisting on the individual's right of access to courts and due process.[11] Indirectly and incrementally, the emerging symbiotic cooperation between national and international courts has presented itself as potentially one of the most effective avenues, if not *the* most effective one, for promoting democratic accountability within states and also globally.

In Chapter 6, we suggest that this growing assertiveness of national courts in global affairs holds the key to the emergence of an effective system of global checks and balances. This could, in turn, promote a global system of law that both reflects the principles of a rule of law and promises to enhance democracy at both levels. It does this by helping to ensure that decision-makers take account of the interests of a greater proportion of the relevant stakeholders–including the interests of foreign stakeholders–and that the outcomes are therefore better informed and more balanced. We demonstrate how greater interaction and coordination between national courts and international tribunals promote a global rule of law that is accountable to all relevant stakeholders. We also assess the contribution of court cooperation to the evolution of international law as a system that reduces the discretion of state executives.

1.7   How Global Judicial "Countermajoritarianism" Can Be Democracy Enhancing

In Chapter 7, we assess both the negative and the positive political externalities that could potentially arise as a result of the increased judicial activism and the expansion of judicial review on the part of international tribunals and national courts. We first examine the possibility that expansive judicial review, while seemingly improving accountability and transparency, might gradually replace executive discretion with a countermajoritarian judiciary that may operate to stifle deliberations and confuse voters. While we acknowledge that this is a possibility, we suspect that the likelihood of it occurring is relatively remote. As we argue in this chapter, traditional democratic worries about countermajoritarianism are exaggerated and the positive externalities of increased judicial review of the policies of international organizations and decision-making procedures are likely to substantially outweigh any negative effects. By contrast, we suggest that judicial review is likely to enhance

---

[11] David Kosař and Lucas Lixinski, *Domestic Judicial Design by International Human Rights Courts*, 109 AM. J. INT'L L. 713 (2015), see infra Chapter 6.

rather than impede democratic deliberation at the domestic and international levels by more systematically ensuring that the interests of larger groups of stakeholders are taken into account by decision-makers and that the outcomes are appropriately informed and balanced.

We believe that this goal will be easier to achieve than many imagine. Even on those occasions when courts represent the will of their domestic constituents less well than do their executives, the disagreement between these institutions frequently generates useful information to which voters would otherwise not have access. Such information is necessary in order to keep political actors accountable to diverse stakeholders and to compensate for the fact that citizens are generally poorly informed about both policy-making at the level of the international institution and the extent to which their interests are being reliably represented. Greater transparency and deliberation are virtues independent of the representativeness or purity of the motivations of the institutions promoting them.

2

International Political Economy and the Fragmentation of International Law

International regulatory institutions have proliferated since the end of the Cold War. Narrowly tailored to address specific areas of regulation, they nevertheless had overlapping jurisdictions and ambiguous boundaries. While initially concerned about the adverse consequences of this increased fragmentation of international law, most international legal theorists came to belittle this concern. In fact, many extolled the resulting competition for influence among multiple institutions as a generative, market-like pluralism that promises to promote global economic integration and to strengthen the rule of law beyond what could ever have been achieved through more formal, comprehensive institutions. In this chapter we argue that the problem of fragmentation is more serious than is commonly assumed, because it operates to sabotage the evolution of a more democratic and egalitarian international regulatory system and to undermine the reputation of international law for integrity. Powerful states labor to maintain and even actively promote fragmentation because it enables them to preserve their dominance (or the dominance of the interest groups they are supporting) in an era in which hierarchy among states is increasingly viewed as illegitimate, as well as to break the rules at will without seriously jeopardizing the global regulatory system they have created. The chapter closes with a discussion of private standard setting in the form of transnational private regulation. This can be viewed as an even more extreme form of fragmentation, as it tends to be generated and overseen by private parties with narrow interests rather than by government bodies.

2.1 The Phenomenon

In recent years, there has been a growing debate in international legal circles about the importance of what is termed "fragmentation:" the increased proliferation of international regulatory institutions with overlapping jurisdictions and ambiguous boundaries. Practicing jurists, in particular, have expressed the concern that increasing the number of international courts will lead to forum shopping, create inconsistency within case law, and "may jeopardize the unity of international law and, as a consequence, its role in inter-State relations."[1] By contrast, international legal scholars have tended to dismiss such concerns. Some point out that, despite the appearance of fragmentation, regulatory coordination among institutions is now better than ever, the result of the growth in informal, market-like coordination mechanisms, such as networks of governmental organizations.[2] Others argue that fragmentation is a largely harmless side effect of the "institutional expression of political pluralism internationally"[3] or of the increased demand for expertise in international institutions.[4] From this perspective, the ongoing competition among international regulatory institutions for jurisdiction and influence will ultimately be as beneficial for the international regulatory regime as the competition among political interests is for democracy.

In what follows, we argue that fragmentation is a more serious problem than either group suggests because it disrupts the evolution of more democratic and egalitarian international regulatory systems and undermines the normative integrity of international law. Fragmentation does this in three ways. First, it limits the ability of weaker states to engage in the logrolling that is necessary for them to bargain more effectively with more powerful states. Weaker actors are, in addition to being far more numerous, more institutionally, economically, and geographically diverse than powerful states, suggesting that their preferences, too, are more diverse. This diversity makes it more difficult for them to reach a consensus on a particular issue. At the domestic level, weaker actors often manage to overcome this problem by logrolling or trading votes across issues. However, logrolling requires a venue such as a legislature, where policy decisions are made on a wide range of issues. And such venues are rare at the fragmented international level.

To the extent that powerful parties are able to forestall the emergence of such multi-issue venues by creating a fragmented system of multiple, issue-specific treaties, they can preserve and even increase their current

---

[1] Martti Koskenniemi & Päivi Leino, *Fragmentation of International Law? Postmodern Anxieties*, 15 LEIDEN J. INT'L L. 553, 555 (2002) (citing H.E. Judge Gilbert Guillaume, President of the Int'l Court of Justice, Speech to the General Assembly of the United Nations (Oct. 30, 2001)).

[2] Anne-Marie Slaughter, *A NEW WORLD ORDER* (2004).

[3] See Koskenniemi & Leino, *supra* note 1, at 553.

[4] Martti Koskenniemi, *The Fate of Public International Law: Between Technique and Politics*, 70 MOD. L. REV. 1, 4 (2007).

bargaining advantages.[5] Decentralized mechanisms such as networks possess a host of virtues and are capable of greatly facilitating coordination among states within a given regulatory arena. As we shall see, however, they are not well suited to promoting coalition building across issues in a fragmented system.

Second, by creating a multitude of competing institutions with overlapping responsibilities, fragmentation provides powerful states with the opportunity to abandon–or threaten to abandon–any given venue for one more sympathetic if their demands are not met. This further exacerbates the competition between institutions and effectively marginalizes the weaker states, which do not enjoy the same leverage. This is not the kind of environment in which a bottom-up process of constitution making by international tribunals is likely to thrive.

Third, a fragmented system's piecemeal character suggests an absence of design and obscures the role of intentionality. As a result, it is often considered to be merely the accidental by-product of historical events and broad social forces. This has helped to mask the fact that fragmentation is in part the result of a calculated strategy by powerful states to create a legal order that closely reflects their interests and that only they have the capacity to alter.[6] In recent years, as hierarchical strategies have become contested and delegitimized, powerful states have increasingly relied on fragmentation strategies as an alternative means of achieving the same end in a less visible and politically costly way. Historical contingency and the strategic self-interest of powerful states have long been intertwined in connection with fragmentation. The narrow, functionalist design of the institutions that the Allied powers created in the aftermath of World War II was, for the most part, an accident of history. The policy problems that they were designed to address (for example,

---

[5] John Gray makes a related point in connection with the creation of free trade: "Those who seek to design a free market on a worldwide scale have always insisted that the legal framework which defines and entrenches it must be placed beyond the reach of any democratic legislature... The rules of the game of the market must be elevated beyond any possibility of revision through democratic choice." John Gray, *FALSE DAWN: THE DELUSIONS OF GLOBAL CAPITALISM* 18 (1998).

[6] Although our account of how powerful states employ international law emphasizes the role of fragmentation strategies, it shares much in common with other instrumentalist-oriented accounts of hegemonic behavior. This is particularly true of Nico Krisch's account; see Nico Krisch, *International Law in Times of Hegemony: Unequal Power and the Shaping of the International Legal Order*, 16 EUR. J. INT'L L. 369, 371 (2005), which provides what in many ways is a complementary account of how powerful states employ international law to stabilize their dominance and adapt to changing conditions.

economic stabilization, collective security, and containment) emerged at different times in connection with specific historical events, and each required a high degree of expertise that could be found only in the domestic bureaucracies of the Allied powers that were themselves organized along functionalist lines. In such an environment, it was natural to respond to problems in a piecemeal way and to repeat the process as new problems and issues emerged. To a considerable extent, fragmentation was unavoidable.

Yet even during the early stage in the post–World War II development of the international system, strategic considerations were always at work. Historical accounts of the period are clear that the Western powers wanted to insulate key regulatory institutions, particularly economic ones, from the influence of other states, from the newly created United Nations, and from potential cross-contamination from other policy spheres.[7] It is not unlikely that architects of the new international system saw in the mission creep associated with the League of Nations[8] a model to be avoided. Paul Kennedy's history of the UN suggests that the great powers from the outset selectively employed fragmentation to prevent the Economic and Social Council (ECOSOC) from competing with the Security Council for dominance over the integration of security and economic policies. The great powers did nothing to facilitate the UN Charter's requirement that all of the various specialized agencies such as the International Monetary Fund, the International Labor Organization, and the Universal Postal Union were to be "brought into relationship" with the UN and coordinated through the ECOSOC. Instead, they chose to preside passively over a situation of increasing overlap and confusion among the growing number of newly created UN bodies.[9]

---

[7] *See* Paul Kennedy, THE PARLIAMENT OF MAN 113–42 (2006).

[8] Mark Mazower, GOVERNING THE WORLD: THE HISTORY OF AN IDEA 144, 149 (2012); Patricia Clavin & Wilhelm Jens, *Transnationalism and the League of Nations: Understanding the Work of Its Economic and Financial Organisation*, 14 CONTEMP. EUR. HIST. 465 (2005).

[9] *See* KENNEDY, *supra* note 7, at 114–15: "Without being completely cynical about the motives of the Great Powers, then, it is obvious that their governments really did not regard the Economic and Social Council as a principal organ that was a full equivalent to the Security Council. All of them were heavily invested in international security matters, as they showed by putting themselves at the heart of the new system through their permanent membership and veto powers." Kennedy goes on to make clear that weighted voting in the IMF and the permanent membership of the world's five largest economies in the World Bank ensure great power dominance of economic policy-making as effectively as the Security Council ensures it in the security sphere.

As a host of new regulatory problems emerged in the intervening decades, numerous multilateral agreements and specialized institutions were created to deal with them. This situation, in turn, led to a growing number of jurisdictional disputes and mounting concerns about the international regulatory regime's lack of consistency and coherence that are the forerunners of the current preoccupation with fragmentation. In response, at each step along the way, there have been frequent calls for better policy integration and coordination, and in recent years these calls have increasingly been accompanied by demands on the part of the developing states for better representation of their interests in key regulatory institutions.

Yet progress toward a more integrated and democratized international regulatory system and toward the necessary redistribution of influence to bring it about has been virtually nonexistent. We argue that this lack of progress stems from the fact that the powerful states, and particularly the United States, have chosen to rely on four strategies that promote fragmentation. These four fragmentation strategies include (1) avoiding broad, integrative agreements in favor of a large number of narrow agreements that are functionally defined; (2) formulating agreements in the context of onetime or infrequently convened multilateral negotiations; (3) avoiding whenever possible the creation of a bureaucracy or judiciary with significant, independent policy-making authority and circumscribing such authority when its creation is unavoidable; and (4) creating or shifting to an alternative venue (including informal or private ones) when the original one becomes too responsive to the interests of weaker states and their agents.

These four strategies increase the transaction costs to weaker states for engaging in the political coordination necessary to form coalitions capable of bargaining more effectively with their more powerful counterparts. Testament to the success of these strategies is the archipelago of narrowly focused and poorly coordinated treaties and multilateral organizations that characterizes the international legal system, the slow rate with which international institutions have been democratized, and the lack of redistribution between North and South.

At the same time, however, weaker states and those bureaucrats and judges who staff international institutions have not remained completely passive in the face of increasing fragmentation. These actors have occasionally attempted to resist it by developing countervailing or "anti-fragmentation" strategies designed to lower rather than raise the transaction costs associated with strategic coordination by diffuse constituencies. These strategies operate by increasing the repeated game aspects of the institutional context, expanding the independence and role of tribunals and the bureaucratic components of multilateral institutions, and creating linkages between agreements that can serve to create coalitions. The fact that these strategies are at least intermittently successful is indicated by the growing frequency with which powerful states find themselves forced to resort to the fourth fragmentation strategy of venue shifting, including informalization and privatization.

The chapter is organized into five sections. In Section 2.2, we briefly review the international legal literature dealing with fragmentation. In Section 2.3, we examine the strategies that incumbent elites use to maintain their dominance at the domestic level. We argue that many of these strategies operate by suppressing political coordination, and we provide a theoretical framework for analyzing how powerful states use fragmentation to suppress the ability of weaker states to engage in political coordination at the international level. In Section 2.4, we employ this theoretical framework to understand the operation and impact of the four prevalent fragmentation strategies. In Section 2.5, we describe the countervailing efforts of weaker states and international bureaucrats and assess their impact. Section 2.6 concludes.

2.2 The Effects of Fragmentation

As we have already noted, few legal theorists view growing fragmentation as a serious problem, despite the theoretical centrality of institutional integration in the self-narrative of international law. International legal theorists in the neoliberal, institutionalist tradition have argued that fragmentation is not so much a problem as it is part of a gradually evolving solution to the demands imposed on the international system by globalization. Globalization puts a premium on efficiency, and decentralized processes are simply more efficient than more formal, centralized ones.

Jonathan Charney is one of those theorists who view fragmentation as a market-like response to pluralist diversity that is vastly superior to more hierarchical alternatives:

> In conclusion, I am not troubled by the multiplicity of dispute settlement systems established by the [Law of the Sea] Convention. I encourage all to embrace and nurture them so that they may fulfill their laudable objectives. We should celebrate the increased number of forums for third-party dispute settlement found in the Convention and other international

agreements because it means that international third-party settlement procedures, especially adjudication and arbitration, are becoming more acceptable. This development will promote the evolution of public international law and its broader acceptance by the public as a true system of law... Hierarchy and coherence are laudable goals for any legal system, including international law, but at the moment they are impossible goals. The benefits of the alternative, multiple forums, are worth the possible adverse consequences that may contribute to less coherence. This risk is low and the potential for benefits to the peaceful settlement of international disputes is high.[10]

Other theorists in the institutionalist tradition who stress the growing role of intergovernmental and other social networks also consider the problem of fragmentation to be overblown.[11] From their perspective, the term "fragmentation" denotes a degree of isolation and a lack of coordination that simply do not apply to today's increasingly networked world. William Burke-White acknowledges that "the rise of [multiple] international courts does increase the possibility of conflicting judgments, but it does so within the context of a more, rather than less, important role for international law."[12] Burke-White goes on to describe how this interconnected system operates:

> Counterbalancing the danger of fragmentation is an increasingly loud interjudicial dialogue. This dialogue has important implications for the unity of the international legal order as it provides actors at all levels with means to communicate, share information, and possibly resolve potential conflicts before they even occur. This interjudicial dialogue has been relatively well documented and occurs at three distinct levels. Supranational courts are engaged in dialogue with one another, national courts are citing to supranational courts, and national courts are in direct conversation with one another... The significance of this interjudicial dialogue cannot be overstated, for it has the potential to preserve the unity of the international legal system in the face of potential fragmentation. Such dialogue, of course, relies heavily upon international judges themselves. If national and supranational judges consider themselves part of

[10] Jonathan I. Charney, *The Implications of Expanding International Dispute Settlement Systems: The 1982 Convention on the Law of the Sea*, 90 Am. J. Int'l L. 69, 73–75 (1996). *See also* James Crawford, Chance, Order, Change: The Course of International Law, General Course on Public International Law 291 (2014) ("fragmentation poses no real threat to international law as a system").

[11] *See* Slaughter, *supra* note 2; Kal Raustiala, *The Architecture of International Cooperation: Transgovernmental Networks and the Future of International Law*, 43 Va. J. Int'l L. 1 (2002).

[12] William W. Burke-White, *International Legal Pluralism*, 25 Mich. J. Int'l L. 963, 967 (2004).

a common enterprise of international law enforcement, they can, through informal agreements, dialogue, and respect, avoid conflicts before they occur, help to minimize their effects when they do arise, and ensure the development of a unified system.[13]

Legal theorists coming from a postmodern or constructivist tradition have tended to view fragmentation even more positively, as a welcome alternative to the formal, top-down-driven integration advocated by mainstream theorists.[14] The latter, they argue, allowed themselves to be trapped in the ideational framework of domestic law. As a result, they had created a concept of integration that privileged hierarchy and stasis over pluralist competition and adaptation. Such a structure was fundamentally unsuited to meeting the needs of a rapidly changing and more egalitarian international environment, increasingly reliant on technical expertise applied in specialized international institutions.[15] Worse, by suggesting that the progress of international law was inextricably bound to the degree to which the international system was formally integrated, neoliberals had created a standard that critics of international law could seize upon to mistakenly judge it a failure.

Given the imperfections of formal integration, several theorists have been dismissive about anxieties expressed regarding the potential ill effects of fragmentation. Thus, in response to what they clearly view to be excessive concern displayed by the president of the International Court of Justice in making "three consecutive speeches before the United Nations General Assembly," Martti Koskenniemi and Päivi Leino lamented that "one may feel puzzled that among all aspects of global transformation, it is *this* they should have enlisted their high office to express anxiety over."[16] Rather than constituting a legitimate source of anxiety, fragmentation and the proliferation of courts were "either an unavoidable minor problem in a rapidly transforming international system, or even a rather positive demonstration of the responsiveness of legal imagination to social change."[17]

Although the full impact of the resulting system of competing normative structures was not yet clear, its appearance was viewed as a positive development. As Koskenniemi states in his essay "What Is International

[13] *Id.* at 971–73.   [14] Koskenniemi & Leino, *supra* note 1.

[15] *See* Koskenniemi, *supra* note 4, at 2 ("[T]he problems faced by public international law today–marginalization, lack of normative force, a sense that the diplomatic mores that stand at its heart are part of the world's problems–result in large part from [the] strategy, the effort of becoming technical.").

[16] Koskenniemi & Leino, *supra* note 1, at 553.   [17] *Id.* at 575.

22   INTERNATIONAL POLITICAL ECONOMY

Law For?" "[T]he proliferation of autonomous or semi-autonomous normative regimes is an unavoidable reflection of a 'postmodern' social condition and a beneficial prologue to a pluralistic community in which the degrees of homogeneity and fragmentation reflect shifts of political preference and the fluctuating successes of hegemonic pursuits."[18]

Despite their significant differences in emphasis, each of these defenses of fragmentation displays a tendency to embrace assumptions that are widespread among international legal theorists but that we believe to be suspect. The first of these assumptions is that the rate at which international law and international institutions are being created is a reliable indicator of the strength and importance of international law and that the problems associated with fragmentation represent little more than transient costs of adjustment.[19] Yet the fact that this assumption is often appropriate when viewing the evolution of international law over long periods of time does not mean that it is true generally. At both the domestic and the international levels, the proliferation of regulatory laws and institutions often signals incapacity and ineffectiveness, as institutions generate new bodies and mandates in response to the failure of existing ones. In the United States, the protracted "war on drugs" and its associated legislation are a classic domestic example of this, and there are countless examples of this same tendency at the international level as well. Consider the following description by Paul Kennedy of how the General Assembly added to the problem of fragmentation out of frustration with its own incapacity:

> Concerned in part by what it saw as unmet needs and frustrated by its own restricted powers, the General Assembly was already developing the habit of creating newer bodies that would report to it, even if this created policy overlap and bureaucratic overload. Moreover, at least two of the Assembly's own main committees–the Second Committee (economic and financial) and the Third Committee (social)–already could not resist the temptation to move from being broad framers of policy to making executive recommendations in those domains and thus duplicating the ECOSOC. All were in danger of choking the system.[20]

Equally prevalent is the implicit assumption that fragmentation represented a major advance over hierarchy because its very multiplicity was

[18] Martti Koskenniemi, *What Is International Law For?*, in INT'L L. 89, 110 (Malcolm D. Evans ed., 2003) (internal citation omitted).
[19] See, e.g., Burke-White, *supra* note 12, at 967 ("An alternate perspective on the increasing number of fora for international legal adjudication is that international law is today more relevant than it has ever been in the past.").
[20] Kennedy, *supra* note 7, at 120.

considered to be inherently pluralistic and hence a harbinger of the emergence of a more democratic international legal order. Yet while it is reasonable to argue that the proliferation of multilateral agreements has created an institutional environment that is less hierarchal than that which existed during the Cold War, it is not clear that the resulting order is any more pluralistic than the previous one with respect to the range or even the number of interests that it represents. At the national level, no one would argue that the number of domestic laws or institutions a state possesses is a reliable indicator of the number or range of interests that influenced their creation. Autocracies that by definition represent a narrow set of interests frequently have elaborate legal systems and countless regulations.

Also tenuous, for similar reasons, is the assumption that greater fragmentation will be characterized by a heightened level of connectedness that will, in turn, lead to greater democratization. One can acknowledge the growing and often positive role played by transgovernmental networks and still remain concerned about the extent to which the right of traditionally marginalized actors to participate actually leads to their being able to significantly influence policy decisions.[21] As we shall see in the next section, while the decentralized coordination processes that emerge organically out of a fragmented institutional structure might lead to improvements in the quality of policy-making within a given issue-area, these processes are not particularly well suited to the task of building coalitions across issue-areas, a task that is necessary if weaker actors are to bargain with powerful states on a more equal footing.

Finally, there is the assumption reflected in the Koskenniemi and Leino quotes above[22] that the fragmentation of international law is either an unintended side effect of the natural evolution of the international system or the result of judicial creativity in the face of change. While both of these factors have played an important role in creating fragmentation, no broad aspect of international law is likely to emerge without being shaped in a significant way by the strategic interests of powerful states. Just as the strategic preoccupations of powerful states played a major role in determining and reifying the hierarchical character that still persists within many international institutions, so they also played—and continue to play—a major role in fostering fragmentation, and their motivations for doing so are quite similar.

---

[21] On this point, see Eyal Benvenisti, THE LAW OF GLOBAL GOVERNANCE 34–40 (2014).

[22] See supra notes 14–17 and accompanying text.

2.3   Strategic Coordination in the Domestic and International Context

In this section we describe the strategies that domestic elites use to suppress political coordination among potential competitors. We argue that a simple game devised by Barry Weingast to account for the problematic emergence of political rights in a simplified three-actor "state" provides a useful framework for examining how fragmentation strategies help powerful states perpetuate their dominance at the international level.[23]

To challenge the political status quo effectively in any institutional environment, marginalized groups and individuals must collectively engage in a host of political coordination activities. These vary considerably from one context to another, but they characteristically involve such tasks as recruiting new members, fund-raising, selecting leaders, establishing strategic goals, and building coalitions with other groups. Incumbent groups and elites maintain their relative power by devising strategies that directly or indirectly limit the ability of prospective opponents to engage in these activities or by increasing the level or "threshold" of coordination that must be achieved in order to remove them from power.[24]

Over the past two centuries, political elites within democratic states have tended to rely heavily on the manipulation of electoral and legislative rules to accomplish these tasks. Complicated voter registration procedures, lengthy residency requirements, and literacy tests directly limit the ability of marginalized groups to participate in elections. Devices such as poll taxes, the lack of public funding of elections, and the requirement of permits for public demonstrations and assemblies have accomplished the same goal more indirectly by increasing the costs of engaging in political coordination. Strategies such as gerrymandering legislative districts, requiring a large number of signatures for a candidate to appear on a ballot, creating a bicameral versus a unicameral legislature, choosing a presidential rather than a parliamentary system, and adopting majority rule rather than proportional representation tend to perpetuate the political status quo by increasing the effective threshold of coordination required to wrest control of the government.

---

[23] Barry R. Weingast, *The Constitutional Dilemma of Economic Liberty*, J. Econ. Persp. Summer 2005, at 89, 91–96.

[24] *See* Gary W. Cox, Making Votes Count: Strategic Coordination in the World's Electoral Systems 62–63, 197–98, 269–78 (1997).

A substantial institutionalist literature in political science and economics describes how incumbents in different countries during different historical periods have employed these and similar strategies to protect their political power in the face of expected changes in political demand. For example, Stein Rokkan describes how ruling elites in European states supported a shift to proportional representation to protect their power in the face of growing demands for universal suffrage and the threat of working-class solidarity.[25] More recently, Carles Boix has shown that the strategies employed by elites were even more refined and context-dependent than Rokkan suspected.[26] Instead of embracing proportional representation systems wholesale, incumbent parties would condition their strategies on the strength and coordinating capacity of the new parties relative to that of their own.

Autocratic incumbents and leaders of emerging democracies operate in a context different from that of their counterparts in liberal democracies, with the result that the suppression of political coordination takes a different form. In these states, political opponents tend to operate outside the formal political process, which they view as illegitimate, and work to topple the government by sowing political discontent among the general population or by organizing a political or military coup in times of political or economic crisis.[27] Since structural strategies involving electoral and legislative rules are inadequate in the face of such threats, leaders of autocratic regimes and illiberal democracies concentrate on the direct suppression of what can be termed "coordination goods."[28] This is a category of public goods or quasi–public goods that facilitates political coordination among potential opponents of the incumbent regime. It includes political rights and civil liberties, media freedom and access, freedom of assembly, government transparency, and freedom of information. To the extent that these leaders can successfully restrict the supply of these coordination goods, they increase the likelihood of their political survival.

The past few years have been witness to abundant examples of the suppression of coordination goods by modern autocrats and the leaders

[25] *See* Stein Rokkan et al., CITIZENS, ELECTIONS, PARTIES: APPROACHES TO THE COMPARATIVE STUDY OF THE PROCESSES OF DEVELOPMENT (1970).

[26] *See* Carles Boix, POLITICAL PARTIES, GROWTH AND EQUALITY (1998).

[27] In such societies, leadership transitions usually take place as the result of a political or military coup following a political or economic crisis. *See* Bruce Bueno de Mesquita et al., THE LOGIC OF POLITICAL SURVIVAL 354–402 (2003).

[28] Bruce Bueno de Mesquita & George W. Downs, *Development and Democracy*, FOREIGN AFF., Sept.-Oct. 2005, at 77, 80–83.

of emerging democracies. China has introduced a host of Web-restricting activities such as blocking access to Google's English-language news and creating a special police unit. Russia has nationalized the major television networks and placed them under strict government control, and Putin has engineered the arrest and prosecution of Mikhail Khodorvosky, one of the government's most prominent critics. The Vietnamese government has imposed strict controls over religious organizations and branded leaders of unauthorized religious groups as subversives. Venezuela has passed the Law of Social Responsibility in Radio and Television, which critics charge will allow the government to ban news reports of violent protests or government crackdowns.[29]

Given this history, it would be surprising if powerful states did not also engage in a variant of coordination suppression to preserve their dominance at the international level and if the strategies that they employed to accomplish this did not involve the use of international law and the tools the law offers.[30] As Nico Krisch observes in his insightful analysis of how hegemons shape and instrumentalize international law, international law provides major powers (and the interest groups that shape their foreign policies)[31] with a powerful tool for pacification and the stabilization of their dominance.[32] Further, as Krisch also points out, these international norms that hegemons are instrumental in creating come with significant additional drawbacks for those very hegemons, by placing constraints on the hegemon as well as on weaker states. The result is that "new rules can only be created in a relatively egalitarian setting."[33]

Neither of these drawbacks is particularly important in a relatively static international environment of the sort that prevailed during much of the Cold War. However, the volatile environment in the post–Cold War era could potentially jeopardize a powerful state's dominance. Thus, the norms that a powerful state has itself created can limit the state's

---

[29] *Id.* at 81–85. Such strategies appear to be surprisingly effective. Bueno de Mesquita and Downs show that leaders who suppress civil liberties and reduce the freedom of the press increase the chance that they will survive for another year by 15 to 20 percent. *See id.* at 84.

[30] *See* W. Michael Reisman, THE QUEST FOR WORLD ORDER AND HUMAN DIGNITY IN THE TWENTY-FIRST CENTURY CONSTITUTIVE PROCESS AND INDIVIDUAL COMMITMENT 285–88 (2013) (international organizations "always remain policy instruments of States. [. . .] They . . . continue to be arenas of the larger political process.") For related analyses, see G. John Ikenberry, AFTER VICTORY (2001); Joseph S. Nye Jr., THE PARADOX OF AMERICAN POWER (2002); and Robert Jervis, *The Remaking of a Unipolar World*, WASH. Q. Summer 2006, at 7.

[31] On the shaping of international norms by domestic interests, see *infra* Chapter 3.

[32] Krisch, *supra* note 6, at 378.   [33] *Id.*

ability to respond quickly to changing conditions and to selectively reward friends and punish emerging rivals. The requirement that new rules must be created in a relatively egalitarian setting is even more problematic in a dynamic environment, because it can provide opportunities for weaker states to engage in political coordination and act collectively.

To understand the strategies that a dominant group of states might employ to cope with such challenges, it is useful to consider a simple three-person game devised by Barry Weingast.[34] The game was originally designed to illustrate the barriers to cooperation faced by citizens who wish to limit the power of a sovereign, but it is equally useful in understanding how a hegemon or a group of powerful states might employ international law to prevent weaker states from cooperating in order to erode the hegemon's dominance. The three players in the game are a sovereign, S, who is the most powerful figure in the three-person "society," and two citizens, A and B. In order to remain in power, the sovereign needs the support of at least one of the two citizens. If both citizens oppose him, he is deposed and loses power.[35]

The basic game involves a sequence of two moves. S moves first and may choose to honor both citizens' rights or to transgress against the rights of one or both. If S chooses to honor both citizens' rights, the game ends, and S remains in power. If S violates the rights of either or both, A and B have the opportunity to choose whether to acquiesce or challenge the sovereign. If A and B both choose to challenge the sovereign (that is, if they cooperate), the attempted transgression fails and the game ends. If one or both choose to acquiesce (that is, if they fail to cooperate), S's transgression succeeds and the game ends.

Similar to the outcome in the familiar prisoner's dilemma, there are three noncooperative equilibria in which S challenges either one or both of the citizens and they both acquiesce. The cooperative outcome in which A and B cooperate to maximize their collective gain is not an equilibrium.[36] However, if the game is repeated, the game becomes more complicated and virtually any equilibrium is possible, because A and B might find that it is worth incurring the costs of cooperation in the onetime game to avoid a string of future transgressions.[37] Weingast singles out two equilibria arising from the repeated game as being especially noteworthy. One is an asymmetric equilibrium, in which S and one of the citizens repeatedly exploit the second citizen.

[34] *See* Weingast, *supra* note 23, at 91.   [35] *Id.*   [36] *Id.* at 93.   [37] *Id.* at 94.

The other is the cooperative equilibrium, in which both citizens cooperate and challenge the sovereign.[38]

Weingast's stylized game is characterized by two features that corre-
spond to important aspects of the contemporary international
system–and its impact on international law–as well as to the domestic
context of an earlier era. The first is that the sovereign possesses a notable
first-mover advantage. This corresponds to the agenda-setting power
that hegemons and coalitions of powerful states frequently enjoy at the
international level, whereby the final outcome of multilateral negotiations is usually strongly anchored to their initial bargaining position.[39]

The second feature of the game, also typical of the international
system, is that the task facing the two citizens is far more difficult than
that facing the sovereign, so cooperation requires two special conditions.
Because cooperation is never an equilibrium in the single-shot version of
the game, one condition is the familiar requirement that the game must
be repeated. The second, more subtle, requirement is that the citizens
must be able to resolve their differences about the rights they prefer and
be able to agree on a specific package of rights that leaves each better off
than it would be by colluding with S. These can be very difficult conditions to meet when there are a number of different rights to choose from
and the preferences of the citizens differ. In fact, Weingast views them as
being so formidable that the most likely outcome of the game is one in
which the citizens fail to cooperate, and S and one of the citizens exploit
the other citizen. Weingast supports this expectation with data revealing
that over 50 percent of the twenty-four interwar European democracies
failed prior to World War II.[40]

For our purposes, the primary significance of Weingast's game lies in
its message that a hegemon (or small group of powerful states) interested
in preventing weaker states from cooperating can do so by using its first-
mover advantage to (1) limit the perception of weaker parties that they
are involved in a repeated game and (2) limit the opportunities that
weaker states have to resolve the differences in their preferences. As we
shall see in the next section, there are a number of strategies that
hegemons and powerful states employ to accomplish each goal.

---

[38] *Id.*

[39] For a discussion of the role of bargaining power in bargaining, see Ken Binmore, GAME
THEORY AND THE SOCIAL CONTRACT II: JUST PLAYING 78–80 (1998). For a historical analysis of
the dominant role of the great powers in shaping the Universal Declaration of Human
Rights, see Mary Ann Glendon, A WORLD MADE NEW (2001).

[40] Weingast, *supra* note 23, at 89.

Creating detailed agreements in onetime multilateral settings and avoiding the creation of permanent bureaucracies or tribunals with independent policy-making authority are effective ways of accomplishing the first goal. Creating a large number of narrowly focused or bilateral agreements and switching to a competing venue when weaker states threaten to gain control of an existing one are effective ways to accomplish the second. Fragmentation of one sort or another is a hallmark of each of these strategies.

We believe that the growing pace with which fragmentation has occurred in the last decade of the twentieth century and its coincidence with the expansion of US power testify to the fact that powerful states appreciated the benefits that accrued to them from fragmentation and therefore were constantly seeking new avenues by which to promote it. The section that follows attempts to document this intentionality with selected examples. However, we want to reiterate that we are not claiming that all or even most fragmentation arises as the direct result of conscious strategizing on the part of powerful states–only that some of it does and that this has important consequences.

We also think that too great a preoccupation with the role of intentionality comes with its own pitfalls–a tendency to underestimate the impact and importance of fragmentation. As we have seen, much of the existing literature tends to downplay the significance of fragmentation by stressing the ingenuousness and even praiseworthiness of those who bring it about. The message looks to be: to the extent fragmentation is the result of generally beneficial processes such as a competition among pluralist interests or the application of expertise, as opposed to the result of a malevolent strategy, there is no point in getting exercised about it.

While this principle might lead to the correct conclusion in a particular case, it clearly fails to hold true in general. A host of problems that plague modern societies, ranging from global warming to legislative gridlock, have also arisen as side effects of largely positive processes, rather than through the active malevolence of a set of actors or as the result of a deliberate strategy. If we step outside of the formal context of Weingast's game, there exists the possibility–even the likelihood–that each of the hegemonic or powerful state "strategies" discussed in the next section represents a state of the world that is likely to have the same detrimental impact on weaker state cooperation, regardless of whether it occurs as the result of an intentional action on the part of a hegemon or as the result of broader historical processes.

In addition, the genesis of a particular instance of fragmentation may have little or no bearing on how it might be reversed or even the likelihood that it will be. Once a substantial amount of fragmentation has occurred, even if more or less naturally, powerful states may come to see that it serves their interests and therefore work to maintain it. The United States, for example, played no role in precipitating the dissolution of the Multilateral Agreement on Investment and the initial fragmentation that followed in its immediate aftermath. But the United States quickly discovered that it stood to benefit disproportionately from the ensuing rush to replace the agreement with bilateral and minilateral agreements[41] and as a result has become a staunch supporter of the highly fragmented system.[42] Because we suspect that the role intentionality plays in both the genesis and the maintenance of fragmentation varies directly with the concentration of power, this pattern has become increasingly common, we believe, as the United States has attempted to consolidate its position as the world's sole superpower and prepare for subsequent challenges to its authority. The US launch of negotiations over the mega-regional agreements (the Transatlantic Trade and Investment Partnership, TTIP, the Trans-Pacific Partnership, TPP, and the Trade in Services Agreement, TISA) epitomizes a US strategy that seeks on the one hand to sideline China, India, and Brazil, while at the same time to maintain a division between the Pacific Rim states and the EU.[43]

2.4   Four Fragmentation Strategies

2.4.1   The Creation of a Large Number of Narrow, Functionally Defined Agreements

The first of the four prominent fragmentation strategies is deceptively simple: create a large number of narrowly focused agreements rather

---

[41] *See infra* notes 66–68 and accompanying text.

[42] On the evolving US policy regarding the protection of foreign investments, see Gilbert Gagné & Jean-Frédéric Morin, *The Evolving American Policy on Investment Protection: Evidence from Recent FTAs and the 2004 Model BIT*, 9 J. INT'L ECON. L. 357 (2006).

[43] On the rise of new powers at the WTO and their challenges to the dominance of the United States and other states of the Global North, which eventually motivated the latter to pursue the new partnerships see Kristen Hopewell, *Different Paths to Power: The rise of Brazil, India and China at the World Trade Organization*, 22 REV. INT'L POL. ECON. 311 (2015). On the motivations for the TPP and TTIP, see Eyal Benvenisti, *Democracy Captured: The Mega-Regional Agreements and the Future of Global Public Law*, 23 CONSTELLATIONS 58 (2016).

than a small number of broad agreements, each of which oversees regulation in a number of functional areas (for example, a single agreement that regulates trade, labor standards, and the environment). Powerful states are drawn to this strategy because they know not only that weaker states are more numerous than they are but also that they are far more diverse with respect to size, wealth, and their level of development.[44] This diversity makes it difficult for weaker states to agree on any particular issue. At the domestic level, the traditional way to surmount this problem and achieve cooperation is through logrolling: a given legislator agrees to support the policy position of another legislator for whom that issue is very important in exchange for her doing the same in connection with a different issue.

Thus, to the extent that powerful states can narrow the range of issues that will be negotiated in connection with a given agreement and isolate the negotiation of different agreements from each other, they can reduce the likelihood that weaker states will be able to create a countervailing coalition by logrolling. Over time, this strategy has the further advantage for powerful states of creating a world legal order composed of a maze of narrow agreements that would be enormously costly for weaker states or their bureaucratic and judicial allies to overcome by reaching out to other weak states and setting up even temporary coalitions.

Examples of narrow multilateral agreements are prevalent in virtually every area of international law. There are dozens of environmental treaties dealing with specific issues. In connection with labor standards, the International Labour Organisation alone has produced more than two hundred treaties.[45] In the security area, there are numerous agreements related to the banning of specific weapons and numerous conventions prohibiting different types of terrorist actions. International human rights law is also fragmented among several conventions and additional and optional protocols. The popularity of the treaty/protocol framework

---

[44] On the difficulties of even large developing countries such as Brazil and India to forge and maintain coalitions and the success of the United States to divide them, and also about the need to diversify efforts beyond a single regime to strengthen brittle coalitions of developing countries, see Hopewell, *supra* note 43. Hopewell cites Indian negotiators at the Doha Round who said that "Brazil can't be trusted . . . they have a history of abandoning developing country positions" and whose "fears that [India] would not be able to count on Brazil in the endgame stage of the Doha negotiations motivated it to invest in developing other alliances." (at 323).

[45] For the list of conventions see *conventions and recommendations*, Int'l lab. org., http://ilo .org/global/standards/introduction-to-international-labour-standards/conventions-and-recommendations/lang–en/index.htm.

that is widely used in a number of these areas simply compounds the problem; that is, the proliferation of narrow agreements with few, if any, linkages makes logrolling and cooperation among weaker state parties difficult, if not impossible.

As we have already noted, this maze of agreements is the result of any number of factors, and it is rarely possible to reliably isolate the impact of the powerful states' desire to create narrow negotiation venues as a means of limiting the ability of weaker states to form countervailing coalitions. Yet the tendency of powerful states to engage in what might be termed "serial bilateralism"–the negotiation of separate bilateral agreements, with different states all dealing with the same issue when multilateral negotiations threaten to get out of control–suggests that fragmentation is often strategic.[46] Serial bilateralism is being used with increasing frequency by powerful states to shape the evolution of norms in areas such as intellectual property protection and drug pricing, where they have vital interests and where their position on issues is far different from those of the vast majority of states.[47]

The impact of serial bilateralism is particularly significant regarding the protection of foreign investments. Since the end of the Cold War, thousands of bilateral investment treaties (BITs) have been signed. The breadth of their effect stemmed from the fact that while each BIT was negotiated separately (and thus reflects the bilateral power relations between the negotiating parties), the outcomes of the various BITs reflected many similarities.[48] This similarity in the nature of their provisions established a claim that their terms reflect an emerging customary

---

[46] The negotiation histories of regimes such as the Third United Nations Convention on the Law of the Sea (UNCLOS), the World Trade Organization (WTO), and the failed Multilateral Agreement on Investment (MAI), also attest to the intentionality and creativity with which powerful states have structured venues in order to frustrate weaker state cooperation in recent years. *See infra* notes 58–65 and accompanying text.

[47] *See* Eyal Benvenisti & George W. Downs, *Distributive Politics and International Institutions: The Case of Drugs*, 36 CASE W. RES. J. INT'L L. 21 (2004) (discussing the impact of the unregulated intellectual property regime on drug-pricing policies of Northern countries).

[48] Jeswald W. Salacuse & Nicholas P. Sullivan, *Do BITs Really Work?: An Evaluation of Bilateral Investment Treaties and Their Grand Bargain*, 46 HARV. INT'L L.J. 67, 89 (2005) ("[D]espite divergences among individual treaties, BITs as a group also demonstrate many commonalities, including their coverage of similar issues and their use of equivalent or comparable legal concepts and vocabulary. It is these commonalities that are contributing to the creation of an international framework for investment. Moreover among more recent BITs, one detects increasing consensus on certain points; for example, all BITs now require the payment of compensation for expropriation.").

international law, as did the fact that the rulings of arbitral tribunals that enforced these BITs issued decisions that "although not systematically made public, tend[ed] to take the form of lengthy, reasoned, and scholarly decisions that form part of the jurisprudence of this emerging international investment law and serve to solidify and give force to BIT provisions."[49] As a result, powerful states and arbitral tribunals were beginning to treat the similar BIT terms as reflecting customary international law[50] or at least common expectations.

2.4.2 Agreements Formulated in Specially Convened Onetime or Infrequently Convened Settings

A second fragmentation strategy that powerful states use to limit political coordination among weaker states is to create detailed agreements in onetime multilateral settings, with little prospect that they will be renegotiated or significantly amended in the near future. Such venues provide a less congenial setting for engaging in political coordination than does the ongoing legislative process that takes place within most states. They limit the amount of time that weaker states have to discover their common ground as the agreement is being created, and there is thus little prospect that weaker states will have an opportunity to modify the agreement in the future. While in theory the weaker states have the right to propose convening another round of negotiations to update or amend the agreement, actually doing so is rarely possible without the support of the powerful states. In effect, this strategy transforms what is formally a repeated game into what for all practical purposes is a one-shot game.

The web of agreements that collectively constitute the World Trade Organization (WTO) (for example, General Agreement on Tariffs and Trade, General Agreement on Trade on Services, Sanitary and Phytosanitary Measures Agreement, Technical Barriers to Trade, Trade-Related Aspects of Intellectual Property Rights) all contain detailed provisions that insulate the features valued by powerful states from strategic misinterpretation at a later time by national courts or by

---

[49] *Id.*

[50] *Id.* at 114–15 ("[T]he process of creating an international law of investment has seemingly evolved from a situation where the absence of appropriate custom prompted the creation of over 2200 BITs, which in turn has led to the creation of custom."); see also Andreas F. Lowenfeld, *Investment Agreements and International Law*, 42 COLUM. J. TRANSNAT'L L. 123, 129 (2003) ("[T]he BIT movement has moved beyond *lex specialis* (or better, *leges speciales*) to the level of customary law effective even for non-signatories.").

international bureaucrats and tribunals. Whatever is left unregulated is relegated to private and semiprivate standard-setting institutions, which the stronger states dominate.[51] While it is the case that the WTO regime establishes several councils and committees that discuss various aspects of the WTO law, the rule-making authority of these committees is significantly curtailed compared with that enjoyed by the original GATT 1947 bodies.[52] The one important exception is the Appellate Body, which gradually assumed a quasi-legislative role in addition to its dispute-settlement activities.[53] However, the subsequent, if vain, attempts by the major powers to reduce the Appellate Body's independence by careful attention to the appointment process suggest that this expanded role was not at all what they had intended.[54]

The multilateral agreements concerning the laws of war in general (the Hague Regulations of 1907,[55] The Geneva Conventions of 1949,[56] and

[51] *See* Armin von Bogdandy, *Law and Politics in the WTO–Strategies to Cope with a Deficient Relationship*, in 5 MAX PLANCK Y.B. OF U.N. L. 609, 633–41 (J.A. Frowein & R. Wolfrum eds., 2001) (referring to "outsourced rule-making").

[52] *Id.* at 626.

[53] *See* Sol Picciotto, *The WTO's Appellate Body: Legal Formalism as a Legitimation of Global Governance*, 18 GOVERNANCE 477 (2005); Joel P. Trachtman, *The Domain of WTO Dispute Resolution*, 40 HARV. INT'L L.J. 333 (1999).

[54] On the composition of the Appellate Body, see *infra* notes 99–100 and the accompanying text. There is ample evidence to suggest that many government negotiators failed to realize the constitutional and distributive implications of creating this institution. *See* Richard H. Steinberg, *Judicial Lawmaking at the WTO: Discursive, Constitutional, and Political Constraints*, 98 AM. J. INT'L L. 247, 251 n.27 (2004) ("A few WTO DSU negotiators contemplated the possibility that in interpreting WTO agreements, the Appellate Body would engage in expansive lawmaking. However, most trade ministers consistently underestimated or dismissed that possibility, focusing instead on the virtues of its function of applying the rules."); Joseph. H.H. Weiler, *The Rule of Lawyers and the Ethos of Diplomats: Reflections on the Internal and External Legitimacy of WTO Dispute Settlement* 11 (Harv. Jean Monnet Working Paper No. 9/00, 2000), available at www .jeanmonnetprogram.org/papers/00/000901: "From interviews with many delegations I have conducted it is clear that... they saw the logic of the Appellate Body as a kind of Super-Panel to give a losing party another bite at the cherry, given that the losing party could not [sic] longer block adoption of the Panel. It is equally clear to me that they did not fully understand the judicial let alone constitutional nature of the Appellate Body." See also Peter Van den Bossche, *From Afterthought to Centerpiece: The WTO Appellate Body and Its Rise to Prominence in the World Trading System* (Maastricht Fac. Law, Working Paper No. 2005/1, 2005), available at http://ssrn.com/abstract=836284 (analyzing the success of the Appellate Body despite the early modest expectations).

[55] Convention Respecting the Laws and Customs of War on Land, Oct. 18, 1907, 36 Stat. 2277, 1 Bevans 631.

[56] *See, e.g.,* Geneva Convention Relative to the Protection of Civilian Persons in Time of War, Aug. 12, 1949, 6 U.S.T. 3516, 75 U.N.T.S. 287.

the Additional Protocols of 1977[57]) and the agreements concerning the use of specific weapons in particular provide another set of examples of agreements that lack mechanisms for updating in response to changing circumstances (for example, terrorism or the privatization of the military) and to new technological developments.[58]

2.4.3 Narrowly Circumscribing the Authority of Treaty-Based Agents

A third coordination-suppression strategy that powerful states employ is to avoid, whenever possible, the creation of a bureaucracy or judiciary with significant, independent policy-making authority and, when their creation is unavoidable, to circumscribe their authority. Like the previous strategy, this one is easy to justify in terms of widely held values such as transparency and the desire to avoid excessive bureaucratization, and to some extent, these concerns are real. However, powerful states often also appear to be attracted to the political advantages of minimizing the power and creation of independent policy-making bodies, such as reducing the likelihood that bureaucrats and judges will have any opportunity to influence the implementation of an agreement or its subsequent interpretation. This, in turn, limits what weaker states can achieve even if they succeed in cultivating these actors as allies and convince them to work on their behalf.

The aversion of powerful states to regulatory independence and formal institutional infrastructure is well illustrated by WTO agreements. References to judicial proceedings are rare and they tend to establish "panels" and "bodies" rather than courts. "Members" rather than offices issue "reports" that are then "adopted" by the state parties. As mentioned above, the WTO regime does establish several councils and committees

---

[57] Protocol Additional to the Geneva Conventions of 12 August 1949, and Relating to the Protection of Victims of International Armed Conflicts (Protocol I), opened for signature Dec. 12, 1977, 1125 U.N.T.S. 3, 16 I.L.M. 1391; Protocol Additional to the Geneva Conventions of 12 August 1949, and Relating to the Protection of Victims of Non-International Armed Conflicts (Protocol II), *adopted on* June 8, 1977, 1125 U.N.T.S. 609, 16 I.L.M. 1442.

[58] The United Nations is, of course, the most prominent exception to the rule that powerful states resist creating international organizations that are organized along the lines of a national legislature. However, its uniqueness in this regard and the democratic promise that it suggests tend to be more than offset by the UN hierarchical character, which is exemplified by the disproportionate power of the Security Council and the veto power wielded by the five permanent members. The UN Charter also contains a host of detailed rules concerning the responsibilities of the various institutions within the UN system that are difficult to amend.

that discuss various aspects of the WTO law, but the rule-making competence of these committees is significantly limited compared with that which was delegated to the General Agreement on Tariffs and Trade bodies, and much of the institution's standard setting is, as suggested above, relegated to private and semiprivate institutions that are dominated by the stronger states.[59]

2.4.4 Threatening to Exit a Regime or Switching Regimes

Finally, in the event that the three strategies described above fail to accomplish their goal and that weaker states and their agents are successful over time in altering the character of a particular agreement or institution so that it better reflects their interests, powerful states often resort to a strategy of withdrawing from it or switching to a competing venue.

As Krisch has noted, from a historical standpoint one of the most prominent aspects of hegemonic behavior has been that the same powerful actors who employ the law as a handmaiden withdraw from it when they find themselves faced with "the hurdles of equality and stability that international law erects."[60] This same tendency still exists, but in today's world, the act of withdrawal is less visible and only rarely takes the form of formal abrogation. More typically, it manifests itself in the use of less aggressive strategies such as delays in compliance, partial noncompliance, regime switching, and objections about the appropriateness of venue, all of which strategies possess the great virtues of being far more flexible and generating fewer political and legal side effects. When tied to the agenda-setting power of the dominant states, these strategies enable them to escape the consequences of a particular ruling without seriously undermining an agreement that for the most part continues to benefit them disproportionately.

Regime or venue shifting has become increasingly common and can take place at any point in the life cycle of a given agreement. It occurs most frequently when a particular agreement is initially negotiated or during the renegotiations that have been convened to deal with a new problem or political crisis. Typically, one or more powerful states become dissatisfied with the trajectory of negotiations and decide to exit the negotiations and exploit their agenda-setting power to set up a parallel and competing set of negotiations with other powerful states. Once they

---

[59] *See* von Bogdandy, *supra* note 51.   [60] Krisch, *supra* note 6, at 371.

have created the alternative venue and reached a consensus among themselves about the character of the agreement they desire, they approach weaker states with a proposal to restart negotiations. This simple two-step maneuver or some closely related variant has enabled the powerful states to break the coordinated resistance of the weaker parties during several multilateral negotiations.

One example occurred in connection with the negotiation of the United Nations Convention on the Law of the Sea (UNCLOS). Following nine years of negotiation, an ambitious agreement was drafted that included elaborate redistributive provisions designed to benefit developing states, including those that were landlocked. The Reagan administration, upon assuming office, expressed its dissatisfaction with these provisions and decided to walk away from the final technical rounds of negotiations.[61] Although it was too late for the United States to obstruct the finalization of the Convention in 1982, the United States set about undermining the Convention's seabed-mining regime by creating a parallel regime within a group of "like-minded states" (including the United Kingdom, West Germany, France, Japan, Italy, and the USSR) through the promotion of comparable domestic legislation that conflicted with the 1982 Convention.[62] The resulting conflict had to be resolved through negotiations that culminated in a so-called Implementation Agreement, signed in 1994, which basically replaced the arrangement under UNCLOS with one that was more attuned to the interests of the developed states.[63] A second example involving the renegotiation of existing treaties took place during the move from the GATT to the WTO. The United States and the European Union soon

---

[61] In his Oceans Policy Statement issued in 1983, President Reagan announced that the United States would act in accordance with the Convention's principles relating to traditional uses of the oceans, but would not abide by the provisions in Part XI concerning deep seabed mining. *See Accession to the 1982 Law of the Sea Convention and Ratification of the 1994 Agreement Amending Part XI of the Law of the Sea Convention: Hearing Before the S. Environment and Public Works Comm.*, 107th Cong. (2004) (testimony of John F. Turner, Assistant Secretary of State, Oceans, and International Environmental and Scientific Affairs), *available at* http://2001-2009.state.gov/g/oes/rls/rm/2004/30723.htm.

[62] *See* R. R. Churchill & A. V. Lowe, THE LAW OF THE SEA 232–35 (3rd edn. 1999).

[63] Agreement Relating to the Implementation of Part XI of the Convention on the Law of the Sea, Jul. 28, 1994, 33 I.L.M. 1309; *see also* Peter Prows, *Tough Love: The Dramatic Birth and Looming Demise of UNCLOS Property Law* (N.Y.U. L. Sch. Pub. L. & Legal Theory Research Paper Series, Paper No. 06–19, 2006), *available at* http://papers.ssrn.com/sol3/papers.cfm?abstract_id=918458. According to Prows, "[t]he [Implementation] Agreement abrogated many of the operating provisions most problematic for industrialized countries." *Id.* at 30.

realized that the Uruguay Round negotiations, which were open to all
GATT members and where decisions were subject to the tradition of
consensus, would never produce the kind of agreement on the protection
of intellectual property rights that they, especially the United States,
desired.[64] To overcome this resistance, the two powers agreed to exit
the GATT. They set up the WTO as a "modified" GATT regime with the
features that they desired and then invited the remaining GATT members to join the new body. The two powers made it clear that they would
assume no obligations toward countries that did not join the new regime.
As Richard Steinberg describes:

> This maneuver, which closed the Uruguay Round by means of a single
> undertaking, presented the developing countries with a fait accompli:
> either sign onto the entire WTO package or lose the legal basis for
> continued access to the enormous European and U.S. markets. From
> the time the transatlantic powers agreed to that approach in 1990, they
> definitively dominated the agenda-setting process, that is, the formulation
> and drafting of texts that would be difficult to amend.[65]

Another example of shifting venues–this time from multilateral to bilateral regimes–involves the protection of foreign investments. Following
the end of the Cold War, the Western powers mounted an effort to push
for a multilateral agreement on the protection of foreign investments, an
area they regarded as having the same paramount importance as trade or
intellectual property protection. In 1995, the United States initiated,
under the auspices of the Organisation for Economic Co-operation and
Development (OECD), negotiations on a Multilateral Agreement on
Investment (MAI). However, these efforts were frustrated by a coalition
made up of Southern governments and Northern nongovernmental
organizations that together managed to create a divide within the ranks
of Northern governments. As a result, the negotiations on MAI
collapsed.[66] The BITs, described above,[67] were the response. Through

[64] See Richard H. Steinberg, In the Shadow of Law or Power? Consensus-Based Bargaining
and Outcomes in the GATT/WTO, 56 INT'L ORG. 339 (2002).
[65] Steinberg, supra note 54, at 265. It is worth noting that the story of the establishment of
the WTO regime itself reflects another exercise in fragmentation, that of the World
Intellectual Property Organization (WIPO) regime. The United States and the
European Commission incorporated the TRIPS agreement into the new WTO regime
after they had failed, in the early 1980s, to obtain similar protection for intellectual
property under the auspices of WIPO with its wide membership. See also Steinberg,
supra note 64, at 349.
[66] David Henderson, THE MAI AFFAIR: A STORY AND ITS LESSONS (1999).
[67] See supra notes 48–50 and accompanying text.

bilateral negotiations of essentially similar contracts, the powerful states succeeded in setting new global standards. The opposition to the MAI crumbled once the developing countries were forced to negotiate separately.[68]

Finally, the choice to pursue the mega-regional track (the TPP, the TTIP, and TISA) rather than the multilateral one has been attributed to the failure of the Doha Round. Whether intended or not, the simultaneous negotiations reduced the bargaining power of America's partners. The EU, otherwise almost an equal power to the United States in bilateral negotiations, was undercut by the parallel TPP track.[69] European economists have noted that the very existence of the TPP talks has put considerable pressure on the EU to negotiate the TTIP. They have expressed the immediate worry that the TPP might discriminate against European firms,[70] as well as the more long term concern that "the rules enshrined in the TPP could possibly be held as a model to be emulated" in future agreements.[71]

2.4.5   Turning to Informal International Law and Informal Institutions

The communications revolution added urgency to the powerful states' quest for flexibility to cope with the rapidly changing policy environment, pushing them to coordinate more closely and effectively with each other. The availability of and the need for communications bring

---

[68] *See* Salacuse & Sullivan, *supra* note 48, at 75–78 (describing the dramatic increase in BITs signed between developed and developing states during the late 1990s and the motivations of both groups of states for concluding them); Zachary Elkins, Andrew T. Guzman & Beth Simmons, *Competing for Capital: The Diffusion of Bilateral Investment Treaties, 1960–2000*, U. Ill. L. Rev. 265 (2008), *available at* http://ssrn.com/abstract=1001169 (arguing that the spread of BITs is driven by international competition among potential host countries–typically developing countries–for foreign direct investment).

[69] Xinyuan Dai, *Who Defines the Rules of the Game in East Asia? The Trans-Pacific Partnership and the Strategic Use of International Institutions*, 15 Int'l Relations of the Asia-Pacific 1, 8 (2014) (arguing that "in a region where no intraregional institution binds all regional powers, it is easier to imagine new institutions [like the TPP] that attempt to reshape political and economic geography and rewrite regional governance structure.")

[70] Patrick Messerlin, *The Much Needed EU Pivoting to East Asia*, 10 Asia Pacific J. EU Stud. 9 (2012), *available at* http://gem.sciences-po.fr/content/publications/pdf/Messerlin_EU-Pivot112012.pdf ("[t]he main risk of discrimination against EU firms comes, in the short and medium term, from the Transpacific Partnership.").

[71] Billy A. Melo Araujo, *Regulating Services through Trade Agreements – A Comparative Analysis of Regulatory Disciplines Included in EU and US Free Trade Agreements*, 6 Trade L. & Dev. 393 (2014).

diverse parts of national bureaucracies into direct contact with their foreign counterparts on an almost daily basis, leading to an increasing reliance on informal arrangements to facilitate coordination without subjecting them to long-term commitments and rigid rules that could constrain them in the future.[72] As a result, there is a growing temptation to evade the formal requirements of international treaty making (and of the domestic law that requires formal ratification of treaties) and to operate, instead, outside the boundaries of international law. This is apparent in the deliberate tendency on the part of governments of powerful states to avoid both international legal claims and multilateral agreements.

We see this aversion to formal legal processes and institutions explicitly expressed in a 2000 directive of the German federal government instructing all ministries to avoid international obligations as much as possible. Negotiators, the directive stipulated, should explore alternatives to formal international undertakings before committing to such.[73] Similarly, in 2006, the National Security Strategy of the United States stated that one of its three priorities in working with its allies was the "Establish[ment of] results-oriented partnerships."[74] The document states that "[t]hese partnerships emphasize international cooperation, not international bureaucracy. They rely on voluntary adherence rather than binding treaties. They are oriented towards action and results rather than legislation or

---

[72] On the turn to informality, see Nico Krisch, *The Decay of Consent: International Law in an Age of Global Public Goods*, 108 AM. J. INT'L L. 1 (2014); Joost Pauwelyn, Ramses A. Wessel and Jan Wouters, *When Structures Become Shackles: Stagnation and Dynamics in International Lawmaking* 25 EJIL 733 (2014).

[73] *See* DIE BUNDESREGIERUNG, GEMEINSAME GESCHÄFTSORDNUNG DER BUNDESMINISTERIEN § 72(1), (Joint Rules of Procedure of the Federal Ministries) (2006): "Vor der Ausarbeitung und dem Abschluss völkerrechtlicher Übereinkünfte (Staatsverträge, Übereinkommen, Regierungsabkommen, Ressortabkommen, Noten- und Briefwechsel) hat das federführende Bundesministerium stets zu prüfen, ob eine völkervertragliche Regelung unabweisbar ist oder ob der verfolgte Zweck auch mit anderen Mitteln erreicht werden kann, insbesondere auch mit Absprachen unterhalb der Schwelle einer völkerrechtlichen Übereinkunft." [Before the planning and the conclusion of international agreements (international treaties, agreements, interministerial or inter-agency agreements, notes and exchanges of letters) the responsible federal ministry must always inquire whether the conclusion of the international undertaking is indeed required, or whether the same goal may also be attained through other means, especially through understandings which are below the threshold of an international agreement.] *available at* www.bmi.bund.de/cae/servlet/contentblob/150474/publicationFile/13399/Moderner_Staat_-_Moderne_Id_23340_de.pdf. (translated by the authors).

[74] Nat'l Sec. Council, THE NATIONAL SECURITY STRATEGY OF THE UNITED STATES (2006).

rule-making."[75] The same document also extols the so-called coalitions of the willing, suggesting that "[e]xisting international institutions have a role to play, but in many cases coalitions of the willing may be able to respond more quickly and creatively, at least in the short term."[76] President Obama's 2010 U.S. National Security Strategy refers to the "shortcomings of international institutions that were developed to deal with the challenges of an earlier time" and undertakes "to spur and harness a new diversity of instruments, alliances, and institutions."[77]

Bureaucrats in other relatively strong and affluent nations have suggested similar expectations, though stopping short of issuing formal directives. In 2011 the Canadian government expressed its preference that "if a matter is of a routine or technical nature, or appears to fall entirely within the existing mandate and responsibility of a department or agency, and if it does not contain substantive matter which should be legally binding in public international law, it is often preferable to deal with the matter through the use of a non–legally binding instrument."[78] Anthony Aust, a former legal adviser at the British Foreign Office, reported in 2000 that "[b]ecause the use of MOUs is now so wide-spread, some government officials may see the MOU as the more usual form, a treaty being used only when it cannot be avoided. The very word 'treaty' may conjure up the fearsome formalities of diplomacy."[79]

By resorting to informal mechanisms to coordinate their policies, rather than treaties that are subject to domestic ratification processes, the stronger powers also prevent their own citizens (as well as those in other countries) from having the opportunity to voice their opinions during the processes of domestic ratification and incorporation.

At least four types of alternatives to formal international law and institutions have crystallized. First, there are informal government-to-

---

[75] This new term–partnerships–was absent in the 2002 NSS statement. It connotes something more stable than the older term "coalitions of the willing" (which appears only once, in reference to the Tsunami aid) and less than a formal institution. As in: "To confront the threat of a possible pandemic, the Administration took the lead in creating the International Partnership on Avian and Pandemic Influenza, a new global partnership of states committed to effective surveillance and preparedness that will help to detect and respond quickly to any outbreaks of the disease." *Id.*, at 48.

[76] *Id.* at 48.

[77] Nat'l Sec. Council, THE NATIONAL SECURITY STRATEGY OF THE UNITED STATES, 3, 46 (2010).

[78] *Policy on Tabling of Treaties in* Parliament, Global Affairs Canada, Annex C (2011), *available at* www.treaty-accord.gc.ca/procedures.aspx (last visited Jul. 23, 2016).

[79] Anthony Aust, MODERN TREATY LAW AND PRACTICE 26 (2000).

government coordination efforts in most if not all spheres of activity of contemporary governmental action, including by many regulatory agencies in the realms of financial regulation, central banking, antitrust regulation, securities regulation, criminal enforcement, nonproliferation of WMD, combating terrorism, and environmental protection. All of these government bodies coordinate, indeed even harmonize, their activities through informal consultations in informal venues and implement them through their authority under their respective domestic laws. Second, there are nonbinding institutions that enable governments that have common interests to coordinate vis-à-vis other states (prevalent in the context of nonproliferation of weapons, such as most recently the Financial Action Task Force [FATF][80] and the Proliferation Security Initiative [PSI]).[81] Third are joint ventures between governments and private actors, as in the case of the Global Fund to Fight AIDS, Tuberculosis, and Malaria, an entity that is constituted as an independent Swiss foundation.[82] Another example is the International Conference on the Harmonization of Technical Requirements for Registration of Pharmaceuticals for Human Use (ICH), which is a public/private institution set up to harmonize technical requirements for ensuring the quality, efficacy, and safety of drugs.[83] The final type of informal global regulation is done through private standard-setting bodies that operate in areas where governments have been reluctant to act or have simply preferred to let private actors perform such tasks, ranging from letters of credit and insurance to facilitation of transnational trade, credit rating, safety standards, accounting standards, environmental protection, resource management, food safety, and even core labor rights for developing countries.[84]

---

[80] Financial Action Task Force (FATF), www.fatf-gafi.org/ (last visited Aug. 25, 2016); On the FATF and other informal global financial systems see Chris Brummer, SOFT LAW AND THE GLOBAL FINANCIAL SYSTEM: RULE MAKING IN THE 21ST CENTURY (2012).

[81] Bureau of Nonproliferation's webpage on the Proliferation Security Initiative www.state .gov/t/isn/c10390.htm (last visited Aug. 25, 2016); See also Michael Byers Policing the High Seas: The Proliferation Security Initiative, 98 AM. J. INT'L L. 526 (2004).

[82] The Global Fund, www.theglobalfund.org/en/.

[83] On the ICH see Ayelet Berman, The Role of Domestic Administrative Law in the Accountability of IN-LAW: The Case of the ICH, in INFORMAL INTERNATIONAL LAWMAKING 468 (Joost Pauwelyn, Ramses A. Wessel, Jan Wouters, eds., 2012).

[84] On these alternatives, see Slaughter, supra note 2; Eyal Benvenisti, "Coalitions of the Willing" and the Evolution of Informal International Law, in "COALITIONS OF THE WILLING"–AVANTGARDE OR THREAT? 1 (C. Calliess, G. Nolte & T. Stoll eds., 2008). For elaboration on these structures see Benvenisti, supra note 21, at 34–48.

Intergovernmental action among powerful states can be based on their individual authority under their respective domestic laws or on relegating authority to private actors. The coordinated practices that emerge do not betray *opinio juris* (the belief that a certain act is grounded in a legal obligation) and hence cannot serve as evidence for an emerging customary law that binds the states; in fact, the participating governments emphasize the opposite, namely, their self-interest and lack of legal commitment. Outsiders to these clubs, the uninvited governments, inevitably adapt to these practices and rules not because they are formally bound to do so but because incentives are tacitly attached to their observance and disincentives are attached to their nonobservance. Over time, these informal rules modify the expectations of other actors and the range of possible actions open to them in the same ways that are often associated with soft law, but the character of operation is far less subtle. Their requirements are usually unambiguous and the costs of ignoring them all too tangible.

Transnational private regulation has potential geopolitical implications that further diminish the bargaining power of developing countries. For example, private standard setting in the food safety context concentrates power in the hands of large Northern retailers[85] and creates an imbalance between them and producers, who are mainly in the South.[86] Developed countries refuse to regard these private standards as barriers to trade, while Southern countries express concerns about them as the North's devious way of evading WTO obligations.[87] Such suspicions are not allayed by the fact that the modest amount of positive evidence that the developed state defenders of TPRs have marshaled in defense of their democratizing effects often collapses under close scrutiny. As David Vogel has observed, for example: "[a]dvocates of civil regulations claim that, by providing nonbusiness constituencies with new political and market mechanisms to affect business decisions, these regulations can

---

[85] Eyal Benvenisti & George W. Downs, *National Courts and Transnational Private Regulation*, in ENFORCEMENT OF TRANSNATIONAL REGULATION: ENSURING COMPLIANCE IN A GLOBAL WORLD 131 (Fabrizio Cafaggi ed., 2012) [hereinafter Benvenisti & Downs, *National Courts*]; Eyal Benvenisti, Coalitions of the Willing, INFORMAL INTERNATIONAL LAWMAKING (Joost Pauwelyn, Ramses Wessel & Jan Wouters eds., 2012)).

[86] Benvenisti & Downs, *National Courts, id.*; G. Chia-Hui Lee, *Private Food Standards and Their Impacts on Developing Countries*, European Commission – DG Trade Unit G2 Paper (2006).

[87] *See* Axel Marks et al., PRIVATE STANDARDS AND GLOBAL GOVERNANCE: ECONOMIC, LEGAL AND POLITICAL PERSPECTIVES (2012).

help address the democratic deficit in global governance. But virtually all these nonbusiness constituencies are located in developed countries."[88]

2.5   Countervailing Efforts to Reduce the Fragmentation of International Institutions

Like citizens living under an authoritarian regime that controls the media and lacks representative institutions, weaker states are forced to resort to strategies and tactics that are more reactive and opportunistic than those employed by more powerful states. Because the odds that any given strategy will fail are relatively high, weaker states tend to employ a number of them simultaneously and are constantly revising them as the situation changes. Consequently, their tactics are less likely to succeed than are those employed by more powerful states.

One strategy employed by weaker states is a counterpart to the regime switching of stronger states. Rather than promote policies in venues that are currently the focus of powerful state attention, they turn to preexisting ones that developed states have largely abandoned but whose decisions they remain formally committed to following. The fact that they are no longer competing directly with stronger states reduces the level of cooperation that they must engage in to make their collective presence felt, and it makes it easier for them to cultivate agency bureaucrats who may be nervous that the "flight" of the developed states will irreparably damage the prestige of their organization.

Laurence Helfer has described how developing states, looking to minimize the adverse consequences to them of the Trade-Related Aspects of Intellectual Property Rights agreement, have employed this tactic in connection with a number of preexisting institutions, including the Convention on Biological Diversity, the World Intellectual Property Organization, and the World Health Organization.[89] More generally, the developing countries have turned to the UN and its subsidiary bodies for assistance. Although the law that then emerges from these institutions typically has little binding force, it can engender claims about "soft law" that subsequently shape the "evolutionary" interpretation of treaty obligations and international law in general. One can take strong encouragement for the continuation of such efforts from outcomes such as the

---

[88] David Vogel, *Private Global Business Regulation*, 11 ANN. REV. POL. SCI. 261, 276 (2008).
[89] Laurence R. Helfer, *Regime Shifting: The TRIPs Agreement and New Dynamics of International Intellectual Property Lawmaking*, 29 YALE J. INT'L L. 1, 27–28, 51–52 (2004).

WTO's Appellate Body (AB) decision in the *Shrimp/Turtle* case, which held that the GATT agreement had to be interpreted "in the light of contemporary concerns of the community of nations" reflected in non-GATT-related treaties and even in nonbinding declarations.[90]

Weaker states also employ a strategy resembling "divide and conquer," such as the tactic of trying to exploit temporary divisions that occasionally crop up among the core group of powerful states. The negotiations of the UNCLOS, GATT, and the Additional Protocols of the Geneva Conventions[91] demonstrate the ability of developing countries to exploit East/West competition. One of the most significant successes of this strategy was the recognition under UNCLOS that the deep-ocean resources are the "common heritage of mankind" and that in principle these resources should benefit all states.[92] Like other such cases, this achievement depended on the existence of an atypical, even unique, negotiating environment where the regular divisions between states collapsed and where the developing countries could exploit East/West Cold War tensions.[93] Several years later, and under similarly idiosyncratic conditions, there emerged at the UNESCO Convention on Cultural

---

[90] Appellate Body Report, *United States–Import Prohibition of Certain Shrimp and Shrimp Products*, STET 129–30, WT/DS58/AB/R (Oct. 8, 1998).

[91] On the negotiations leading up to the Law of the Sea Convention, see William Wertenbaker, *The Law of the Sea-I*, THE NEW YORKER, Aug. 1, 1983, at 38 [hereinafter Wertenbaker, *The Law of the Sea-I*], and William Wertenbaker, *The Law of the Sea-II*, THE NEW YORKER, Aug. 8, 1983, at 57. *See also supra* notes 60–62 and accompanying text. On the WTO negotiations, see *supra* notes 63–64 and accompanying text. On the success of the developing countries during the drafting of the 1977 Additional Protocols (and the subsequent reinterpretation of the same norms by international courts), see Allison Marston Danner, *When Courts Make Law: How the International Criminal Tribunals Recast the Laws of War*, 59 VAND. L. REV. 1, 13–17, 24–33 (2006).

[92] Surabhi Ranganathan, STRATEGICALLY CREATED TREATY CONFLICTS AND THE POLITICS OF INTERNATIONAL LAW (2014).

[93] *See* Wertenbaker, *The Law of the Sea-I, supra* note 91, at 49–54 (describing the coordination during the negotiations of UNCLOS among the United States and the Soviet Union who became members of the informal and secretive so-called "Group of Five"). According to Wertenbaker, both superpowers wished to keep their coordination secret (each side being concerned with criticism from its allies). *See id.* at 50. This might explain why they did not at that time exit the UNCLOS to form together a new venue for negotiations. Another explanation might be that the Cold War competition between the United States and the Soviet Union for the allegiance of developing states put the two superpowers in a Prisoners' Dilemma in connection with the treaty. Although each would have been better off cooperating with the other to exit the agreement and create one that they jointly preferred, both were fearful that the other would back out of such a scheme at the last minute in order to appear to be the champion of the developing states and score a major political victory. As a result, both states remained in the treaty.

Diversity a coalition of developing governments and developed states headed by Canada and France that set the goal of impeding the spread of American culture.[94] The BRICS (Brazil, Russia, India, China, and South Africa) have tried to set up their own institutions as a counterpoint to Western-dominated institutions, but experts anticipate that, given the differences among the five members, the prospects for successful community building will remain elusive.[95]

Developing democratic states also employ their own unique brand of soft-balancing strategies designed to produce a gradual shift in practices and eventually outcomes that will benefit weaker states over the long run. But these strategies are also politically unthreatening and even attractive to powerful states because they embody principles that the powerful states have publicly embraced and that would be costly to renounce. For example, weaker states might advocate that a given international institution be designed to reflect the same overarching principles, structures, and procedures that are embodied in the domestic institutions of democratic states. It is far more difficult for powerful states to object to the institutionalization of such widely held ideals as equality, democracy, and procedural due process than to the adoption of specific reforms such as reduced agricultural subsidies.[96]

The two most prominent and successful of these strategies, which are closely interrelated, involve pushing for more inclusive and representative personnel policies on the part of international institutions and judiciaries and for an expansion of their policy-making roles.[97] The fruits of the first strategy are evident in the move to make the

---

[94] U.N. Educ., Sci., & Cultural Org. [UNESCO], *Convention on the Protection and Promotion of the Diversity of Cultural Expressions*, U.N. Doc. CLT-2005/Convention Diversite-Cult Rev. (Oct. 20, 2005), http://unesdoc.unesco.org/images/0014/001429/142919e.pdf; *see also* Joost Pauwelyn, *The UNESCO Convention on Cultural Diversity, and the WTO Diversity in International Law-Making*, AM. Soc'y INT'L L. INSIGHT, Nov. 15, 2005, www.asil.org/insights/2005/11/insights051115.html.

[95] Christian Brutsch and Mihaela Papa, *Deconstructing the BRICS: Bargaining Coalition, Imagined Community, or Geopolitical Fad?* 6 CHINESE J. INT'L POL. 299 (2013).

[96] The study of the possibilities for structuring the decision-making processes in international institutions–the project on global administrative law–reflects and assesses such efforts. *See* Benedict Kingsbury, Nico Krisch & Richard B. Stewart, *The Emergence of Global Administrative Law*, 68 LAW & CONTEMP. PROBS. 15, 15–18 (2005).

[97] *See* Eric Posner & Miguel de Figueiredo, *Is the International Court of Justice Biased?* (U. Chicago L. & Econ., Olin Working Paper No. 234), *available at* http://ssrn.com/abstract=64258 (discussing evidence that judges in the ICJ have favored the states that appoint them, the states whose wealth level was close to that of the judges' own states, the states whose political system was similar to that of the judges' own states, and the states whose culture (language and religion) was similar to that of the judges' own states).

composition of multimember international tribunals such as the International Court of Justice (ICJ) and the WTO Appellate Body broadly representative of the membership of the institutions. It is widely perceived that the ICJ "reflects complex cleavages: north versus south; east versus west; wealthy versus poor; and so forth."[98] The panelists in the WTO panels also reflect different nationalities and interests. The 585 panelists recruited between 1995 and 2015 included 251 from seven countries: New Zealand, Australia, Switzerland, Canada, Brazil, Chile, and South Africa. Because the United States and the EU tend to be the biggest users of the WTO dispute-settlement system, and given the rule that citizens of parties to disputes could serve as panelists in such disputes only with the agreement of the parties, panelists tend to come from other countries, and only 14 positions were taken by US citizens, and 73 positions were held by citizens of countries who were EU members in 2015.[99] Of the seven members of the WTO's Appellate Body, the United States and the EU have had one national each. The other five members came from five OECD countries (Japan, New Zealand, Australia, Mexico, and South Korea) and eight non-OECD countries (Egypt, the Philippines, China, India, Uruguay, South Africa, Brazil, and Mauritius). Arguably, this helps explain why the influence of weaker states in international institutions that have central bureaucracies and tribunals, while still small in proportion to their number and populations, has been growing in recent years, and it attests to the soft-balancing strategies mentioned earlier.[100]

Weaker states are aware that even when bureaucrats and judges are drawn from developing states, they will bring their own personal and professional interests to bear. These can range from a personal or professional commitment to promoting greater equality in the international system to narrower interests such as expanding the influence of the

---

[98] *See* Eric A. Posner, *The Decline of the International Court of Justice* 23 (U. Chicago L. & Econ., Olin Working Paper No. 233, 2004), *available at* www.law.uchicago.edu/files/files/233.eap_.icj_.pdf.

[99] Kara Leitner & Simon Lester, *WTO Dispute Settlement 1995–2015 – A Statistical Analysis*, 19 J. INT'L ECON. L. 289, 300 (2016).

[100] WTO Appellate Body Members, www.wto.org/english/tratop_e/dispu_e/ab_members_descrp_e.htm. These informal quotas are not determined by the text of the agreement, which states that "[t]he Appellate Body membership shall be broadly representative of membership in the WTO." Understanding on Rules and Procedures Governing the Settlement of Disputes, Apr. 15, 1994, Marrakesh Agreement Establishing the World Trade Organization, Annex 2, 33 I.L.M. 1125, 1236 art. 17(3), *available at* www.wto.org/english/docs_e/legal_e/28-dsu.doc.

institutions that they represent and enhancing their own careers. Weaker states have learned, however, that in the pursuit of such goals these agents will often act in ways that erode the discretion of powerful states.

Beyond the personal background of the bureaucrats and judges, there are systemic factors that prompt defragmentation efforts. Weaker states–particularly democratic weaker states–recognize that international bureaucrats and judges have a vested interest in rationalizing their environments and that this tendency should work to their benefit over time. By creating generalizable principles and by privileging consistency and precedent, these actors not only reduce their own decision costs and increase their efficiency but they also reduce the coordination costs of weaker states by reducing the level of fragmentation. This process of rationalization provides weaker states with a stable hierarchy of claims that they can then employ in a variety of venues, and it increases the likelihood that a victory in one particular venue will have wide-ranging ramifications.

As we shall see in Chapter 4, weaker states know that international bureaucrats and judges will tend to support their claims on the grounds that any erosion in the hegemony of the powerful developed states increases their own discretion and authority. The interests of bureaucrats and judges are best served when they operate in a multipolar environment in which they are viewed as a critical part of any winning coalition, rather than merely as the agent of the great powers. Supporting the claims of weaker states is a strategy that promotes the emergence of such multi-polarity even if it does not guarantee it. This phenomenon has been observed in national legal systems, where the courts systematically supported the weaker political branch of government in its conflicts with the relatively stronger branch in order to enhance their own prestige.[101]

Finally, while the weak states' defragmentation efforts have demonstrated modest success, the more effective response to the democratic deficits of fragmentation came with the increased demand by various civil society groups for transparency, participation, and other accountability mechanisms within international bodies.[102] Although direct voice

---

[101] Nicos C. Alivizatos, *Judges as Veto Players, in* PARLIAMENTS AND MAJORITY RULE IN WESTERN EUROPE 566 (Herbert Doering ed., 1995) (suggesting that divisions between the political branches strengthen the courts); Eyal Benvenisti, *Party Primaries as Collective Action with Constitutional Ramifications: Israel as a Case Study,* 3 THEORETICAL INQUIRIES L. 175 (2002) (suggesting that the Israeli Supreme Court was supporting the legislature in its relationship with the executive).
[102] *See* Benvenisti, *supra* note 21.

was still acutely missing, these marginalized actors could benefit at least indirectly from more disciplined and public decision-making processes within international institutions and from review of their decisions.

The countervailing efforts by weaker states reflect their acknowledgment of the adverse consequences of an international legal regime that is becoming increasingly arbitrary and even biased against them. Ultimately, weaker states are almost defenseless against the proliferation of the fragmentation strategy, including the tendency of international institutions to outsource enforcement to ad hoc "coalitions of the willing." These coalitions lend legitimacy to the resort to coercion on the part of wealthier and more powerful states at the expense of the poorer and weaker ones, a situation that seems likely to further increase frustration on the part of the weaker states.

Over time, these effects of fragmentation threaten to erode the reputation of international law as a system striving to ensure normative integrity and evenhandedness. The irony, unfortunately, is that if this fragmentation leads weaker states to stop viewing international law as a source of hope, they are likely to be the losers in the long run. As potentially the most important "coordination good"[103] available to weaker states, international law is one of the few tools that, as the German law professor August Wilhelm Heffter suggested in 1855, provides an association of unequal states with the opportunity to collectively resist the "supremacy of one."[104]

2.6 Conclusion: The Deeper, Domestic Roots of Fragmentation

International legal theorists have tended to view fragmentation as either a harmless by-product of broad social forces or as the embodiment of a new pluralist legal order that better represents the diversity of global interests than did the postwar order that preceded it. We have argued, by contrast, that the functional specialization and atomistic design of fragmentation are, at least in part, the products of a calculated effort on the part of powerful states to protect their dominance and discretion by creating a system that only they have the capacity to alter. Fragmentation helps them accomplish these goals by making it difficult for weaker states to create coalitions through cross-issue logrolling and by dramatically

---

[103] *See* Bueno de Mesquita & Downs, *supra* note 28.
[104] August Wilhelm Heffter, *Das Europaische Volkerrecht der Gegenwart* 7 (3d edn., Berlin, E.H. Schroeder, 1855) (translated by the authors).

increasing the transaction costs that international bureaucrats and judges face in trying to rationalize the international system or to engage in bottom-up constitution building. The turn to informal mechanisms erodes the voice of domestic constituencies to resist governmental policies.

The strategies used by powerful states to promote fragmentation are familiar and well developed. Regimes are constructed out of narrow, functionally based agreements that are negotiated in separate, onetime settings. Regulatory responsibility is virtually never assigned to ongoing, deliberative bodies that are systematically representative, and whenever possible, significant, independent policy-making authority is withheld from those bureaucracies or judiciaries whose creation cannot be avoided. When these strategies fail to accomplish their goal and weaker states or agents of international institutions appear to be gaining enough control to threaten their interests, powerful states switch to a competing institution or venue.

The "pluralism" produced by this fragmentation is less representative, less diverse, and less generative than that term normally implies. With only a few exceptions, the design and operation of the resulting international legal order reflect the interests of only a handful of developed states and their internal constituencies, and they are hostile to redistribution. Instead of operating to bring about democratization in a more decentralized way, as many had hoped, the resulting order has effectively undermined any movement toward it.[105]

In the preceding sections, we have argued that the ability of weaker states to cooperate in order to stay or reverse the fragmentation process is undermined by multiple factors: the substantial agenda-setting power of the dominant states, the high transaction costs that fragmentation has already exacted, and the wide diversity among weaker states with respect to their policy preferences. Important sources of this diversity that we have not yet discussed are domestic factors that undermine coordination among weaker states. An important factor contributing to the division among weaker states is whether the government is democratic or not. Apart from the area of defense spending, where resources are often used to maintain internal rather than external security, nondemocratic regimes in developing states also generally invest a much lower portion

---

[105] United Nations Millennium Declaration, G.A. Res. 55/2, at 4, U.N. GAOR, 55th Sess., Supp. No. 49, U.N. Doc. A/55/49 (Sept. 9, 2000), *available at* www.ohchr.org/english/law/millennium.htm. In this declaration the state parties also resolve "[t]o work collectively for more inclusive political processes, allowing genuine participation by all citizens in all our countries." *Id.* at ¶ 25.

of tax revenue than their democratic counterparts in the provision of public goods such as education and healthcare.[106] Bueno de Mesquita *et al.* argue that this is the case because the power base of nondemocratic incumbents consists of small, economically privileged, and/or militarily powerful elite groups that stand to benefit far more from receiving special government subsidies, contracts, and tax privileges than they would from the increased provision of general public goods.[107] This same logic suggests that with the exception of free trade, which often disproportionately benefits elites, autocratic developing states will also be less interested than their democratic counterparts in supporting or even influencing those international institutions that provide global public goods such as peacekeeping, public health services, or environmental regulation.

These differences in the priorities of democratic versus nondemocratic small states, on top of their lack of agenda-setting power, leave the group of mostly democratic developing states and the NGOs that support them at a distinct strategic disadvantage in their attempts to expand their policy-making role in international institutions. But even those democratic states often find it difficult to coordinate among themselves. This is due to the unequal political power of domestic interest groups that can benefit from fragmentation and in fact take an active role in promoting it. In fact, to fully understand the motivations for fragmentation and its pernicious effects on the domestic distribution of political and economic power, it is necessary to delve into the domestic sources of global fragmentation, the topic of Chapter 3.

---

[106] *See* Bueno de Mesquita et al., *supra* note 27, at 174–213.   [107] *Id.* at 8, 174–213, 279.

3

The Impact of Domestic Politics on Global Fragmentation

The fragmentation of the international legal space and the plurality of global governance bodies have most obviously benefited the small group of powerful Northern states. If we look behind the veil of state sovereignty, however, we see that fragmentation operated above all to secure the interests of powerful interest groups within those states, as the emerging global space insulated and thus freed them from otherwise constraining domestic regulation and scrutiny. These actors had little appetite for robust accountability mechanisms within global institutions that could render the global bodies inconveniently accountable to the wider publics. For these groups, international law has always provided both opportunity and cover. Treaties are negotiated by state executives, traditionally with little domestic scrutiny by the other political branches. And those treaties, once ratified, bind future generations of voters, leaving them with limited ability to unilaterally terminate the treaty. Moreover, the treaty text usually provides easy escape clauses for these groups, and, in addition, the domestic courts have tended to grant their executive branches wide discretion in interpreting the texts.[1] The fragmentation of the global legal space, in freeing these narrow interests from the constraints of adverse regulation and from accountability, has afforded them new opportunities to reap benefits. This chapter elaborates on the motivations of domestic interests and their contributions to the evolution of the fragmented and unaccountable global regulatory space.

3.1 Domestic Actors in a Transnational Economic and Legal Space

Political economists long ago made the convincing case that state institutions provide an effective means for certain domestic interest groups to exploit less organized domestic groups in the competitive market for

---

[1] George W. Downs & David M. Rocke, *Optimal Imperfection?* (1995).

political goods (such as taxes, subsidies, and favorable market regulation).[2] In this market, better organized groups, namely, those composed of a relatively smaller number of individuals, can outbid larger groups of diffuse constituencies because the former realize higher per capita benefits from cooperation with fellow group members and incur lower costs in monitoring and sanctioning free riders.[3] Hence, other things being equal, smaller groups, such as producers and employers, will obtain collective goods more efficiently than larger groups of consumers or employees, thereby securing a disproportionate share of the aggregate social welfare while externalizing part of their production costs to the larger groups.[4]

These greater organizational capabilities also provide small groups with a competitive edge in obtaining and assessing information on policies.[5] More effective monitoring of the government prompts politicians and bureaucrats to bias policy in favor of those who can appreciate their efforts. The larger body of ill-informed voters either hardly notices its relative loss or attributes the loss to random factors.[6] Thus, the information rationale suggests that small-group policy bias stems not

---

[2] *See* George J. Stigler, *The Theory of Economic Regulation*, 2 BELL J. ECON. & MGMT. SCI. 3 (1971).

[3] As a result, the political influence of groups is inversely related to their size. *See* Mancur Olson, THE LOGIC OF COLLECTIVE ACTION 22–36 (1965). Ethnic, national, racial, and indigenous minorities are usually excluded from this definition of small groups. Although numerically inferior relative to the larger community, their organizational costs may be relatively higher than those of the majority. But there may be political circumstances in which they in fact obtain political influence that outweighs their relative size. *See* Bruce A. Ackerman, *Beyond Carolene Products*, 98 HARV. L. REV. 713 (1985) (suggesting that not all minorities are "discrete and insular").

[4] This does not mean that small groups will achieve optimal amounts of a potential collective good. Collective losses still result from the unequal incentive of individuals within that group to contribute to the collective effort (determined by the relative stake each individual has in the collective pie). But it does suggest that "the larger the group, the farther it will fall short of providing an optimal amount of a collective good." Olson, *supra* note 3, at 35.

[5] For an explanation of information as a collective good, see Susanne Lohmann, *An Information Rationale for the Power of Special Interests*, 92 AM. POL. SCI. REV. 809 (1998); *See also* Michael D. Rosenbaum, *Domestic Bureaucracies and the International Trade Regime: The Law and Economics of Administrative Law and Administratively-Imposed Trade Barriers*, 42 TEX. INT'L L.J. 241 (2006) (arguing that administrative procedures that lower the costs of access to information shift power over policy-making from more organized to less organized groups).

[6] In developed countries, for example, policies are biased in favor of the relatively few farmers, whereas in developing countries the large agricultural sector is heavily taxed. *See* Gary S. Becker, *A Theory of Competition among Pressure Groups for Political Influence*, 98 Q. J. ECON. 371, 385 (1983).

only from more effective lobbying but also from more efficient monitoring of policies once they are adopted.[7] It also accounts for the growing influence of NGOs, which advance the cause of larger groups by promoting, for example, human rights or protection of the environment. The information they gather and disseminate improves the effectiveness of monitoring bodies, such as the legislature, and reduces the incentive to adopt policies that are biased against the larger groups.[8]

This observation can also be tested historically. As Mancur Olson elaborates in *The Rise and Decline of Nations*, because smaller groups could organize themselves more quickly within the nascent Westphalian system of sovereign states, they were able to use the states as instruments for obtaining a disproportionate share of resources for themselves.[9] Indeed, the political institutions of the emerging nations have reflected just such a skewed power relationship between the smaller and larger groups. Constitutions insulated the smaller groups' share from majority vote[10] without restricting the opportunities for small groups to influence lawmakers.[11] Politicians, whose immediate interest is election or reelection, broker public goods in exchange for campaign contributions or other political support (in nondemocratic regimes) or, too often, personal financial gain.

To the extent that bureaucrats and judges proved more resistant to interest-group capture, or if voters have managed to overcome barriers to cooperation, the small groups' ultimate retreat has been international

---

[7] *See* Lohmann, *supra* note 5, at 812.

[8] *See* Helen V. Milner, INTERESTS, INSTITUTIONS, AND INFORMATION 247–48 (1997).

[9] Mancur Olson, THE RISE AND DECLINE OF NATIONS ch. 3 (1982).

[10] Landowners were particularly concerned that a landless majority would use its numerical superiority to redistribute property. *See* THE FEDERALIST No. 10 (James Madison) (discussing property ownership as a basis for conflict of interests among voters and legislators). The installation of a complex and diversified system of government, supermajority amendment requirements, and judicial review to protect constitutional rights such as the right to property responded to such concerns. *see id.*; THE FEDERALIST No. 51 (Alexander Hamilton or James Madison) (discussing the political structures for curbing such conflict of interests), No. 78 (Alexander Hamilton) (explaining the rationale of judicial review); *see also* William M. Landes & Richard A. Posner, *The Independent Judiciary in an Interest-Group Perspective*, 18 *J.L. & ECON.* 875 (1975) (presenting constitutional guarantees as securing legislative deals among diverse interest groups).

[11] Marx, of course, made a stronger claim–namely, that small groups, the bourgeoisie, invented the state system to exploit the masses. For Marxist-oriented historiography of the emergence (and possible demise) of the nation-state that corroborates the Olsonian thesis, see generally Ernest Gellner, NATIONS AND NATIONALISM (1983); Eric J. Hobsbawm, NATIONS AND NATIONALISM SINCE 1780 (2nd edn. 1992).

law. History shows that those small groups realized early on the benefits accruing from global cooperation under the auspices of international law. Briefly stated: the international legal realm, dominated by state executives who enjoyed unfettered discretion in the sphere dubbed "foreign affairs," proved particularly vulnerable to domestic capture. The bureaucrats and the judges hesitated to formulate an independent view of the "national interest," deferring instead to the vision of the state executive. Courts in all jurisdictions have developed an array of doctrines–such as the political question doctrine, justiciability, and act of state–to conceal their role as effective keepers of the rule of law in the international arena.[12]

This strong judicial deference hints at the strategy developed by small groups to provide themselves with cover from the vagaries of the domestic democratic vote. Whereas no constitution is beyond legislative interpretation and, ultimately, popular amendment to the detriment of small groups,[13] international law and the court's deference in the international arena ensured the continued domination by small-group of policy-making.[14] When larger constituencies have ultimately succeeded in mobilizing and imposing restrictions, such as antitrust regulations and higher labor standards, on producers and employers, the latter have reacted by shifting their activities to foreign markets and societies and to international law and institutions as their regulators.[15]

The next section shows how the laissez-faire nature of international law continues to enable smaller groups to evade national regulations and exploit the global commons. In fact, these smaller groups have had an even greater influence on the development of international law than on the development of domestic law, primarily because information gathering and assessment costs are much higher in the international arena. Since antiquity, international negotiations have always sought to operate in relative secrecy, a practice reinforced by public and judicial approval of a Hobbesian view of sovereign states as struggling to survive in an

---

[12] *See infra* Chapter 5 Section 5.1.

[13] Thus, Landes and Posner's suggestion that constitutional guarantees were the tools to secure the interests of the smaller interest groups, notably their property rights, presented only part of the institutional guarantees of small-group interests–arguably the less significant part. *See supra* note 10.

[14] *See* Albert O. Hirschman, EXIT, VOICE AND LOYALTY (1970); *cf.* Richard A. Epstein, *Exit Rights Under Federalism*, 55 LAW & CONTEMP. PROBS. 147 (1992) (discussing exit as a check on states' power in a federal system).

[15] International law did so through the creation of international organizations (IOs), which are immune to national regulation. *See infra* text accompanying notes 34–37.

anarchic and intimidating global environment. Shielded from public scrutiny, small groups (producers, importers, and so on) often exercise disproportionate influence on the executive branch's conduct of external affairs. The edge enjoyed by small groups can be traced historically by following the development of international norms. The following section examines the actual influence these groups have had on the formulation of policies in several areas of law.

3.2   How Domestic Actors Shape International Law

3.2.1   Early Cases

Smaller groups have been successful in influencing international nego-tiations and international law since the very inception of the Westphalian order of sovereign states. In fact, a small but effective group of Dutch merchants that sought to secure access to the high seas was responsible for the birth of modern international law. In 1604 these merchants, who collectively formed the Dutch United East India Company, commis-sioned a legal brief from a young lawyer, Hugo Grotius–now widely regarded as the founder of international law.[16] His opinion, *Mare liberum* (published as a book in 1609),[17] a brilliant defense of the notion of the high seas as a shared resource, set the course for the development of international law.[18]

---

[16] On the Grotian legacy in international law, see David Kennedy, *Primitive Legal Scholarship*, 27 HARV. INT'L L.J. 1, 76–95 (1986); Hersch Lauterpacht, *The Grotian Tradition in International Law*, 23 BRIT. Y.B. INT'L L. 1 (1946). But see the fierce critique in Giorgio del Vecchio, *Grotius and the Foundation of International Law*, 37 N.Y.U. L. REV. 260 (1962).

[17] The Dutch company ordered publication of an anonymous version in connection with negotiations between the Netherlands and Spain, and possibly for reasons related to *domestic* political conflict in the Netherlands. *See* C.G. Roelofsen, *Grotius and the International Politics of the Seventeenth Century, in* HUGO GROTIUS AND INTERNATIONAL RELATIONS 95, 109 (Hedley Bull et al. eds., 1990). For the background of the treatise, see C.G. Roelofsen, *Grotius and International Law: An Introduction to Some Themes in the Field of Grotian Studies, in* GROTIUS READER 3, 9–10 (L.E. van Holk & C.G. Roelofsen eds., 1983) [hereinafter Roelofsen, *Themes*]. *See also* Hamilton Vreeland, HUGO GROTIUS – THE FATHER OF THE MODERN SCIENCE OF INTERNATIONAL LAW 45–47 (1917); J.K. Oudendijk, STATUS AND EXTENT OF ADJACENT WATERS 15–16 (1970).

[18] Grotius envisioned a world order based on sovereign states subject to nothing but their free will. State consent, rather than God's commands or Papal grants, was therefore the basis of international obligations. Accordingly, Grotius's reasoning refrained from allud-ing to religious text and instead emphasized utilitarian arguments, such as economic efficiency: "[W]hen it can be done without any prejudice to his own interests, will not one person share with another things which are useful to the recipient, and no loss to the

The early seventeenth century witnessed several commercial disputes among merchants from different European countries. Grotius's treatise related to a conflict between Portuguese and Dutch merchants over the right to navigate the high seas en route to the coveted spice markets of the Far East.[19] At the same time, Dutch fishing fleets argued with their English competitors over the right to fish in the waters of the North Sea, or what King James I called the "British Seas."[20] When English merchants grew interested in tapping the profitable markets of the Far East, only to be rebuffed by Dutch competitors who had managed to secure exclusive contracts with the foreign rulers, intergovernmental talks were begun in London.[21] The merchants arguably could have resolved these commercial disputes themselves through transnational negotiations and contracts rather than interstate agreements.[22] But some influential competitors preferred to alter the game by mobilizing the support of their own state and the strength of its army in their efforts to eliminate competition and ensure private capture. In other words, these merchants sought to externalize the costs of creating a trade monopoly to the state apparatus by enlisting the state's military resources to secure the desired goal.[23] This was a cozy deal for the ruling elites: In

---

giver?" Hugo Grotius, THE FREEDOM OF THE SEAS 38 (James Brown Scott ed., Ralph van Deman Magoffin trans., Oxford Univ. Press 1916) (1633).

[19] See Vreeland, *supra* note 17, at 51–52.

[20] See Oudendijk, *supra* note 17, at 33–40; Roelofsen, *Themes, supra* note 17, at 13–14.

[21] See Oudendijk, *supra* note 17, at 37–40.

[22] In those days, merchants across political boundaries had been using a shared law, called *lex mercatoria* or Law Merchant. This law was a cosmopolitan law, beyond states' control. Its development through fairs, its reliance on customs, and its avoidance of formalities reflected a reliance on reputational sanctions and hence close ties between merchants. The Dutch East India and the British East India companies could have resorted to this law for resolving their emerging differences. For a discussion of the Law Merchant, see Clive M. Schmitthoff, *International Business Law: A New Law Merchant, in* CLIVE M. SCHMITTHOFF'S SELECT ESSAYS ON INTERNATIONAL TRADE LAW 20, 22–25 (Chia-Jui Cheng ed., 1988) and Daniel R. Coquillette, *Legal Ideology and Incorporation II: Sir Thomas Ridley, Charles Molloy, and the Literary Battle for the Law Merchant, 1607–1676,* 61 B.U. L. REV. 315, 346–63 (1981). For a discussion of the Law Merchant's underlying logic, see Lisa Bernstein, *Merchant Law in a Merchant Court: Rethinking the Code's Search for Immanent Business Norms,* 144 U. PA. L. REV. 1765 (1996) and Lisa Bernstein, *Opting Out of the Legal System: Extralegal Contractual Relations in the Diamond Industry,* 21 J. LEGAL STUD. 115 (1992).

[23] Similar efforts of local merchants to tap the legislative resources of the state to change the rules of the game and drive out foreign competitors can also explain the demise of Law Merchant in England. *See* 4 William Holdsworth, *A HISTORY OF ENGLISH LAW* 332–36 (3rd edn. 1945) (describing how, in the latter part of the sixteenth century, English trading companies began to drive out foreign merchants, sharing with Queen Elizabeth their

addition to added prestige, these dignitaries could benefit from their merchants' increased revenues.

In attempting to elevate commercial disputes to the international level, merchants contracted with lawyers who offered different visions of international law. Grotius's *Mare liberum*, with its open-access thesis that benefited Dutch merchants seeking access to ports in Southeast Asia, was soon challenged by other founding fathers of international law. John Selden's treatise *Mare clausum* highlighted the interests of British merchants, who could rely on Britain's naval superiority.[24] Commissioned to provide the antithesis to Grotius's work, the book so pleased King Charles that he ordered it to be placed among the public records of the courts.[25] Alberico Gentili, an Italian-born Oxford professor who represented Spanish interests in the English Court of Admiralty, took a middle course that reflected the objectives of his clients.[26] Thus, then as now, interest groups devised general arguments intended to advance their sectarian interests. As a result, international law quickly became a tool for externalizing small-group costs on to the larger segments of society.

3.2.2   Contemporary Conflicts

The history of early seventeenth-century commercial disputes shows how quickly the dominant domestic interest groups adjusted to, and learned to exploit, the emerging Westphalian order of sovereign states. They used their strong influence on their states' external relations not only to shape the outcomes of specific treaty negotiations but also, more generally, to influence the development of both domestic and international law that maintained a laissez-faire international legal environment.[27] Such an environment facilitates competition among states that

---

proceeds in return for public regulation of exports and imports); *see also* Coquillette, *supra* note 22, at 362 & n.271.

[24] John Selden, MARE CLAUSUM: OF THE DOMINION, OR, OWNERSHIP OF THE SEA, (Marchamont Nedham trans., London, William Du-Gard, 1652) (1635).

[25] *Id.* at 5; Eric G.M. Fletcher, *John Selden (Author of* Mare clausum*) and His Contribution to International Law*, 19 TRANSACTION GROTIUS SOC'Y 1, 8–9 (1934).

[26] *See* Gezina H.J. Van der Molen, ALBERICO GENTILI AND THE DEVELOPMENT OF INTERNATIONAL LAW 165–67 (1937).

[27] *See* Markus Lampe, *Explaining Nineteenth-Century Bilateralism: Economic and Political Determinants of the Cobden–Chevalier Network*, 64 ECON. HIST. REV. 644 (2011); Ronen Palan, *Tax Havens and the Commercialization of State Sovereignty*, 56 INT'L ORG. 151, 168–69 (2002).

small groups, whose relocation costs are relatively low, continue to exploit.

In the early twenty-first century, international law continues to afford small groups essentially the same exit options that existed in earlier times. Despite the growing effectiveness of improved labor conditions and human rights norms, producers can still shop around for jurisdictions that provide them with virtually unprotected workforces. Even though early awareness of the need to cooperate in promoting labor standards led to the establishment of the International Labour Organisation in 1919 and to considerable pressure from civil society in developed economies, current mechanisms still fall short of effectively monitoring countries and ensuring compliance.[28] Developments in human rights law have emphasized civil and political rights rather than economic and social rights, thereby constraining governments while leaving multinational employers relatively unfettered.[29] Here, too, efforts to impose obligations on multinational companies, while increasingly becoming more effective,[30] still face formal legal hurdles.[31]

Another, even more effective, exit option has been the creation of international regulatory institutions through state-brokered agreements, either agreements that are formally subject to international law or– recently an even better option–informal agreements that evade both domestic law and international law. While private law contracts are often costly to negotiate and enforce because of monitoring and compliance problems, reliance on the state machinery for negotiation and monitoring may lower transaction costs or at least externalize them.

---

[28] The idea of international action in promoting labor standards was raised by the British industrialist Robert Owen in the Holy Alliance Congress in 1818. For discussion of labor rights as human rights and the machinery for their protection, see generally Hector Bartolomei DE LA Cruz et al., THE INTERNATIONAL LABOR ORGANIZATION (1996); HUMAN RIGHTS, LABOR RIGHTS, AND INTERNATIONAL TRADE (Lance A. Compa & Stephen F. Diamond eds., 1996); Laura Ho et al., *(Dis)assembling Rights of Women Workers along the Global Assembly Line: Human Rights and the Garment Industry*, 31 HARV. C.R.-C.L. L. REV. 383 (1996); Klaus Samson, *The Standard-Setting and Supervisory System of the International Labour Organisation*, in AN INTRODUCTION TO THE INTERNATIONAL PROTECTION OF HUMAN RIGHTS 149 (Raija Hanski & Markku Suksi eds., 1997).

[29] *See* Ho *et al.*, *supra* note 28, for a critical analysis of the employers' impunity under international law.

[30] The United Nations Guiding Principles on Business and Human Rights, A/HRC/17/31 (2011).

[31] Akpan v. Royal Dutch Shell Plc, No. 337050/IIA ZA 09–1580 (District Court of the Hague, Jan. 30, 2013).

Moreover, domestic norms that regulate private law contracts, such as antitrust or consumer-protection regulations, impose significant limitations on certain transactions and hence increase costs dramatically. By signing international treaties, governments can enable producers and other small interests to avoid these cumbersome limitations by shifting certain transactions to the international arena.[32] International law, which governs these treaties, remains virtually oblivious to the adverse effects treaties might have on the interests of nonstate third parties, such as consumers and workers.[33]

The fragmented legal space explored in Chapter 2 provides small interest groups with an even greater level of insulation from both domestic and international scrutiny by domestic politicians, regulators, and civil society. Moreover, the fact that international organizations (IOs, that is, bodies set up by treaties) have an independent legal personality under international law also grants them immunity from judicial scrutiny.[34] These bodies enjoy immunity from suits in national courts and are not subject to any national rules prohibiting antitrust activity or protecting creditors against insolvency.[35] More importantly (from the perspective of participating states), international law shields state parties to such organizations from direct or vicarious liability for acts of the

---

[32] *See* in greater detail, Chapter 2. For a specific discussion of the International Coffee Organization, which illustrates the phenomenon, see *infra* notes 49–51 and accompanying text.

[33] Treaties are subject only to an elusive concept of *jus cogens*, which renders void only those commitments that constitute grave breaches of international human rights law such as slavery, genocide, etc. *See* Theodor Meron, HUMAN RIGHTS AND HUMANITARIAN NORMS AS CUSTOMARY LAW 31, 220–21 (1989); Michael Byers, *Conceptualising the Relationship between* Jus Cogens *and* Erga Omnes *Rules*, 66 NORDIC J. INT'L L. 211, 219 (1997).

[34] *See* Reparation for Injuries Suffered in the Service of the United States, Advisory Opinion, 1949 I.C.J. Rep. 174, 178–79 (Apr. 11); Peter H.F. Bekker, THE LEGAL POSITION OF INTERGOVERNMENTAL ORGANIZATIONS 54–61 (1994); Henry G. Schermers & Niels M. Blokker, INTERNATIONAL INSTITUTIONAL LAW §§ 1562–1574 (3rd rev. edn. 1995).

[35] In the wake of the collapse of the London-based International Tin Council, claims of individual debtors were rejected owing to the immunity enjoyed by the organization. *See* J.H. Rayner Ltd. v. Dep't of Trade & Indus., [1989] 3 W.L.R. 969, 81 I.L.R. 670 (H.L.) [hereinafter *The ITC Litigation*]; *see also* International Ass'n of Machinists v. OPEC, 649 F.2d 1354 (9th Cir. 1981) (dismissing a suit by a US labor union against OPEC and the individual member states of OPEC under the Sherman Act on procedural grounds). For more in-depth discussion of this issue, see generally Bekker, *supra* note 34; Michael Singer, *Jurisdictional Immunity of International Organizations: Human Rights and Functional Necessity Concerns*, 36 VA. J. INT'L L. 53 (1996); and Romana Sadurska & Christine M. Chinkin, *The Collapse of the International Tin Council: A Case of State Responsibility?*, 30 VA. J. INT'L L. 845 (1990).

institutions[36] and recognizes the immunity of international organizations from domestic adjudication.[37] Through its laissez-faire approach to treaties and IOs, international law continues to provide an advantageous legal environment for small domestic interest groups seeking to pursue transnational commercial transactions sheltered from the reach of the growing number of national regulations. And to the extent that this avenue becomes clogged by intensifying demands for accountability, the formal organization is shunned in favor of more informal and even private regimes.

Domestic influences are particularly noticeable in environmental disputes. From the first international litigation related to transboundary environmental damage–sulfur dioxide emissions from a Canadian smelting company at Trail in British Columbia[38]–to current debates over mitigating climate change and protecting the ozone layer, sectarian domestic interests hold sway in international negotiations and influence the development (or lack thereof) of international law. Thus, for example, the governments of the upper-riparian states tolerated the continuous pollution of the Rhine River throughout the 1970s and 1980s by industries that treated the river as their private dumping area.[39] These governments, yielding to the interests of the domestic

---

[36] *Responsibility of International Organizations: Titles and Texts of the Draft Articles on the Responsibility of International Organizations*, U.N. Doc. A/CN.4/L.778, art. 62 (2011). *See also The ITC Litigation, supra* note 35, 3 W.L.R. at 980, 81 I.L.R. at 671; *see also* Arab Org. for Industrialization v. Westland Helicopters Ltd., 80 I.L.R. 622 (Fed. Sup. Ct. 1989) (Switzerland) (finding the insolvent AOI legally distinct from the state parties and hence finding the latter not liable for the AOI obligations).

[37] On this question of immunity see Eyal Benvenisti, Law of Global Governance 110 (2014) [hereinafter Benvenisti, GG Law]; Eric De Brabandere, *Belgian Courts and the Immunity of International Organizations*, 10 Int'l Org. L. Rev. 464 (2014); August Reinisch, *The Immunity of International Organizations and the Jurisdiction of Their Administrative Tribunals*, 7 Chinese J. Int'l L. 285 (2008); August Reinisch, International Organizations before National Courts (2000).

Marc Cogen, *Human Rights, Prohibition of Political Activities and the Lending Policies of the World Bank and International monetary Fund, in* The Right to Development in International Law 387 (Chowdhury et al. eds., 1992).

[38] The Trail Smelter Case (U.S. v. Can.), 3 R.I.A.A. 1905 (1938).

[39] *See* Aaron Schwabach, Comment, *The Sandoz Spill: The Failure of International Law to Protect the Rhine from Pollution*, 16 Ecology L.Q., 443 (1989) (discussing the disastrous consequences of the 1986 toxic waste contamination of the Rhine from a warehouse in Basel and examining the failure of the Rhine treaty regime). For background on the litigation in Dutch courts with respect to pollution of the Rhine by a French mining company in Alsace, see Handelskwekerij G.J. Bier B.V. and Stichting "Reinwater" v. Mines de Potasse d'Alsace S.A. (MDPA), 11 Neth. Y.B. Int'l L. 326 (1980); for subsequent litigation in this dispute, see Handelskwekerij G.J. Bier B.V. and Stichting "Reinwater" v.

industries and their workforce, colluded to stall effective plans to reclaim and protect the river by giving sustained support to a largely ineffective system of international protections.[40] Similarly, Finland and Sweden, whose cooperation is usually cause for envy and emulation,[41] failed to reach an agreement on jointly reducing pollution from pulp mills because of resistance to regulatory initiatives mounted by their respective pulp industries.[42]

Domestic interest groups shaped also the US position in international negotiations. US leadership in global efforts to curb production of CFC emissions to protect the ozone layer throughout the 1980s and early 1990s was motivated primarily by the five American CFC producers. Although the firms were responsible for 30 percent of the world production of CFC emissions, their CFC sales were not a significant part of their revenue. Once they developed substitutes for most CFC

Mines de Potasse d'Alsace S.A. (MDPA), 15 NETH. Y.B. INT'L L. 471 (1984), and *Mines de Potasse d'Alsace S.A. (MDPA)/Onroerend Goed Maatschappij,* 19 NETH. Y.B. INT'L L. 496 (1988) [hereinafter *MDPA III*]. For similar litigation in the French courts, see La Province de la Hollande septentrionale contre Etat ministre de l'Environnement, Tribunal Administratife de Strasbourg, Jul. 27, 1983, *reprinted in* 4 REV. JUR. ENVN'T 343 (1983) (annulling the permit to pollute), *overturned* Conseil d'tat, Apr. 18, 1986, *reprinted in* 2-3 REV. JUR. ENVN'T 296 (1986) (finding no manifest error in granting the permit) [hereinafter *French Pollution Permit Case*]. For a discussion of an "unsatisfactory" 1994 decision of another local court in the Netherlands concerning pollution by a Belgian company of the River Meuse, see Jan M. van Dunn, *Liability in Tort for the Detrimental Use of Fresh Water Resources Under Dutch Law in Domestic and International Cases, in* THE SCARCITY OF WATER 196, 205 (Edward H.P. Brans et al. eds., 1997). The fact that these cases of pollution had to be brought to court, and by Dutch NGOs, suggests the political constraints involved.

[40] The polluting industries along the Rhine, from Basel, Switzerland, to the heavily industrialized Ruhr in Germany, opposed stringent controls that would increase production costs. Their workers shared this interest, fearing for their jobs. These groups shaped their governments' positions in negotiating the Rhine treaty regime. *See* Schwabach, *supra* note 39, at 469–70. Following the 1986 major spill of toxic chemicals into the Rhine from the Sandoz warehouse in Basel, the West German opposition party, the Social Democrats, justified its decision to remain silent by the fear of industry relocation: "We can't pull out of the industrial society . . . We don't want to." Russel Watson *et al., The Blot on the Rhine,* NEWSWEEK, Nov. 24, 1986, at 58 (quoting Harold Schaefer, spokesperson of the Social Democrats). In 1986 the Dutch court of appeal determined that the level of salt allowed by the 1976 Bonn Salt Convention was exceedingly high, damaging the river and the environment in the Netherlands, and constituting a breach of Dutch tort law. *See MDPA III, supra* note 39.

[41] For a comprehensive account of the Swedish-Finnish Frontiers River Commission see Malgosia Fitzmaurice, *The Finnish-Swedish Frontier Rivers Commission,* 5 HAGUE Y.B. Int'l L. 33, 44 (1992).

[42] *See* Matthew R. Auer, *Geography, Domestic Politics and Environmental Diplomacy: A Case from the Baltic Sea Region,* 11 GEO. INT'L. ENVTL. L. REV. 77 (1998).

uses, they stood to gain from a global CFC ban.[43] In contrast, the contemporaneous US failure to join the Convention on Biological Diversity was a function of the adverse economic consequences it portended for private American companies.[44] Negotiations over a Biosafety Protocol under the Biological Diversity Convention collapsed in February 1999.[45] The protocol, which would have restricted trade in genetically modified agricultural products, was blocked by a coalition of six states whose industries had strong interests in such trade.[46]

Domestic interest groups shape international trade law and negotiations. They have driven governments into both trade wars and violations of trade agreements.[47] Trade agreements, informal understandings, and even elaborate institutional regimes help producers from different countries establish and maintain cartels that are detrimental to consumers.[48]

---

[43] See Todd Sandler, GLOBAL CHALLENGES 112–13 (1997); see also Richard Elliot Benedick, OZONE DIPLOMACY (1998).

[44] See Kal Raustiala, The Domestic Politics of Global Biodiversity Protection in the United Kingdom and the United States, in THE INTERNATIONALIZATION OF ENVIRONMENTAL PROTECTION 42, 48–52 (Elizabeth Economy & Miranda A. Schreurs eds., 1997).

[45] See Christopher S. Zalewski & Paul F. McQuade, A Stalemate on Biosafety Pact, THE NAT'L L.J., May 24, 1999, at C1; U.S. and Allies Block Treaty on Gene-Altered Goods, N.Y. TIMES, Feb. 25, 1999, at A1 [hereinafter U.S. and Allies].

[46] These states included the United States, Canada, Australia, Argentina, Chile, and Uruguay–all of them major agricultural exporters. See Zalewski & McQuade, supra note 45; U.S. and Allies, supra note 45.

[47] Ongoing trade disputes between the United States and the European Union over EU restrictions on the importation of genetically modified food, hormone-treated beef, and bananas from Central America, as well as US retaliatory measures in the form of 100% tariffs on certain EU exports to the US, reflect competition, rather than collusion, among rival domestic interests. But they also reflect the direct influence these domestic groups have on their respective governments' positions. This influence has prompted the EU to disregard the rulings of the World Trade Organization, which had found the EU in breach of trade agreements in both the banana and beef hormone disputes. See The WTO Appellate Body Reports: European Communities–Regime for the Importation, Sale and Distribution of Bananas, Rep. No. WT/DS27/AB/R, Sept. 9, 1997; EC Measures concerning Meat and Meat Products (Hormone), Rep. No. WT/DS26/AB/R, WT/DS48/AB/R, Jan. 16, 1998) [hereinafter WTO Appellate Reports]. These violations persisted despite the findings and the US retaliatory measures. See U.S. – Europe Trade War Looms over Bananas, N.Y. TIMES, Dec. 22, 1998, at A1; Imports Face Higher Tariffs on Beef Issue, N.Y. TIMES, Mar. 23, 1999, at C1.

[48] During the 1980s, protective US trade policies restricted, among others, the import of Japanese cars, of textile and apparel, of steel, and of semiconductors. These policies benefited some US as well as foreign industries, while American consumers bore the costs. See William A. Niskanen, US Trade Policy, in 3 REGULATION 34 (1988), reprinted in William A. Niskanen, POLICY ANALYSIS AND PUBLIC CHOICE 183 (1998). For an analysis of the International Coffee Organization, see Robert H. Bates, OPEN-ECONOMY POLITICS (1997); infra notes 49–51 and accompanying text.

Other treaties reflect complex give-and-take between producers and bureaucrats. Take, for example, Robert Bates's in-depth study of the International Coffee Organization (ICO). It explores a contemporary example of an international market failure that the prevailing Westphalian paradigm is incapable of addressing.[49] The ICO was a cartel of coffee-producing states controlled by the two leading producers, Brazil and Colombia. During the almost three decades of its operation, from the early 1960s to late 1989, the ICO set quotas for participating states, thereby restricting competition and raising the price of coffee. The United States supported the ICO. In fact, the support of the United States, the destination for over 50 percent of the world's coffee imports, was integral to the ICO's enforcement because the monitoring and policing of quotas was left to the consuming states' customs offices. In other words, for almost three decades the US government spent public resources to police a scheme that actually imposed a significant but hidden tax on American coffee consumers and encroached on certain US businesses. These actions cannot be understood without lifting the veil of national sovereignty to reveal that political considerations rather than economic factors were the motivators of this behavior and that the US position was the result of a comfortable deal among a small domestic interest group (the large coffee roasting firms), legislators, and bureaucrats. The higher price for raw materials gave the larger roasters an economic advantage over the smaller ones. In exchange for long-term contracts with deferred rebates, these large roasters lobbied and testified before Congress to win its endorsement of the ICO regime.[50] A complacent Congress benefited the executive bureaucracy whose dominant goal was to prevent domestic challenges to the US-backed Latin American regimes, a threat they called "Castroism."[51] The ICO deal provided an opportunity to shift funds surreptitiously from the US economy to Latin America, making some influential producers happy.

A final example in support of the transnational conflict paradigm is the treatment of global tax competition by the Organisation for Economic Co-operation and Development (OECD). In view of "the distorting effects of harmful tax competition," the OECD created a committee in 1996 to report on the situation and recommend possible measures to

---

[49] See Bates, *supra* note 48.

[50] For the role of the large roasters, see *id.* at 129–33, 150–53.

[51] For the motivations of the administration, see *id.* at 121–29. Although one could say that the US executive pursued here a general anti-Soviet interest, this interest was not subject to scrutiny by Congress.

address it.[52] Two years later, the OECD Council approved the committee's report and adopted its modest and controversial recommendations.[53] The report makes clear that pervasive tax competition is not only economically inefficient but also inequitable, as it shifts the tax burden from mobile capital to less mobile labor–that is, from the smaller groups to the larger ones.[54] The report specifically identifies domestic business interests as responsible for the ever-expanding competition. The committee, adopting a rather diplomatic tone, hints at the political complexity of the issue: From 1985 to 1994, foreign direct investment from G7 countries in low-tax jurisdictions increased more than fivefold, well above the growth rate of total outbound foreign direct investments.[55] In other words, although the heads of the G7 claimed to be troubled by what they see as "harmful tax competition . . . carrying risks of distorting trade and investment [that] could lead to the erosion of national tax bases,"[56] they have not committed to taking action that would adversely affect their respective domestic actors.[57] With Luxembourg and Switzerland critical of the "partial and unbalanced approach" of the report and recommendations, the challenge to implement the recommendations remained.[58] It was only after the 2008 financial crisis, and following the US lead, that efforts to combat tax havens started to bear fruit.[59]

3.3 The Transnational Conflict Paradigm and the Law: Sustaining Norms, Procedures, and Institutions

Not only have smaller domestic interest groups used their relative edge over other, more diffuse, domestic groups to secure specific gains and a comfortable global legal environment, but they have also invested in

---

[52] *See* Organisation for Econ. Co-operation and Dev., HARMFUL TAX COMPETITION para. 1, at 7 (1998) [hereinafter OECD].

[53] Luxembourg and Switzerland criticized the recommendations and abstained. *See id.* at 73–78. For criticism, see Reuven S. Avi-Yonah, *Globalization, Tax Competition and the Fiscal Crisis of the State*, 113 HARV. L. REV. 1573 (2000).

[54] *See* OECD, *supra* note 52, para. 30, at 16. "The Committee is aware that many of the preferential tax regimes referred to in this Report have been put in place in response to pressures by the business community on those parts of government that have the responsibility for economic development." *Id.* para. 32, at 17.

[55] *See id.* para. 35, at 17.

[56] *Id.* para. 1, at 7 (quoting the Ministerial Communiqué of the G7 Heads of State in the Lyon Summit, 1996).

[57] For criticism of the recommendations' effectiveness, see Avi-Yonah, *supra* note 53.

[58] *See* OECD, *supra* note 52, at 73 (reporting statement by Luxembourg); *id.* at 76 (reporting statement by Switzerland).

[59] Tsilly Dagan, *Community Obligations in International Taxation in* COMMUNITY INTERESTS ACROSS INTERNATIONAL LAW (Eyal Benvenisti & Georg Nolte eds., forthcoming).

establishing a legal framework that ensured their continuing control over international negotiations and secured the durability of negotiated treaties, while leaving open the option for low-cost, temporary evasions of treaty obligations. This section delineates the relevant norms, procedures, and institutions that constitute this framework.

3.3.1   Treaty Negotiation and Ratification

Smaller domestic interest groups enjoy a great deal of control over the treaty negotiation process and outcome and therefore risk little in shifting these transactions from the private to the international sphere. As proposed by Robert Putnam, the structure of international negotiations is a two-level game played by government representatives simultaneously at the international level with representatives of foreign governments and at the domestic level with representatives of domestic interest groups.[60] The smaller domestic interest groups, because of their particularly strong influence on the negotiation and ratification processes, are poised to dominate the game at the domestic level. They will either capture the executive or instead delay, weaken, or block negotiations that could encroach on their interests.[61] The domestic level of the game is composed of two phases: the negotiation phase and the ratification phase that follows. The influence of the smaller interest groups is particularly strong during the opaque negotiation phase, at which time they are better positioned than other groups to act collectively to monitor the government's representatives and furnish them with partial data.[62] Should they fail to persuade the executive, they can move to the second line of defense–the ratification phase, where they can exert effective influence on lawmakers and where they can exploit the

---

[60] See Robert D. Putnam, *Diplomacy and Domestic Politics: The Logic of Two-Level Games,* 42 Int'l Org. 427, 436 (1988). On this two-level game, see generally Double-Edged Diplomacy: International Bargaining and Domestic Politics (Peter B. Evans et al. eds., 1993) (analyzing eleven cases of two-level bargaining); George W. Downs & David M. Rocke, Optimal Imperfection? (1995); Milner, Interests, *supra* note 8. For an argument for a "three-level game"–including an additional "transnational/transgovernmental bargaining" level, see Thomas Risse-Kappen, *Structures of Governance and Transnational Relations: What We Have Learned?, in* Bringing Transnational Relations Back In 280, 300 (Thomas Risse-Kappen ed., 1995).

[61] See Milner, Interests *supra* note 8, ch. 3.

[62] See Jeffrey L. Dunoff, *The Misguided Debate over NGO Participation at the WTO,* 1 J. Int'l Econ. L. 433, 446–47 (1998) (describing the information assistance Kodak and Fuji provided to their governments in their trade dispute).

information they collected during the negotiation phase, over which they have a virtual monopoly.

The particular vulnerability of the process of treaty negotiation and ratification to interest-group influence becomes clearer when it is compared to garden-variety domestic legislation. In contrast to the relatively transparent and accessible legislative process, international negotiations are less susceptible to serious domestic deliberation and scrutiny. Moreover, unlike legislative proposals, of which the legislature is in control from the initial introduction of bills through the discussion of amendments to the final product, the treaty to be ratified is a completed transaction essentially immune to subsequent unilateral alterations.[63] The sequential process of treaty ratification gives the government a free hand to set the agenda, formulate the policies, and choose among alternatives.[64] The ex post "take it or leave it" option presented to the ratifying body erects a high hurdle for those who wish to oppose or amend the international transaction.[65]

In many states the ratification process does not require legislative approval at all and hence permits even fewer opportunities to scrutinize the treaty.[66] In Commonwealth countries and in Scandinavia, the government, rather than the legislature, ratifies the treaty and thereby commits the state to international obligations.[67] In theory, such

---

[63] For an analysis of the political advantages presidents have over the legislature through the exclusive power to initiate, to make take-it-or-leave-it proposals, and to control information, see Matthew S. Shugart & John M. Carey, PRESIDENTS AND ASSEMBLIES 139–40 (1992).

[64] There are profound advantages to the party who can decide how to sequence the voting process when there are more than two options open to the voters (and when there are more than two voters). As was formally demonstrated in Kenneth J. Arrow, SOCIAL CHOICE AND INDIVIDUAL VALUES (1951), the agenda-setter can virtually dictate the final vote simply by deciding the order of votes.

[65] Reservations, understandings, and declarations and interpretations, attached to treaties at the time of ratification or made thereafter, could alter somewhat the contours of the agreement without breaching it. Note, however, that such pronouncements may be limited by the treaty or by general international law, which proscribes reservations that are "incompatible with the object and purpose of the treaty." Vienna Convention on the Law of Treaties, May 23, 1969, S. TREATY DOC. NO. 92-1 (1969), 8 I.L.M. 679, art. 19(c).

[66] See Stefan A. Riesenfeld & Frederick M. Abbott, Foreword: Symposium on Parliamentary Participation in the Making and Operation of Treaties, 67 CHI.-KENT L. REV. 293, 303 (1991). For a comparative survey of the practices of treaty ratification, see THE EFFECT OF TREATIES IN DOMESTIC LAW (Francis G. Jacobs & Shelley Roberts eds., 1987) [hereinafter EFFECT OF TREATIES].

[67] For the British procedure, see R. Higgins, United Kingdom, in EFFECT OF TREATIES, supra note 66 at 123–24, and Lord Templeman, Treaty-Making and the British Parliament, 67 CHI.-KENT L. REV. 459 (1991). For the situation in Denmark, see Claus Gulmann, Denmark, in EFFECT OF TREATIES, supra note 66, at 29–30; in Iceland, see Ragnar

ratification does not carry any domestic implications, because ratification cannot change national law. But, in fact, unless there is a statute
that specifically conflicts with the treaty obligations, the government is
not deterred from implementing these obligations domestically
through regulations or other acts. The onus falls on the legislature to
pass a statute that would explicitly invalidate the treaty's internal
effect. But the legislature may hesitate to do so, because such
enactment could amount to a breach of the state's international
obligations.

In the United States, the interplay between Congress and the executive
in the treaty-ratification process is more complicated. On the one hand,
the constitutional requirement of a two-thirds majority in the Senate for
"advice and consent" to treaties essentially grants veto power to a minority of thirty-four senators,[68] thereby enabling interest groups to concentrate their efforts on fewer legislators.[69] Executive agreements
compromise this strategy, however, by allowing a presidential bypass of
the Senate in concluding international obligations.[70] On the other hand,
therefore, small groups must also invest in influencing the executive. In
recent years, the United States has developed a so-called fast track
procedure with respect to trade agreements. In such cases, the president
agrees to involve Congress in the negotiations in return for a bicameral
congressional commitment to vote the agreement up or down without

Adalsteinsson, *The Current Situation of Human Right in Iceland*, 61/62 NORDIC J. INT'L L.
167, 168–70 (1992–93); in Sweden, see Michael Bogdan, *Application of Public
International Law by Swedish Courts*, 63 NORDIC J. INT'L L. 3, 8–11 (1994).

[68] *See* Stefan A. Riesenfeld & Frederick M. Abbott, *The Scope of U.S. Senate Control over the
Conclusion and Operation of Treaties*, 67 CHI.-KENT L. REV. 571, 601 (1991).

[69] The involvement of Congress does not necessarily result in the representation of the
larger constituency. Indeed, sometimes Congress is captured by small interests, while at
the same time the executive promotes general interests.

[70] Executive agreements take one of two forms: unilateral acts by the President, and
executive actions requiring approval by a bicameral majority of Congress rather than a
supermajority of the Senate. *See* Dames & Moore v. Regan, 453 U.S. 654 (1981); United
States v. Pink, 315 U.S. 203 (1942); United States v. Belmont, 301 U.S. 324 (1937);
RESTATEMENT (THIRD) OF THE FOREIGN RELATIONS LAW OF THE UNITED STATES §303 & cmt. g
(1986) [hereinafter RESTATEMENT] ("Presidents have asserted a broad authority to make
many other international agreements [in addition to recognition of states and armistice
agreements], at least in the absence of inconsistent legislation or of Congressional action
restricting such agreements."). On executive agreements, see generally Louis Henkin,
FOREIGN AFFAIRS AND THE UNITED STATES CONSTITUTION 215–30 (2nd edn. 1996); John H.
Jackson, *United States, in* EFFECT OF TREATIES, *supra* note 66, at 141, 142–44; Joel R. Paul,
The Geopolitical Constitution: Executive Expediency and Executive Agreements, 86 CAL. L.
REV. 671 (1998); and Riesenfeld & Abbott, *supra* note 68, at 635–41.

amendment.[71] Congressional involvement at the negotiation phase limits the discretion of government negotiators at the international bargaining process and provides more voice to groups that are less influential with the executive, although the president continues to control the agenda.[72]

National courts, especially during the Cold War era, traditionally deferred to the executive and embraced the principle that legislative supervision of international negotiations should be limited. In the celebrated case of United States v. Curtiss-Wright Export Corp., the United States Supreme Court affirmed that

> [i]n this vast external realm, with its important, complicated, delicate and manifold problems, the President alone has the power to speak or listen as a representative of the nation. He *makes* treaties with the advice and consent of the Senate; but he alone negotiates. Into the field of negotiation the Senate cannot intrude; and Congress itself is powerless to invade it.[73]

The logic of this argument holds as long as the distinction between domestic and international affairs remains sharp. But when international negotiations impose significant burdens on domestic policies and individuals, executive power must be limited.

For the same reasons, courts have tended until very recently to be reluctant to assert their own powers to review ratified treaties. As a result, treaties enjoyed greater immunity from judicial review than did statutes. In some countries, the constitution itself accords treaties a higher status than statutes, and sometimes a status even higher than the constitution itself, thereby immunizing treaties from judicial scrutiny.[74] In those

---

[71] See Harold H. Koh, *The Fast Track and United States Trade Policy*, 18 Brook. J. Int'l L. 143 (1992); Riesenfeld & Abbott, *supra* note 68, at 637–38; Detlev F. Vagts, *The Exclusive Treaty Power Revisited*, 89 Am. J. Int'l L. 40, 41–42 (1995). *See generally* George A. Bermann, *Constitutional Implications of U.S. Participation in Regional Integration*, 46 Am. J. Comp. L. 463 (1998).

[72] Regarding Congress's role in implementing the Basel II recommendations, see discussion in Benvenisti, *GG Law*, at 38.

[73] United States v. Curtiss-Wright Export Corp., 299 U.S. 304, 319 (1936). The Court used Congress's relative lack of information as an argument against its involvement in decision-making: "[The President], not Congress, has the better opportunity of knowing the conditions which prevail in foreign countries, and especially is this true in time of war. He has his confidential sources of information. He has his agents in the form of diplomatic, consular and other officials. Secrecy in respect of information gathered by them may be highly necessary, and the premature disclosure of it productive of harmful results." (*id.* at 320).

[74] See, e.g., J.D. de la Rochère, *France, in* Effect of Treaties, *supra* note 66, at 42 (discussing article 55 of the French constitution); Henry G. Schermers, *Netherlands, in* Effect of Treaties, *supra* note 66, at 109, 111 (discussing article 120 of the Dutch constitution).

jurisdictions where treaty ratification is deemed a governmental (formerly a royal) prerogative, treaties are insulated from judicial review, somewhat paradoxically, because they have no direct effect in the domestic legal system and hence no effect on individual rights.[75] In other states, national courts are, in theory, competent to review the constitutionality of treaties (or of statutes implementing treaties), but only a few national courts, such as the constitutional courts of Italy, Germany, and the United States, have asserted such authority and then have exercised it only in rare and exceptional cases.[76]

The judicial hesitation to constitutionally scrutinize treaties accorded well with the traditional inclination of national courts to defer to the discretion of the executive in conducting the country's foreign affairs.[77] Until the late 1990s, judicial interference with treaty obligations was deemed an intervention in international affairs, regardless of the domestic implications. The basic approach has been that in international affairs, "[o]ur State cannot speak with two voices on such a matter, the judiciary

---

[75] This applies to Britain and other Commonwealth countries, as well as to the Scandinavian countries. *See* Templeman, *supra* note 67, at 461; sources cited *supra* note 67.

[76] The single US case striking down a treaty (domestically classified as an executive agreement) as incompatible with the Constitution remains Reid v. Covert, 354 U.S. 1 (1957). *Dames & Moore*, 453 U.S. at 662, however, suggests that the Supreme Court is ready to relax constitutional norms in deference to "the never-ending tension between the President exercising the executive authority in a world that presents each day some new challenge with which he must deal and the Constitution under which we all live and which no one disputes embodies some sort of system of checks and balances. . . ." *See also* Missouri v. Holland, 252 U.S. 416 (1920) (holding that Congress and the federal government had power to do by treaty what they could not do by domestic legislation); Louis Henkin, CONSTITUTIONALISM, DEMOCRACY, AND FOREIGN AFFAIRS 71 (1990) ("Where 'balancing' an individual right against the public interest is deemed to be the constitutional order, courts treat foreign affairs differently: private rights are depreciated, while competing public needs are accorded compelling weight."). *But see* Curtis A. Bradley, *The Treaty Power and American Federalism*, 97 MICH. L. REV. 390 (1998) (arguing for greater federalism constraints on the treaty power). The German Constitutional Court "will spare no effort and, in fact, will go out of its way, to reconcile Germany's treaty obligations with its internal legal order." Jochen Abr. Frowein & Michael J. Hahn, *The Participation of Parliament in the Treaty Process in the Federal Republic of Germany*, 67 CHI.-KENT L. REV. 361, 385 (1992). Thus, it has found a treaty incompatible with the constitution only once. *See id.* at 384–85. The Italian constitutional court "took the attitude of undervaluing conflicts between treaties and the Constitution." Giorgio Gaja, *Italy, in* EFFECT OF TREATIES, *supra* note 66, at 87, 101. The constitutional courts of Germany and Italy have also upheld their authority to review Parliamentary decisions to transfer sovereign powers to the European Union (but never exercised it). *See also infra*, Chapter 6, Section 6.3.

[77] For an analysis of this question *see* Chapter 5.

saying one thing, the executive another,"[78] and the executive's voice is preferred because of an inherent "advantage of the diplomatic approach to the resolution of difficulties between two sovereign nations, as opposed to the unilateral action by the courts of one nation."[79] Hence, only the executive's voice would be heard. Therefore, not only did courts abstain from reviewing international treaties for compatibility with domestic prescriptions, but when interpreting them they also deferred to the executive's interpretation.[80] Furthermore, a variety of judicially developed "avoidance doctrines" permitted the courts to dodge petitions to review treaties against domestic norms or to review domestic policies against international norms.[81] Such extreme deference to the executive is deeply troubling, as it enables a sizable amount of executive activity, having major ramifications for domestic interests, to remain completely beyond judicial reach and effective public scrutiny. As the next two sections will show, the same deferential attitude persisted beyond the ratification stage, in the face of attempts to terminate a treaty unilaterally or to renege temporarily on it. This ensured the executive branch virtually unfettered discretion in deciding whether to comply with treaty obligations.

3.3.2   Ensuring Treaty Durability

Domestic and international norms that insulate treaty obligations from post-ratification domestic challenges by larger political groups further enhanced the stronger domestic effect of treaties vis-à-vis statutes. Once ratified, there was neither the opportunity to revoke a treaty through judicial review nor the possibility of terminating it through unilateral state action by, for example, a statute. Unless the ratifying state chooses to violate the treaty and suffer whatever consequences breach entails, it

---

[78] The Arantzazu Mendi, 1939 App. Cas. 256, 264 (H.L.) (appeal taken from Eng.) (granting immunity to the nationalist government of Spain by the British House of Lords following recognition by the Foreign Office as a de facto government).

[79] United States v. Alvarez-Machain, 504 U.S. 655, 669 n.16 (1992).

[80] See Eyal Benvenisti, *Judicial Misgivings Regarding the Application of International Norms: An Analysis of Attitudes of National Courts*, 4 EUR. J. INT'L L. 159, 166–68 (1993).

[81] *Id.* at 169–73. These doctrines range from the more general ones, such as standing, justiciability, and the political question doctrine, to specific doctrines that reduce the bite of international norms (deference to the executive's interpretation of treaty provisions, failure to recognize the standing of individuals to seek redress for the violation of international obligations) and protect local and foreign governments from judicial proceedings (through sovereign immunity or act-of-state doctrines).

remains bound until the other signatories agree to modify or terminate it.[82] Herein lies the chief benefit of treaties for smaller domestic groups: The treaty proved even more resistant to subsequent modification pressures than constitutional guarantees. Unlike constitutional guarantees, which are subject to modification through constitutional amendments, no subsequent domestic majority can unilaterally change the state's international obligations. Absent the consent of the other parties, future governments would continue to be bound by the same treaty obligations. International law ensures treaty durability by rendering irrelevant all subsequent domestic political developments that might affect a state's international obligations.[83] The International Court of Justice (ICJ) demonstrated the strength of this doctrine in its 1997 judgment concerning a dispute between Hungary and Slovakia.[84] The ICJ determined that the damming of the Danube River, a mammoth project conceived in the bygone communist era, should go ahead despite the momentous political transformations that had taken place in the two states and the intensive and widespread popular opposition to the project in Hungary. Neither domestic political changes nor strong popular opposition to the project could excuse the unilateral termination of the 1977 treaty.[85] The communist legacy, however inefficient or environmentally dangerous, survived the transformation of both regimes and all unilateral contradictory moves of the two governments.[86] Finding the agreement flexible and therefore renegotiable, the ICJ imposed the treaty

---

[82] See Vienna Convention, *supra* note 65, arts. 39–40.

[83] See id. art. 27 ("A party may not invoke the provisions of its internal law as justification for its failure to perform a treaty.").

[84] Gabcikovo-Nagymaros Project (Hung. v. Slovk.), 1997 I.C.J. Rep. 7 (Sept. 25).

[85] For a discussion of the development of the internal environmental-political opposition in Hungary on the planned project on the Danube River, see Fred Pearce, GREEN WARRIORS 107–16 (1991); Judit Galambos, *Political Aspects of an Environmental Conflict: The Case of the Gabcikovo-Nagymaros Dam System, in* PERSPECTIVES ON ENVIRONMENTAL CONFLICT AND INTERNATIONAL POLITICS 72 (Jyrki Kknen ed., 1992).

[86] See Gabcikovo-Nagymaros Project, 1997 I.C.J. at paras. 144–47, at 79–80. In reaching this conclusion, the court deliberately emphasized international undertakings at the expense of domestic pressures. It rejected Hungary's claim that a "state of ecological necessity," even if such existed, precluded the wrongfulness of its unilateral suspension of the project, because Hungary could resort to negotiations to reduce the environmental risks. It similarly rejected Hungary's claims to impossibility of performance, fundamental change of circumstances, and lawful response to Czechoslovakia's earlier material breach (namely, Slovakia's construction of the provisional diversion project). See id. at paras. 101–12, at 63–68. The ICJ was also critical of Slovakia's moves. It found the Slovak diversion of the Danube waters as breaching its obligation to respect Hungary's right to an equitable and reasonable share of the river. See id. at para. 78, at 54.

on both sides and ruled that they should renegotiate its implementation.[87] The judgment clearly seeks to insulate international politics from the influence of domestic politics. Even when one side breaches its obligation to renegotiate in good faith, the government of the other side cannot bow to domestic public pressure and adopt a unilateral response. Instead, it must exhaust all possible means to persuade its counterpart to return to the negotiating table.[88] This international legal doctrine is buttressed in many countries by constitutional or doctrinal guarantees that insulate treaties from efforts by domestic groups to force the government to breach treaty obligations. A judicially created rule of statutory interpretation accepted in many jurisdictions–that statutes should be interpreted as much as possible in conformity with the state's international obligations–will often preempt these efforts.[89] Although the stated justification is the presumed intent of the legislature, courts have resorted to the rule in spite of rather clear indications from the legislature that it wanted the treaty breached. A case in point is the "sad case of the PLO mission," in which the judge disregarded Congress's clear intent to breach the Headquarters Agreement between the United States and the UN by preventing the PLO leader from arriving in New York.[90] The court found the statute vague enough to permit an interpretation that stultified its aim and prevented an international conflict. Of course,

[87] *See id.* at paras. 138–40, at 77–78.

[88] This is the *cumulative* message of the decision, which is captured in President Schwebel's declaration. Although he was "not persuaded that Hungary's position as the Party initially in breach deprived it of a right to terminate the Treaty in response to Czechoslovakia's material breach," the President joined the majority in imposing the resuscitated agreement on the parties. *Id.* at 85 (Declaration of President Schwebel).

[89] A comparative survey of this presumption includes: M. Ann Hayward, *International Law and the Interpretation of the Canadian Charter of Rights and Freedoms: Uses and Justifications,* 23 U. W. ONT. L. REV. 9, 13–16 (1985) (Canada); Gulmann, *supra* note 67, at 36 (Denmark); Regina v. Secretary of State for the Home Dep't, (Ex parte Brind) [1991] 1 A.C. 696, 760 (H.L.), and Derbyshire County Council v. Times Newspapers Ltd [1992] 3 W.L.R. 28, 44 (Eng. C.A.) (United Kingdom); Jochen A. Frowein, *Federal Republic of Germany, in* EFFECT OF TREATIES, *supra* note 66, at 63, 68–69 (Germany); Darusz v. Union of India, 92 I.L.R. 540 (Sup. Ct. 1993) (India); C.A. 25/55, 145/55, 148/55, Custodian of Absentee Property v. Samra, 10 P.D. 1825, 1831, 22 I.L.R. 5 (1956) (Israel); Gaja, *supra* note 76, at 100–01 (Italy); Minister of Defence (Namib. v. Mwandinghi), 91 I.L.R. 341 (High Ct. 1993) (Namibia); State v. Ncube, 91 I.L.R. 580 (1993) (S.C.) (Zimbabwe). For a critical view of this rule from a constitutional law perspective, see Curtis A. Bradley, *The Charming Betsy Canon and Separation of Powers: Rethinking the Interpretive Role of International Law,* 86 GEO. L.J. 479 (1998).

[90] *See* United States v. PLO, 695 F. Supp. 1456 (S.D.N.Y. 1988); W. Michael Reisman, *An International Farce: The Sad Case of the PLO Mission,* 14 YALE J. INT'L L. 412, 429–32 (1989).

Congress can overcome this hurdle by stating explicitly its breach of a treaty obligation. But only in extreme cases–not even in the "sad case of the PLO mission," where Congress clearly disregarded the Headquarters Agreement with the UN[91]–would Congress issue such an admission.

The combined outcome of these rules insulates many governments from domestic challenges that would require them to renege on treaty obligations against their will. The smaller groups are assured that their gains will last, in one form or another, until the larger groups within all relevant states simultaneously agree to modify their treaty obligations. They also know, as we shall see in the next section, that when *it is* in their interests to commit an international breach, their government will not be effectively constrained from doing so. In other words, the norms pave a one-way street: Governments can hardly be *forced* to renege on treaty obligations, but when they so choose, they can hardly be *prevented* from doing so. This is exactly the outcome desired by small groups that invest in controlling their governments.

3.3.3   Providing Escape Clauses for Unilateral Defections

Most international treaties are "relational," in that the relations they create between parties extend well into the future.[92] During the life of such treaties, conditions often change, and therefore state negotiators take pains to ensure that treaty obligations provide efficient mechanisms for adjusting to these changes. Governments prefer to retain control over their reaction to such changes instead of conferring authority on international institutions to determine what adjustments are necessary. They ensure their discretion through ambiguous texts, insufficient monitoring tools, or suboptimal enforcement mechanisms. Small domestic groups insist on this discretion, as their interests may be affected by strict future compliance with treaty obligations. Thus, as George Downs and David Rocke have explained, international trade law includes weak enforcement norms to accommodate the uncertain future demands of domestic

---

[91] US v. The Palestine Liberation Org. et al 695 F. Supp. 1456 (1988); W. Michael Reisman, *An International Farce: The Sad Case of the PLO Mission*, 14 YALE J. INT'L L. 412, 429–432 (1989).

[92] On the characteristics of "relational contracts," see Ian R. Macneil, THE NEW SOCIAL CONTRACT (1980); Charles J. Goetz & Robert E. Scott, *Principles of Relational Contracts*, 67 VA. L. REV. 1089 (1981); Ian R. Macneil, *Economic Analysis of Contractual Relations: Its Shortfalls and the Need for a "Rich Classificatory Apparatus,"* 75 NW. U. L. REV. 1018 (1981); Ian R. Macneil, *The Many Futures of Contract*, 47 S. CAL. L. REV. 691 (1974); Alan Schwartz, *Relational Contracts in the Courts: An Analysis of Incomplete Agreements and Judicial Strategies*, 21 J. LEGAL STUD. 271 (1992).

interest groups.[93] Parties design enforcement norms strong enough to encourage signatories to observe the agreement most of the time, thereby preventing, for example, trade wars, "but low enough to allow politicians to break the agreement when interest-group benefits are great."[94] Because retaliatory measures often fail to target only the group responsible for the breach, they therefore externalize the costs of the breach to other domestic groups.

Note that escape clauses that offer impunity for the defecting state executive may not be equally available to a legislature that wishes to renege on the treaty. First, the relevant escape clauses are more likely to reflect small-group interests. Justifications for the breach by the larger groups–including such breaches as the interest in sound environmental policies or improved workers' conditions–are less likely to permit defection with impunity. Second, the legislature is less capable than the executive of monitoring other states' violations, a key tool–if only rhetorical–for justifying one's own breach to both the international community and international tribunals. Last, because breaches are followed immediately by international negotiations and possibly adjudication, the executive is more capable than the legislature of finessing the consequences of a breach (or externalizing the costs to the larger public). Due to the relative edge enjoyed by the executive over the legislature, the former is more likely to initiate unilateral defections from international obligations, whereas the latter will likely remain inactive.

Interested small domestic groups also prefer not to seek the courts' protection against their executive's decision to renege on its treaty obligations; their political leverage provides sufficient guarantees against the need to do so. In fact, they are more interested in seeing that domestic courts remain uninvolved and so refrain from demanding compliance of a reneging government; and courts live up to the expectation. National courts have faced numerous petitions for injunctions challenging domestic policies–whether statutes or administrative decisions–on the grounds that they were incompatible with general international law[95] or specific

---

[93] Downs & Rocke, *supra* note 60, at 88. Downs and Rocke extend their observation to other kinds of international agreements in which states desire the ability to respond periodically to domestic interests. *Id.* at 88–104.

[94] *Id.* at 77.

[95] This is notably the case with efforts to invoke international human rights standards in national courts. *See* Harold Hongju Koh, *Transnational Public Law Litigation*, 100 YALE L.J. 2347 (1991); Beth Simmons, MOBILIZING HUMAN RIGHTS: INTERNATIONAL LAW IN DOMESTIC POLITICS (2009). For a comparative perspective, see Benedetto Conforti & Francesco Francioni, ENFORCING INTERNATIONAL HUMAN RIGHTS IN DOMESTIC COURTS (1997).

treaty obligations.[96] Parties have likewise brought suits challenging the domestic recognition of foreign governments' acts, such as the expropriation of private property abroad, which international law regarded as illegal.[97] National courts have generally reacted negatively to such claims, as until the early 2000s judges invariably chose to defer to the executive.[98] Courts in virtually all democracies have shown great ingenuity by inventing an arsenal of "avoidance doctrines" that enables them to align their judgments with the executive's perceived national interests.[99] They sidestepped questioning the international legality of the executive's activities and the fruits of its negotiations.[100] In some jurisdictions, notably that of the United States, courts allowed the executive to violate international customary law lawfully.[101] It was also widely accepted that the executive may terminate treaties unilaterally without legislative or judicial review.[102]

Paradoxically, some have attributed the then prevalent deferential attitude to the lack of democratic legitimacy inherent in international

[96] See, e.g., Sale v. Haitian Ctrs. Council, 509 U.S. 155 (1993) (rejecting claim that repatriation of Haitian refugees at sea violated the UN Convention on Refugees); United States v. Alvarez-Machain, 504 U.S. 655 (1992) (finding the US government's forced abduction of a Mexican citizen to be compatible with the US-Mexican extradition treaty); Harold Hongju Koh, The "Haiti Paradigm" in United States Human Rights Policy, 103 YALE L.J. 2391 (1994) (discussing the Sale case). For a similar decision by a chamber of the German Federal Constitutional Court, see the decision of July 17, 1985 (EuGRZ 1986, 18, at 20) (Federal Republic of Germany).

[97] See, e.g., Banco Nacional de Cuba v. Sabbatino, 376 U.S. 398 (1964) (applying act of state doctrine to expropriation of private assets of US citizens in Cuba).

[98] See supra note 80.   [99] See supra note 81.

[100] Thus, in the Rhine Pollution case discussed above, see French Pollution Permit Case, supra note 39, at 298, the French Conseil d'État upheld the permission to pollute as lawful, finding that international norms (including applicable treaties) did not proscribe it. For criticism of the decision, see Alexandre Kiss, 2–3 REVUE JURIDIQUE DE L'ENVIRONNEMENT, 307–09 (1986) (commentary following the case).

[101] See Garcia-Mir v. Meese, 788 F.2d 1446, 1454–55 (11th Cir. 1986) (holding that cabinet officers, in addition to the President, may violate international customary law); see also Louis Henkin, International Law as Law in the United States, 82 MICH. L. REV. 1555, 1568–69 (1984); Agora: May the President Violate Customary International Law? 80 AM. J. INT'L L. 913 (1986).

[102] On the US law, see RESTATEMENT, supra note 70, § 339(b) ("Under the law of the United States, the President has the power. . . to make the determination that would justify the United States in terminating or suspending an agreement because of its violation by another party or because of supervening events, and to proceed to terminate or suspend the agreement on behalf of the United States.") On German law, see Frowein & Hahn, supra note 76, at 363 (stating that treaty termination power is considered to be within the exclusive domain of the executive). In those countries that do not require parliamentary approval of treaties, executive termination power is obvious.

treaties and other norms.[103] According to this view, because the formulation of international treaties and custom is itself democratically deficient, courts should not regard international obligations as worthy of respect and enforcement, which therefore puts those obligations beyond the proper scope of judicial scrutiny. This explanation, however, only highlights the undemocratic consequences of the courts' hesitation: International treaties, which often entail significant domestic ramifications, bypass the courts' scrutiny because they had already bypassed regular legislative review. Executive power thus reigns supreme.

The national courts' deferential approach was not, however, motivated by a concern for democratic legitimacy. Instead, it stemmed from the same global interjurisdictional competition that affects the other branches of government. An assertive court that was ready and willing to enforce international norms upon recalcitrant governments (which, for example, refrain from imposing environmental standards on polluting industries) invited sanctions on its state for dodging international obligations. Potentially affected firms could then decide to relocate to another jurisdiction, in which courts were more compliant. For the same reason, national courts had little incentive to impinge upon the laissez-faire underpinnings of international law or to develop stringent standards governing the activity of locally based companies that operate abroad. A judicial assertion, for example, that state parties to a bankrupt international organization are responsible for its outstanding obligations to third parties, might lead other international organizations to establish headquarters in jurisdictions where such responsibility is not recognized.[104] Enforcing strict domestic standards on domestic actors

---

[103] The democratic deficiency debate continues to stir scholarly attention. *Compare* Curtis A. Bradley & Jack L. Goldsmith, *The Current Illegitimacy of International Human Rights Litigation*, 66 FORDHAM L. REV. 319 (1997), Curtis A. Bradley & Jack L. Goldsmith, *Customary International Law as Federal Common Law: A Critique of the Modern Position*, 110 HARV. L. REV. 815 (1997), *and* Phillip R. Trimble, *A Revisionist View of Customary International Law*, 33 UCLA L. REV. 665 (1986), *with* Harold Hongju Koh, *Commentary: Is International Law Really State Law?*, 111 HARV. L. REV. 1824 (1998), *and* Gerald L. Neuman, *Sense and Nonsense about Customary International Law: A Response to Professors Bradley and Goldsmith*, 66 FORDHAM L. REV. 371 (1997). On the probable influence of the democracy argument on the court, see Richard A. Falk, THE ROLE OF DOMESTIC COURTS IN THE INTERNATIONAL ORDER (1964); Lea Brilmayer, *International Law in American Courts: A Modest Proposal*, 100 YALE L.J. 2277 (1991); and Thomas M. Franck, *The Courts, the State Department and National Policy: A Criterion for Judicial Abdication*, 44 MINN. L. REV. 1101 (1960).

[104] *See The ITC Litigation, supra* note 35 (refusing to recognize the responsibility of state parties for the debts of the international organization).

operating abroad, such as the famous cases of Union Carbide[105] or Texaco,[106] may prompt them and others to leave the jurisdiction and set up shop abroad, where their competitors are based. National courts, as much as national legislatures and governments, appreciated this threat and joined the race to the bottom. They behaved like any other actor in a prisoner's dilemma scenario as they pursued one dominant strategy: protect domestic interests.[107] This timidity would be overcome only in the early 2000s, when growing external threats to their authority and, simultaneously, improved interjudicial communications enabled courts to generate assurances that their foreign peers would cooperate.

This thesis also extends to courts of regional organizations, such as the Court of Justice of the European Union, where one would expect a similar partisan attitude when dealing with the external relationships of the organization. And indeed, that court dismissed a number of challenges to the European Commission's and Council's discriminatory policies regarding the "Banana War" involving the EU, Central American countries, and the United States.[108]

---

[105] Gasses released from a pesticide plant owned by Union Carbide India (owned by Union Carbide Corp., a US company) killed about 2100 people and injured over 200,000. Lawsuits were brought by both individual claimants and the government of India in the U.S. District Court of the Southern District of New York against the US parent. The court dismissed the cases for forum non conveniens. See In re Union Carbide Corp. Gas Plant Disaster at Bhopal, India in December 1984, 634 F. Supp. 842 (S.D.N.Y. 1986), modified, 809 F.2d 195 (2d Cir. 1986). Despite the Indian government's assertion that Indian courts were unable to cope with the magnitude of this claim, the court opined that litigating in India would better respect Indian sovereignty and judicial self-sufficiency. See id. at 867. The real underlying issue was, of course, the possibility of obtaining the higher US standards of damages including punitive damages.

[106] Two class-action suits filed in US courts by Ecuadorian and Peruvian citizens against Texaco alleged that Texaco had severely polluted rainforests and rivers in Ecuador and Peru as a result of its oil exploitation activities in Ecuador. The suits were again dismissed for forum non conveniens and reasons of international comity. See Aquinda v. Texaco, Inc., 945 F. Supp. 625 (S.D.N.Y. 1996), vacated, 157 F.3d 152 (2d Cir. 1998); Sequihua v. Texaco, Inc., 847 F. Supp. 61 (S.D. Tex. 1994).

[107] See Eyal Benvenisti, Judges and Foreign Affairs: A Comment on the Institut de Droit International's Resolution on "The Activities of National Courts and the International Relations of Their State," 5 Eur. J. Int'l L. 423, 426 (1994).

[108] See Case C-73/97 P, French Republic v. Comafrica SpA & Dole Fresh Fruit Eur. Ltd. & Co., 1999 (Jan. 21, 1999); Case C-280/93, Germany v. Council of the E.U., 1994 E.C.R. I-4973. For criticism of this case (and on the Chiquita Italia case, Case C-469/93, Amministrazione delle Finanze dello Stato v. Chiquita Italia SpA, 1995 E.C.R. I-4533), see Meinhard Hilf, The Role of National Courts in International Trade Relations, 18 Mich. J. Int'l L. 321, 338–43 (1997). But see Case C-122/95, Germany and Belg. v. Council of the E.U., 1998 E.C.R. I-973, in which the court annulled part of the Council's decision approving the conclusion of a trade agreement with third states because it discriminates

The three characteristics of treaties discussed in this section–small-group domination of the negotiation and ratification of treaties, the lack of opportunities for the larger public to challenge existing treaty obligations, and the opportunities for governments and small groups to escape their treaty obligations with relative impunity–combined to ensure small groups a significant edge over other domestic groups in securing their sectarian interests.

3.4   The Externalities of Interest-Group Capture

Why are small groups better than diffuse groups at maneuvering the global space? The answer, in short, is that the inherent collective action problems of consolidating political power in the global regulatory space have become increasingly more challenging for diffuse groups to resolve, whereas small groups have found it increasingly profitable to overcome their impediments to cooperation. The process of globalization, which increases the dependence of most states on a small set of foreign actors, suggests at least four reasons for concern about the deterioration of the effectiveness of traditional mechanisms of domestic political and regulatory accountability. This is a worrisome trend because those are the ways by which citizens can exercise agency and control their political branches. (Those concerns are, of course, in addition to the traditional worries about the internal systemic problems of democracy.)

First, the continuous lowering of the technical and legal barriers to the free movement of people, goods, services, and capital across territorial boundaries has exacerbated the well-known failures already inherent in domestic democratic processes. This situation has strengthened the hand of those domestic actors who can exploit the increased availability of "exit" options from the state made possible by globalization. These include, for example, the option of relocating themselves or their investments. The threatened "exit" by these actors has increased their "voice" at the expense of the diffuse majority. The end of the Cold War also meant the end of external threats to national sovereignty and of internal threats of popular insurrection, two concerns that had led leaders in some countries to create "a broad social base that identified its economic

---

between different exporters of bananas to the EU. Note, however, that at the time of judgment, the relevant agreement was under challenge at the WTO. See *WTO Appellate Reports, supra* note 47 (WTO Appellate Body's decision in the banana dispute).

interests with the success of the regime."[109] Those leaders felt less need to cater to the interests of diffuse voters once those threats had faded and once the alternative to the market economy had been dealt a decisive blow.

A second, related, challenge that globalization poses for the efficacy of democratic processes within many states springs from the proliferation of small and medium-size states that face increasing competition over access to foreign investment and foreign markets. Divided by political boundaries and high levels of political, social, and economic heterogeneity, these states often find it difficult to forge cooperation and instead find themselves competing for foreign investment or having to fend off a foreign state's influence. This often makes it relatively easy for a strong economic or political actor–whether a powerful state or a wealthy investor–to practice "divide and rule" strategies against them, as explored in Chapter 2. These strategies further erode the capacity of weak sovereigns for collective action and effectively confine them to different "cells" in a maze of prisoner's dilemmas (or a large, global prison).

A third challenge to the viability of democratic voice within national boundaries stems from the lack of congruence between the population of enfranchised voters and the population of parties affected by the voters' decisions. The basic assumption of state democracy–that there is a strong overlap between these two populations–might have been correct in a world of "separate mansions," when territorial boundaries defined not only the persons entitled to vote but also the community that was primarily affected by the choices made. Today, however, this condition is rarely met,[110] and the consequences manifest themselves in two negative ways. First, voters in one country define rights that have spillover effects (for example, permitting unabated pollution or imposing cap-and-trade emission regimes on foreigners as well)[111] beyond their

---

[109] *See* Jose E. Campos & Hilton L. Root, THE KEY TO THE ASIAN MIRACLE: MAKING SHARED GROWTH CREDIBLE (1996), at 28 et seq. (explaining the relative success of certain East Asian economies by efforts to respond to the Communist threat emanating from China through land reform, strong and independent bureaucracy, and other welfare promoting measures). In Europe, the Communist threat was certainly one of the main drivers of the rise of the welfare state (*see* James Petras, *The Western Welfare State: Its Rise and Demise and the Soviet Bloc*, GLOBAL RESEARCH (Jul. 4, 2012), *available at* www.globalresearch.ca/the-western-welfare-state-its-rise-and-demise-and-the-soviet-bloc/31753).

[110] Eyal Benvenisti, *Sovereigns as Trustees of Humanity: On the Accountability of States to Foreign Stakeholders*, 107 AM. J. INT'L L. 295, 304 (2013).

[111] *See* Case C-366/10, *Air Transport Association of America and others v. Sec'y of State for Energy and Climate Change*, 2011 E.C.R. I-13755 (regarding the EU emission trading regime which is enforced on foreign airline carriers).

states without the affected stakeholders having the opportunity to participate in the vote or otherwise influence the decisions that are taken.[112]
Second, foreign actors increasingly employ economic leverage to influence markets, politicians, and domestic public opinion in other states.[113]
This phenomenon may distort the domestic democratic process in the
target states and disenfranchise their citizens.

Fourth, the rise of problems in the global commons (global terrorism,
climate change) requires collective responses through regional and international organizations, and this increases the demand for international
governance, which then further reduces the space for national discretion.
In consequence, there is a proliferation of global venues for regulation
that are dominated by the executive branches of a small number of
powerful states. They remain largely inaccessible and quite opaque to
most voters, while enabling better-organized and better-funded groups
to exploit asymmetric information about the goals and consequences of
regulation. Many international organizations have functioned to further
disempower diffuse domestic electorates by expanding the executive
power of powerful states, especially through "fragmentation": setting
up multiple regulatory organizations, each with a narrow scope of
authority, that prevent smaller and developing states from engaging in
the logrolling that is necessary for them to bargain more effectively with
the more powerful states.[114]

These developments render largely improbable any cooperation
among diffuse voters across political boundaries through state legislatures and courts; at the same time they enfranchise small groups that can
concentrate their efforts on the executive branches, especially on those of
the more powerful states. Faced with the inherent weakness of the
legislative and judicial branches to reach out to their peers in other
countries or to second-guess their respective executives in external
affairs, as well as the precarious global standing of most states, the

---

[112] Nadia Urbinati & Mark E. Warren, *The Concept of Representation in Contemporary Democratic Theory*, 11 ANN. REV. POL. SCI., 387, 397 (2008); *see also* Jean Cohen, *Constitutionalism Beyond the State: Myth or Necessity? (A Pluralist Approach)*, 2 HUMANITY: AN INT'L J. HUM. RTS., HUMANITARIANISM, DEVELOPMENT 127 (2011) (discussing the need to reconsider state boundaries when considering sovereignty); Nancy Fraser, *Reframing Justice in a Globalizing World*, 36 NEW LEFT REV. 69, 71 (2005) (arguing that prior conceptions of the nation-state are insufficient to address modern problems that spill over national borders).

[113] David Schneiderman, *Investing in Democracy? Political Process and International Investment Law*, 60 U. TORONTO L.J. 909 (2010).

[114] *See* Chapter 2.

presumption of domestic checks and balances as a means of disciplining the executive and protecting the interests of diffused constituencies through the domestic democratic process has been seriously compromised.

International law has always reflected the interests of the developed world, in particular, in the context of protecting the property of foreign owners. It is international law that is responsible for the invention of the corporation that, on the one hand, is independent of its foreign parent company[115] but, on the other hand, is recognized as owned by the foreign company and hence immune from expropriation by the state of incorporation (or, in the event of expropriation, would entitle the owner to prompt, adequate, and effective compensation).[116] Moreover, if operated from a third country, the tax laws of both the host state and the parent company's home state will not apply, and the entire operation could thus benefit from tax havens. This ingenious legal invention is perhaps no less momentous for global business than the very invention of the company itself. The obligation to accord foreign investments "fair and equitable treatment" has become a keyword for imposing an increasingly demanding set of standards on host states via privatized dispute-resolution mechanisms that were established to insulate foreign investors from the national courts of the host states.[117] The efforts of developing countries to transform political venues such as the General Assembly of the United Nations into serious legislative ones, for example, when trying to promote the so-called New International Economic Order, failed miserably and faded with the disintegration of the Soviet bloc.[118]

---

[115] See Ronen Palan, *Tax Havens and the Commercialization of State Sovereignty*, 56 INT'L ORG., 151, 168–69 (2002).

[116] This wording (in relation to lawful expropriation) is known as the "Hull Formula," named after the American Secretary of State who declared in 1938 that Mexico is obligated to pay compensation for expropriation for any reason whatsoever: "[U]nder every rule of law and equity, no government is entitled to expropriate private property, for whatever purpose without provision for prompt, adequate and effective payment therefor." Green Haywood Hackworth, DIGEST OF INTERNATIONAL LAW 657 (1943).

[117] Julie A. Maupin, *Public and Private in International Investment Law: An Integrated Systems Approach*, 54(2) VIRGINIA J. INT'L L. 367 (2014); Lise Johnson & Oleksandr Volkov, *Investor-State Contracts, Home-State "Commitments" and the Myth of Stability in International Law*, 24(3) AM. REV. INT'L ARB. 361 (2013); Robert Stumberg, *Sovereignty by Subtraction: The Multilateral Agreement on Investment*, 31 CORNELL INT'L L.J. 491 (1998); Andreas F. Lowenfeld, *Investment Agreements and International Law*, 42 COLUM. J. TRANSNAT'L L. 123 (2003).

[118] Doreen Lustig, INTERNATIONAL CORPORATE REGULATION IN THE 20TH CENTURY: A HISTORY OF FAILURE? (forthcoming, 2017), chapter 4. Mark Mazower, GOVERNING THE WORLD: THE HISTORY OF AN IDEA 273–304, 344–377 (2012)

When economic markets became global at the end of the Cold War, property rights came increasingly to be defined by international agreements and decisions of international organizations. International law has become a tool to discipline the majority of states to conform to global standards on various aspects of property definition and use (for example, pollution and use of natural resources, intellectual property rights). Perhaps because the traditional tools of international law have become too public for some, governments of powerful states have further explored the opportunities for fragmentation, such as the use of informal cooperation through "networks" of state executives or the de facto delegation of standard-setting functions to private actors. The global political markets of today are dominated by the executive branches of a small subset of relatively strong states that, in turn, have been responsive to the influence of special interests and opaque to public scrutiny. And, unsurprisingly, the standards set by these informal networks reflect the interests of the powerful states.[119]

Interest-group influence has consequences on the North/South global divide. This is clear, for example, in the struggle to define the global protection of intellectual property rights. Margot Kaminski is among the scholars who have been monitoring the ways in which the United States has "aggressively shifted among various international law and policy-making forums to promote a goal of harmonizing the world's intellectual property laws in its image."[120] The effort began with the creation of the World Trade Organization (WTO) in 1995. The WTO consisted of the old GATT regime and the new General Agreement on Trade in Services, and the Trade-Related Aspects of Intellectual Property Rights (TRIPS). The commitment to protect intellectual property rights globally was imposed by the United States and the EU by making the future of trade liberalization conditional on that.[121] But legislatures and courts in the developing world have interpreted their

---

[119] For example, in antitrust policies *see* Eleanor Fox, *Antitrust without Borders: From Roots to Codes to Networks*, in COOPERATION, COMITY AND COMPETITION POLICY (Andrew T. Guzman ed., 2010), Tristan Feunteun, *Cartels and the Right to Food: An Analysis of States' Duties and Options*, 18 J. INT'L ECON. L. 341, 368 (2015).

[120] Sean M. Flynn, Brook Baker, Margot Kaminski, & Jimmy Koo, *The U.S. Proposal for an Intellectual Property Chapter in the Trans-Pacific Partnership Agreement*, 28 AM. U. INT'L L. REV. 105 (2012).

[121] *See supra* Chapter 2; Richard H. Steinberg, *Judicial Lawmaking at the WTO: Discursive, Constitutional, and Political Constraints*, 98 AM. J. INT'L L. 247 (2004); Richard H. Steinberg, *In the Shadow of Law or Power? Consensus-Based Bargaining and Outcomes in the GATT/WTO*, 56 INT'L ORG. 339 (2002).

obligations narrowly,[122] and intellectual property owners sought to enhance their rights even further. As multilateral negotiations over updating the WTO accords failed, the United States moved to bilateral free trade area (FTA) agreements, to an Anti-Counterfeiting Trade Agreement (defeated by the EU Parliament which refused to ratify it),[123] and most recently to "mega-regional agreements" with twelve Pacific Rim countries (the Trans-Pacific Partnership or TPP) and with the EU (the Trade and Investment Partnership or TTIP).[124] Were these negotiations successful, they would have set new global standards for IP protection that would have entailed significant restrictions on the access to drugs.[125]

Beyond heavily influencing treaty regimes and the decisions of global regulatory bodies, influential Northern interests also operate through virtually unregulated multinational corporations (MNCs) that break up their production chain into different links that operate in discrete localities and offer the advantages of freedom of establishment and the free movement of capital and goods. Thus, not only can they benefit from different standards of production, but they can also shape those standards and impose them on host governments vying for foreign money.[126] Furthermore, interest groups have begun to lobby weaker foreign states directly.[127] Their influence is felt in key areas such as

---

[122] *See* the Indian Supreme Court judgment in Novartis v. The State of India, *infra* note 140 in chap. 5.

[123] Margot E. Kaminski, *An Overview and the Evolution of the Anti-Counterfeiting Trade Agreement*, PIJIP Research Paper Series, paper no. 17 (2011).

[124] Eyal Benvenisti, *Democracy Captured: The Mega-Regional Agreements and the Future of Global Public Law*, 23 CONSTELLATIONS 58 (2016).

[125] Amy Kapczynski, *The Trans-Pacific Partnership–Is It Bad for Your Health?* N. ENGL. J. MED. 201 (2015). On the domination of small interest groups in determining US trade policies see Margot E. Kaminski, *The Capture of International Intellectual Property Law through the U.S. Trade Regime*, 87 S. CAL. L. REV. 977 (2014); Peter Drahos, *Global Law Reform and Rent-Seeking: The Case of Intellectual Property*, 7 AUSTRALIAN J. CORP. L. 1 (1996); Christopher Ingraham & Howard Schneider, *Industry Voices Dominate the Trade Advisory System*, WASHINGTON POST, Feb. 27, 2014, *available at* www.washington post.com/wp-srv/special/business/trade-advisory-committees/.

[126] For an overview of these developments, see Dan Danielsen, *How Corporations Govern: Taking Corporate Power Seriously in Transnational Regulation and Governance*, 46 HARV. INT'L L. J. 411 (2005); Gerald F. Davis, Marina V.N. Whitman & Mayer Nathan Zald, *The Responsibility Paradox: Multinational Firms and Global Corporate Social Responsibility* (Ross Sch. of Bus. Working Paper Series, Working Paper No. 1031, Apr. 2006). For a critical discussion, see Doreen Lustig & Eyal Benvenisti, *The Multinational Corporation as "the Good Despot": The Democratic Costs of Privatization in Global Settings*, 15 THEORETICAL INQUIRIES L. 125 (2014).

[127] For a recent example, see Stavros Gadinis, *Three Pathways to Global Standards: Private, Regulator, and Ministry Networks*, 109 AM. J. INT'L L. 1 (2015).

international taxation (for example, bilateral tax treaties that ensure that the host states do not tax the foreign investors)[128] and foreign investment law (and specifically, bilateral investment treaties that secure foreign investment from host state control),[129] and most recently in the so-called land-grabbing phenomenon, the long-term lease of vast tracts of land for cultivation.[130] For the latter they have sought out states with a poor definition of property rights and weak systems of land governance as their choice for investment.[131] While this comes as a surprise to economists, who assumed that stronger property rights regimes would attract investors,[132] foreign investors apparently rely on their domination of the political market as the framework for protecting their investments.

Finally, the contemporary global legal arena is also conspicuous for the many areas that remain intentionally unregulated. For instance, there are still no effective global regimes–formal or informal–that can overcome global tax competition and tax havens,[133] assign state responsibility for acts or omissions of locally registered corporations that operate beyond the national jurisdiction,[134] or resolve sovereign

---

[128] Tsilly Dagan, *The Tax Treaties Myth*, 32(4) N.Y.U. J. INT'L L. & POL. 939 (2000); Kim Brooks & Richard Krever, *The Troubling Role of Tax Treaties*, 51 TAX DESIGN ISSUES WORLDWIDE, SERIES ON INTERNATIONAL TAXATION 159 (Geerten M. M. Michielse & Victor Thuronyi eds., 2015), *available at* http://papers.ssrn.com/sol3/papers.cfm?abstract_id=2639064 (high-income countries gain from tax treaties with low-income countries because they restrict low-income countries' abilities to collect revenue from income earned in their jurisdictions. For multinational corporations the system offers a simple path to avoid taxation).

[129] Soumyajit Mazumder, *Can I Stay a BIT Longer? The Effect of Bilateral Investment Treaties on Political Survival*, 10(3) REV. INT'L ORG. 1 (2015), *available at* http://shomma zumder.github.io/files/BIT-Survival.pdf.

[130] Jochen von Bernstorff, *The Global "Land-Grab," Sovereignty and Human Rights*, 2(9) EUROPEAN SOC'Y OF INT'L L. REFLECTIONS (2013), *available at* www.esil-sedi.eu/sites/default/files/ESIL%20Reflections%20-%20von%20Bernstorff_0.pdf.

[131] Olivier De Schutter, *How Not to Think of Land-Grabbing: Three Critiques of Large-Scale Investments in Farmland*, 38 J. PEASANT STUDIES 249, 266 (2011); Amnon Lehavi, *Land Law in the Age of Globalization and Land Grabbing*, in RESEARCH HANDBOOK ON COMPARATIVE PROPERTY LAW 25 (Michele Graziadei & Lionel Smith eds., 2015).

[132] Rabah Arezki, Klaus Deininger, & Harris Selod, *What Drives the Global "Land Rush"?* 29 WORLD BANK ECON. REV. 207, 207 (2015). ("this finding contrasts the standard literature insofar as the quality of the destination country's business climate is insignificant, and weak tenure security is associated with increased interest for investors to acquire land in the country.")

[133] Tsilly Dagan, *supra* note 59; Reuven Avi-Yonah, INTERNATIONAL TAX AS INTERNATIONAL LAW: AN ANALYSIS OF THE INTERNATIONAL TAX REGIME (2007).

[134] *See, e.g.*, the Guiding Principles, *supra* note 30; Kiobel v. Royal Dutch Petroleum Co., 133 S.Ct. 1659 (2013).

defaults in ways that provide equitable burden sharing between borrowers and lenders.[135]

3.5   Conclusion

Public choice literature is replete with analyses of the failure of democratic systems to reflect the actual preferences of the individual voter. This chapter complements these analyses by showing an even greater decline in voter power as a result of small-group domination of international politics and of an increasingly interdependent world economy. Moreover, it demonstrates that domestic norms and institutions designed to protect domestic interest groups that are replicated in the global governance space impose significant burdens on foreign stakeholders as well. The resultant democratic deficits affect the diffuse constituencies of developed and developing countries alike.

But herein lies also the promise of the domestic responses to interest-group domination. To the extent that domestic institutions, particularly national courts, are able to constrain national regulators and insulate them from interest-group capture, they can benefit not only their own constituency but also, indirectly, communities in other parts of the world.

These insights are corroborated in the following chapters. Chapters 4 and 5 examine the potential responses of courts, the institutions that traditionally operated to limit capture by special interests and protect the diffuse or discrete and insular voters. We begin with an examination of the potential review functions of international tribunals. For the reasons discussed in Chapter 2 and in this one, we suggest that compared with their national brethren, international courts are less well equipped to serve as bulwarks against powerful state executives. But bolstered by the more robust responses of national courts, there may be reason to hope that, collectively, interjudicial cooperation could prove effective in imposing accountability mechanisms on global regulators.

---

[135] Joseph E. Stiglitz & Martin Guzman, *The Rule of Law for Sovereign Debt*, PROJECT SYNDICATE (Jun. 15, 2015), *available at* www.project-syndicate.org/commentary/sover eign-debt-restructuring-by-joseph-e-stiglitz-and-martin-guzman-2015–06?barrier= true; Michael Waibel, SOVEREIGN DEFAULTS BEFORE INTERNATIONAL COURTS AND TRIBUNALS 163 (2011).

4

The Brittle Independence of International Tribunals and Its Effects on Fragmentation

4.1 Introduction

International tribunals (ITs) can, in principle, enhance democracy both at the level of the state[1] and at the global level.[2] But to ensure that ITs can indeed provide effective checks on unfettered economic and political power of the few who control international institutions, it is necessary to ensure that the tribunals are sufficiently independent of those few powerful actors. Herein lies the main challenge for ITs. While powerful actors operating through international institutions would generally benefit from public perception that the tribunals that review their actions are sufficiently independent,[3] they are less likely to tolerate activist judges who dare to review their reasoning and limit their discretion. Hence the puzzle: Under which circumstances will international institutions agree to concede authority to ITs that would review their policies? When and why will international judges dare to defy their subjects of review and restrain their discretion in a meaningful way?

In this chapter, we offer answers to these questions. We draw upon the theoretical and empirical literatures on the evolution of court independence within modern democratic states to identify the aspects of their political environments that have fostered judicial independence at the domestic level. To date, most of the literature on the independence of international tribunals, like most of the literature dealing with judicial independence at the domestic level, has focused on the rules connected

---

[1] Robert O. Keohane, Stephen Macedo & Andrew Moravcsik, *Democracy-Enhancing Multilateralism*, 63 Int'l Org. 1 (2009).

[2] Ruth W. Grant & Robert O. Keohane, *Accountability and Abuses of Power in World Politics*, 99 Am. Pol. Sci. Rev. 29, 30 (2005).

[3] On the link between judicial independence and legitimacy, *see, e.g.*, Armin von Bogdandy & Ingo Venzke, *In Whose Name? An Investigation of International Courts' Public Authority and International Tribunals Democratic Justification*, 23 Eur. J. Int'l L. 7 (2012); Ruth MacKenzie & Philippe Sands, *International Courts and Tribunals and the Independence of the International Judge*, 44 Harv. Int'l L.J. 271 (2003).

with the ways that judges are nominated, selected, and tenured.[4] While it is true that these formal structural features play an important role in determining judicial independence, they are not sufficient in and of themselves. The freedom of ITs to interpret and develop the law in the ways they deem appropriate is also a function of attributes of the broader political context in which they are embedded. Historically, political division is the principal generator of court independence.

We therefore extend the analysis of domestic courts' independence to examine the role that these or similar factors are likely to play in facilitating the independence of ITs at the global level. We follow the observation that the main factor that determines judicial independence at the domestic level is the extent to which the political branches are divided and require a court that can arbitrate between them in an impartial manner. We then extend that observation to the global regulatory sphere. We seek to identify potential sources for divisions that can enhance the role of ITs as impartial umpires. This leads us to focus on two broad aspects of the global environment not usually associated with the independence of international tribunals: the extent of political division between states that are parties to an international tribunal (what we call "interstate competition") and the extent of political division within states between state executives and national courts (NCs) (what we refer to as "interbranch division"). We submit and prove that interstate competition or interbranch division (and obviously, the juxtaposition of both types of competition) is key to determining the extent to which ITs will feel sufficiently confident to impose legal constraints on global policy-making. This leads us to suggest further that because of increased competition, the conditions that facilitate judicial independence at the global level have increased in recent years.

---

[4] von Bogdandy & Venzke, *supra* note 3; Laurence R. Helfer & Anne-Marie Slaughter, *Why States Create International Tribunals: A Response to Professors Posner and Yoo*, 93 CAL. L. REV. 1, 44–57 (2005) discusses the political and structural factors that motivate states to create and constrain the independence of international tribunals. *See also* Tom Ginsburg, *Political Constraints on International Courts*, in THE OXFORD HANDBOOK OF INTERNATIONAL ADJUDICATION 483 (Cesare PR Romano, Karen J. Alter & Yuval Shany eds., 2014) (distinguishing between *ex ante* such as appointment and tenure of judges and *ex post* constraints, such as the ability to exit a regime), and Robert O. Keohane et al., *Legalized Dispute Resolution: Interstate and Transnational*, 54 INT'L ORG. 457, 460–62 (2000) (referring also to the level of legal discretion that judges may exercise when interpreting a treaty, and the degree of control that governments exert over a tribunal's material and human resources, as also playing a role in determining overall tribunal independence).

4.2   Political Divisions as Determinants of Judicial Independence

4.2.1   The Impact of Political Division between and within States on the Independence of International Tribunals

One of the earliest and most prominent explanations for the evolution of judicial independence and the expansion of court lawmaking power in the domestic setting is the McNollgast theory of judicial independence.[5] The authors argue that court independence is inversely related to the likelihood that its decisions will be ignored or overridden by the political branches. As a result, judicial independence waxes and wanes with the pattern of partisan control that exists in the political branches of government and institutional rules. In the United States, for example, the likelihood of the Supreme Court being overridden tends to be the least and its political independence the greatest during periods when the government is under divided partisan control. This is when court independence is greatest, as the chances are then good that either one of the legislative chambers or the executive branch will veto any attempt to overturn a given decision. An independent judiciary can also emerge and be sustained within the domestic context when two political parties enjoy an alternating or cyclical majority and anticipate that this situation is likely to continue. Conversely, during periods of unified partisan control, the independence of the judiciary and its impact on lawmaking are likely to be modest, in part because the party in power will exploit its dominance to expand the judiciary and stack it with individuals who share its judicial philosophy.[6]

---

[5] McNollgast, *Conditions for Judicial Independence*, 15 J. CONTEMP. LEGAL ISSUES 105 (2006); McNollgast, *Politics and the Courts: A Positive Theory of Judicial Doctrine and the Rule of Law*, 68 S. CAL. L. REV. 1631 (1995). (McNollgast is a collective pen name that is employed by three longtime collaborators: Matthew McCubbins, Roger Noll, and Barry Weingast.) On the political preconditions for judicial independence see also Mark C. Stephenson, *"When the Devil Turns . . . ": The Political Foundations of Independent Judicial Review* 32 J. LEGAL STUD. 59 (2003); Tom Ginsburg, JUDICIAL REVIEW IN NEW DEMOCRACIES: CONSTITUTIONAL COURTS IN ASIAN CASES 21–33 (2003); John Ferejohn, *Judicializing Politics, Politicizing Law*, 65 LAW & CONTEMP. PROBS. 41, 57 (2002); Robert D. Cooter, THE STRATEGIC CONSTITUTION 225 (2000); Mark J. Ramseyer, *The Puzzling (In)dependence of Courts: A Comparative Approach*, 23 J. LEGAL STUD. 721 (1994); William M. Landes & Richard A. Posner, *The Independent Judiciary in an Interest-Group Perspective*, 18 J. L. ECON. 875 (1975).

[6] For a demonstration of this claim in the actual practice of NCs, see Ginsburg, *supra* note 5; Ramseyer, *supra* note 5.

Matthew Stephenson,[7] Clifford Carruba,[8] and other scholars develop a related theory of judicial independence. They suggest that the courts carefully gauge the strength of their public support to question the policies of political branches, as measured by public opinion. The motivations of the public for backing the court's decision when it runs counter to the position of the government can vary. They can range from simply wanting to ensure that government institutions continue to be constrained by the rule of law to believing that the court's policy preferences are more closely aligned with its own.[9] Voters' reliance on judicial findings and positions depends on the relative reliability they assign to the information that the different branches provide voters, where reliability reflects the degree to which the voter can rely on a given branch's support of or opposition to a proposed piece of legislation as evidence that the proposal is in the voter's interest.

Both models suggest that judicial independence thrives on dissension. It is then that the court's impartial referee role is in high demand by the competing political branches. It is then that the voters are seeking nonpartisan information about the rival political branches' compliance with their constitutional obligations.

Both models also set similar limits to the freedom of the court. In the former case, judicial doctrine needs to be moderate in the sense that the judiciary cannot lean too far in favor of either of the contending political parties or else at least one of them will abandon its preference for judicial independence; and in the latter case, the public may regard the information that the court generates as unreliable. If the expected level of political competition diminishes, such that one party becomes overwhelmingly dominant, that party (and the majority of voters who support it) will

---

[7] Matthew Stephenson, *Court of Public Opinion: Government Accountability and Judicial Independence*, 20 J. LAW, ECON. & ORG. 379 (2004).

[8] Clifford James Carrubba, *A Model of the Endogenous Development of Judicial Institutions in Federal and International Systems*, 71 J. POL. 55 (2009). *See also* Lawrence Baum, JUDGES AND THEIR AUDIENCES: A PERSPECTIVE ON JUDICIAL BEHAVIOR (2006).

[9] Tom S. Clark, THE LIMITS OF JUDICIAL INDEPENDENCE (2011); Nuno Garoupa & Tom Ginsburg, *Judicial Audiences and Reputation: Perspectives from Comparative Law*, 47 COLUM. J. TRANSNAT'L L. 51, 51–52 (2008–2009) ("Whether judges are motivated to make good law or maximize policy goals, they need to develop and maintain a good reputation with some audience [...] Whatever it is that judges seek to maximize, their ability to do so depends on certain audiences that react to their decisions: the media, politicians, lawyers and law professors, and the public itself. And judicial ability to communicate with these audiences in turn depends on the institutional structure in which judges operate.")

abandon its support of the existing cooperative equilibrium and judicial independence will perish with it.[10]

The different models are not, of course, directly applicable to the international system, which is made up of different kinds of actors and possesses weaker and more unstable rules and institutions. However, the models' central result, that political competition plays a key role in determining judicial independence, possesses a cross-contextual descriptive robustness. Hegemonic power and severe inequality are rarely if ever compatible with the emergence or sustainability of institutional independence in any political system. Historically, institutional checks and balances such an independent judiciary have often emerged as the result of a political compromise between at least two powerful, relatively equal actors (for example, political parties, coalitions of states, interest groups) who believed that such a body would effectively monitor and assist in enforcing one or more agreements between them.

Given the opaque and uncertain character of political accountability in the international system, the potential contribution of such a public-opinion model for understanding the emergence of independence in the case of ITs is difficult to assess. Just as there is no set of well-defined parties, legislature, or executive branch at the international level, there is also no well-defined court of public opinion. Nonetheless, it seems reasonable to assume that the prospects for judicial independence will be increased if that portion of the transnational "public" composed of weaker states and NGOs believes that ITs will provide them with significantly more reliable information about the consequences and legality of policies of international organizations than they would otherwise have. Once in hand, such information could function to create valuable focal points for weaker state/NGO coordination and reduce the risks associated with collective action. What is less clear is whether judgments of ITs about policies of international organizations and the grounds on which they are based will be able to reliably reach this public; also unclear is the extent to which ITs can help ensure that this occurs.

The models of judicial independence described above emphasize the role of political competition and the ways that courts are able to expand their freedom during periods of division or disunity that unpredictably arise among the political branches of government. However, there is reason to believe that the role of courts is sometimes less passive than

---

[10] Stephenson, *supra* note 5 at 73. On the link between political competition and independent courts, *see also* sources mentioned in *supra* note 5.

most theories suggest. As will be further elaborated below, once political division has emerged, courts often have the ability to sustain it strategically to bolster their independence and increase their discretion by supporting the relatively weaker branch of government when the other, stronger branch threatens to regain dominance. For example, by insisting on parliamentary preapproval of executive action, courts have been able to ensure the input of legislatures that had been short-circuited by the executive. By lowering threshold requirements for initiating proceedings against executives and by allowing civil society to provide information to the court through amicus briefs, courts have enhanced their own opportunities to call the executive to account for its policies. Moreover, faced with global coordination by executive branches that circumvented and weakened the role of national legislatures, NCs have turned to interjudicial cooperation that has strengthened both their legislatures and, indirectly, themselves.[11]

4.2.2   How Political Divisions Influence the Independence of International Tribunals

It might be useful to identify different types of political competition or political division at the global level that facilitate the independence of international tribunals. We can distinguish between two such types. The first and more common type occurs at the interstate level, when countries compete against each other and can challenge each other's attempts to control the tribunal by, for example, punishing judges for their adverse rulings. The second type of political competition, which has only recently shown signs of emerging, is at the intra-state level. It results from interbranch division within states and occurs when executives of state parties are dependent on the support of their respective domestic legislatures or judiciary for the ratification of their preferred policies that have been adopted at the global level. In such scenarios, the international tribunal might be able to rely on the national court (perhaps less on the national legislature) to ensure that its decision is respected and implemented by the state party.

(a)   Interstate Competition

Interstate competition occurs at the level of an international organization, where state parties compete for power and are divided on policies.

---

[11] *See* infra Chapter 5.

These states, although they may be displeased with a ruling by an international tribunal, prefer to remain bound by the agreement that grants authority to the international tribunal. State parties may even accept an adverse ruling by an international tribunal when the benefits of participation outweigh the costs. The more costly the exit from the international tribunal's jurisdiction, the greater would be the independence of the tribunal. The relatively independent functions of the WTO Appellate Body (AB) vis-à-vis the United States and the EU can be explained by the fact that neither of them is seriously considering ignoring the AB's opinions and that attempts to unilaterally punish judges for their adverse judgments might undermine the very legitimacy of the court. The crisis that unfolded when the United States decided to punish Appellate Body members by refusing to renominate them is a case in point.[12] Therefore, the combination of internal division between state parties and high exit costs for either state is likely to grant the relevant tribunal a relatively high measure of independence from the member states.[13]

Regional human rights courts are another example of relatively independent tribunals. Their independence is derived from a division between a majority of states that would welcome the international tribunal's new law and a minority that would not. In such a case (consider, for example, cases where the European Court of Human Rights (ECtHR) criticizes Russia for abusing convention rights), the reputational effects of ignoring rulings of human rights courts weigh more heavily on the responding state than on the court. Those who do not comply with the law made by the international tribunal would suffer the reputational consequences of being noncompliant with an evolving human rights standard that others accept. Because petitions are usually brought consecutively against a specific state rather than simultaneously against several states, the human rights international tribunal has an opportunity to single out the responding state as a violator. By contrast, when a petition raises a matter of concern to most or many member states and the international tribunal cannot single out a sole violator–for example, when suits were brought to the ECtHR against all NATO members[14] or members of

---

[12] Gregory Shaffer, *Will the US Undermine the World Trade Organization?*, Huffington Post, May 23, 2016, *at* www.huffingtonpost.com/gregory-shaffer/will-the-us-undermine-the_b_10108970.html.

[13] Joost Pauwelyn, *The Rule of Law without the Rule of Lawyers? Why Investment Arbitrators Are from Mars, Trade Adjudicators from Venus*, 109 Am. J. Int'l L. 761 (2015).

[14] Bankovic v. Belgium, 2001-XII Eur. Ct. H.R. 333.

KFOR[15]–the international tribunal may find it more difficult to constrain the member states.[16]

The most important interstate competition seems likely to be that created by the growing economic power and political prominence of developing countries. While different from each other in any number of ways, these states possess similar preferences on a wide range of issues, such as climate change and trade, which are likely to continue to dominate the international policy agenda in the coming years. In addition, they possess policy priorities that often differ considerably from those of the postwar coalition of powerful states that has dominated the governance of the international system up until this point. This creates the prospect that in the near future, the coalition of powerful states that will be governing the international system will be markedly less united and more politically competitive and divisive–a situation that, as we have seen, has given rise historically to greater court independence and expanded lawmaking power for the court. The increased competition between developed and developing nations and possibly the growing divisions among the developed nations might therefore result in greater independence for ITs and lawmaking discretion.

(b)   Domestic Interbranch Division

Interbranch division–internal competition between or within the branches of government within a state party–can also facilitate the independence and influence of international tribunals. As discussed in Chapter 3, such interbranch division has been challenged by the expansion of the international regulatory system, which has afforded the executives of powerful states and the domestic interest groups that support them the opportunity to formulate policies that have important domestic repercussions in often opaque and fragmented decision-making apparatuses of international organizations. That is, this policy-making occurs absent the institutional scrutiny that would normally occur at the domestic level and absent the protection that such scrutiny offers to politically weaker domestic stakeholders. As a result, the adoption of policies by state executives at the global interagency level is often viewed by national legislatures and courts as a strategy that executives use to evade domestic

---

[15] Agim Behrami & Bekir Behrami v. France, App. No. 71412/01, Eur. Ct. H.R. (2007); Ruzhdi Saramati v. France, Germany and Norway, App. No. 78166/01, Eur. Ct. H.R (2007).

[16] Shai Dothan, REPUTATION AND JUDICIAL TACTICS: A THEORY OF NATIONAL AND INTERNATIONAL COURTS 105, 145 (2015).

law. As we shall see in the next chapter, increasingly wary of this problem, national legislators and courts have begun to monitor the implementation of, and on occasion to offer resistance to, international agreements[17] and decisions of international organizations,[18] particularly those obtained via inter-executive bargaining that appear to threaten or erode the authority of legislatures and courts or those that challenge the constitutional limitations on state power.

This interbranch tension at the national level can be exploited by ITs to increase their own power and influence. They have an institutional stake in doing so: A decision by a national court that requires its national authorities to follow the instructions of an international tribunal can enhance the latter's independence and authority. As we mention below,[19] not only has the Court of Justice of the European Union (CJEU) exploited the horizontal division that was created by the requirement of consensus for changing EU law but it has also, and perhaps more importantly (although it has been little noticed), benefited from the interbranch division that existed in three smaller members. The interbranch division in the three Benelux countries resulted from domestic constitutional doctrines that ensured the supremacy of the EC law (as interpreted by the CJEU) over regular domestic legislation.[20] As a consequence, the CJEU has been able to rely on the compliance of at least these three member states with its rulings. The important role that domestic support plays in fostering the independence of ITs is

---

[17] *See* the Lisbon Treaty Judgment of the German Constitutional Court, Bundesverfassungsgericht [BVerfG], 2 BvE 2/08, Jun. 30, 2009, *available at* www.bverfg.de/entscheidungen/es20090630_2bve000208en.html; *Brunner* v. *The European Union Treaty*, German Federal Constitutional Court Judgment of Oct. 12, 1993 (trans. in [1994] 57 COMMON MKT. L. REP.); *Treaty of Lisbon II*, 03.11.2009 [Decision of the Constitutional Court of the Czech Republic Nov. 3, 2009], Pl. ÚS 29/09, *available at* www.usoud.cz/en/decisions/20091103-pl-us-2909-treaty-of-lisbon-ii-1/.

[18] Joined Cases C-402/05 P & C-415/05 P, Kadi & Al Barakaat v. Council of the European Union, 2008 E.C.R.I-6351.

[19] *See* Chapter 7 Section 5.

[20] The Dutch Constitution of 1953 provided for the supremacy of international treaties over domestic statutes. The Luxemburg Court of Cassation (in 1950) and its Conseil d'E'tat (in 1951) acknowledged the supremacy of treaty obligations over local laws. In its 1971 *Le Ski* decision, the Belgian Court of Cassation, unable to rely on express provision in the Belgian Constitution, invoked the monist theory of the primacy of international law over national legislation, in determining that treaties supersede subsequently incompatible national laws. Minister for Economic Affairs v. Fromagerie Franco-Suisse "Le Ski" [1972] C.M.L.R. 330. *See* Eyal Benvenisti, *Judicial Misgivings Regarding the Application of International Law: An Analysis of Attitudes of National Courts*, 4 EUR. J. INT'L L. 159, 163 (1993).

demonstrated by what occurs when the basis of such support is absent. For example, in their study of the Andean Tribunal of Justice (ATJ), an international tribunal modeled on the CJEU, Karen Alter and Laurence Helfer attribute its modest lawmaking (compared with the extensive lawmaking by the CJEU) to the ATJ's inability to expect that the NCs of the member states and the other domestic interlocutors would support its rulings.[21]

The European Court of Human Rights is also sensitive to interbranch division and actively seeks to establish a professional rapport with the NCs of the member states. As Yonatan Lupu and Eric Voeten demonstrate,[22] one way of doing this is by increasing the citation of precedents when this is likely to resonate with domestic legal professionals and courts. The authors find that the ECtHR makes more reference to its precedents when it deals with politically sensitive cases (where the national court might face resistance from the other branches of government) and when the international tribunal decides cases from common law countries whose legal systems rely more on precedent.

Of course, it is important to note that while interbranch divisions can enhance the independence of ITs vis-à-vis the states' executives, the ITs will remain quite dependent on the preferences of potential domestic allies–primarily the NCs. This is because the ITs depend on those domestic allies to implement their judge-made law. Because these domestic allies are ultimately accountable to their domestic constituencies, they can usually be expected to give only limited and intermittent support to the IT. There is, after all, no reason to believe that NCs and national legislatures will generally share the same preferences as the IT. Moreover, the impact of interbranch division tends to be limited because it is almost always confined to one state or a small group of states (for example, between the executives and the NCs of a handful of powerful democracies), whereas interstate divisions are far more likely to be global in character. As a result, instances of independence of ITs stemming from interbranch division can usually be expected to be more modest, localized, and transient relative to independence that is driven by interstate competition (for example, by North-South differences).

---

[21] Laurence R. Helfer & Karen J. Alter, *Nature or Nurture? Judicial Lawmaking in the European Court of Justice and the Andean Tribunal of Justice*, 64 INT'L ORG. 563 (2010).

[22] Yonatan Lupu & Eric Voeten, *Precedent on International Courts: A Network Analysis of Case Citations by the European Court of Human Rights* (2010), *available at* www.eisa-net.org/be-bruga/eisa/files/events/stockholm/Lupu%20Voeten%20SGIR%202010%20Paper.pdf.

Interbranch division promises to bolster the independence of ITs vis-à-vis state executives due to the relatively greater independence and domestic legitimacy of NCs (as opposed to those of the ITs). The processes by which judges of NCs are elected and their independence is assured, once tenured, results in national court judges who are more insulated from executive influence than judges of ITs, some of whom can be reappointed.[23] NCs in most democracies also enjoy greater domestic legitimacy than do most ITs. The basis of their authority–the national constitutions–is usually more immune to intragovernmental interference or manipulation. Nor is the legal system NC judges control one that the executive can easily exit. As a result, NCs are almost invariably more independent than ITs, whose compositions and budgets are controlled by governments and who are sometimes viewed as expendable by the most powerful states.

As the CJEU example suggests, NCs, for their part, can also benefit from cooperation with ITs. ITs can facilitate coordination between NCs by endorsing, or at least by not opposing, their shared interpretation of the law. Therefore, while serious areas of potential disagreement exist between NCs and ITs and are likely to persist, it is difficult to escape the conclusion that at this particular stage in their respective developments, ITs and NCs, like the couple in the familiar battle of the sexes game, will both be better off if they coordinate their actions than if they act independently.

(c) Independence of International Tribunals Is Shaped by Both Interstate Competition and Interbranch Division

It follows that the relative dependency of any given international tribunal is shaped both by interstate competition and by interbranch division. An international tribunal can be both interstate-dependent and intrastate-dependent, be relatively independent on both axes, or enjoy only partial (either interstate or interbranch) independence. For example, the

---

[23] This is especially the case with the ICJ where elections are dominated by the P5. *See* Mackenzie & Sands, *supra* note 3; Edward McWhinney, *Law, Politics and "Regionalism" in the Nomination and Election of World Court Judges*, 13 SYRACUSE J. INT'L L. COM. 1 (1986). But this is also the case with time-limited appointments: The Commission on Democracy through Law of the Council of Europe (the "Venice Commission") has determined that "time-limited appointments as a general rule can be considered a threat to the independence and impartiality of judges." (CDL-AD (2002)012 Opinion on the Draft Revision of the Romanian Constitution, para. 57).

International Court of justice (ICJ) is arguably interstate-dependent by virtue of the fact that the P5 control the process of judicial appointments and can veto requests to the Security Council to give effect to its judgments. It is also interbranch-dependent because the implementation of many of its judgments (for example, those regarding the responsibility for armed conflicts, the delimitation of boundaries, and the use of transboundary resources) depend to a very large extent on state executives.[24] By contrast, the CJEU has been both interstate-independent and interbranch-independent. The interstate competition resulted from the different appetites for open markets between the larger and smaller states that constituted the initial six members of the European Economic Community. The interbranch division was driven by the NCs of the Benelux states. These courts exhibited relatively more willingness than the NCs of the larger member states to refer questions of interpretation to the CJEU[25] and to implement its rulings despite executive resistance. The courts of the big three–France, Germany, and Italy–regarded the CJEU with suspicion. They– and the French courts in particular–were significantly less enthusiastic about making referrals to the CJEU and made clear that they would not automatically embrace its rulings.[26]

---

[24] This may also be the case of the Andean Tribunal of Justice. Helfer & Alter, *supra* note 21, emphasize the ADJ's interbranch-dependency, but they also mention that member states have exited from the Andean Community and this would imply that the AGJ was also interstate-dependent. On the procedures for appointing judges in international tribunals from the perspective of democratic theory see Armin von Bogdandy & Ingo Venzke, *IN WHOSE NAME? A PUBLIC LAW THEORY OF INTERNATIONAL ADJUDICATION* 224–30 (2014).

[25] The greater appetite for open markets and more judicial receptivity to satisfy this appetite is reflected in the rate of judicial referrals to the CJEU. The courts of the smaller states referred questions to the CJEU significantly more (relatively to the size of their population) than those of the courts of the bigger states. Belgium and the Netherlands brought many more references per-person than the rest of the member states. Between 1970 and 1979 (after the expansion from 6 to 12 member states), the courts of Belgium and the Netherlands referred 4 cases per 500,000 persons per year (CPPY), while German courts brought 2.2 CPPY and France, Italy, the United Kingdom, and Denmark less than 1; Between 1980 and 1989 (after another expansion) the courts of Belgium and the Netherlands brought 7.1 CPPY each, while Germany 2.8, France 2.6, Italy 1 and the United Kingdom less than 1. Between 1990 and 1998 (yet another expansion) Belgian and Dutch courts brought 6 CPPY (Germany 3 CPPY, France 2, Italy 3, and the United Kingdom 1). While in the total account, the courts of the larger countries contributed the larger number of references, even the absolute numbers are telling, with German courts referring 246 cases during 1980–89 while Dutch courts referred 224 cases during the same period. This information is taken from figure 2.1 in Karen J. Alter, *ESTABLISHING THE SUPREMACY OF EUROPEAN LAW* 35 (2001).

[26] The French and German courts presented the strongest resistance to the CJEU supremacy, *see* Alter, *supra* note 25, chapter 3 (on German courts reaction to the CJEU rulings) and chapter 4 (on the reactions of the French courts).

By capitalizing on a unique confluence of critical circumstances involving interstate competition and interbranch division–the requirement of consensus for overcoming CJEU judgments, the unlikelihood of exit, and inviting a steady flow of cases from member states' NCs–the CJEU offers the most prominent example of an IT that succeeded in making significant modifications to its legal system, by benefiting from–as well as actively promoting–both interstate competition and interbranch divisions. To the extent that a transformation of the European order was achieved through law, it was the product of collaboration between the CJEU and the courts of the smaller member states rather than a collective effort on the part of European judges acting as a class.

4.2.3   Strategies to Enhance the Independence of International Tribunals

As mentioned above, there is reason to believe that the role of courts is sometimes less passive than would be suggested by most theories, which emphasize the role of the political branches in creating or hindering judicial independence. While interstate competition and interbranch division are usually a given from the perspective of the international tribunals, courts at times have the opportunity to strategically sustain it for their own purposes, by supporting the relatively weaker state or domestic actors in states that compete with the executive.

Independent ITs have been able to further increase interstate competition by weighing in on behalf of weaker state interests rather than operating as the agents of powerful states as they would have been forced to do under conditions of dependency. For example, we have documented the countervailing efforts by ITs supported by relatively weak states to confront the adverse consequences (for them) of fragmentation by developing a jurisprudence that is based on a view of international law as a system from which exit is conceptually impossible.[27] Interbranch division can be enhanced by strengthening traditional checks on executive authority and unilateralism, namely, NCs and civil society. This can be

---

[27] On these countervailing efforts see Chapter 2, Section 2. On the lack of exit, see *Fragmentation of International Law: Difficulties Arising from the Diversification and Expansion of International Law*, Report of the Study Group of the International Law Commission finalized by Martti Koskenniemi, Apr. 13, 2006, UN Doc. A/CN.4/L.682, para. 176 ("States cannot contract out from the *pacta sunt servanda* principle – unless the speciality of the regime is thought to lie in that it creates no obligations at all (and even then it would seem hard to see where the binding force of such an agreement would lie).")

achieved primarily by relaxing standing requirements of individuals to initiate suits against governments on the international plane or by increasing opportunities for public participation in judicial proceedings. In general, information that ITs generate can be instrumental domestically vis-à-vis the domestic political branches. The reasoning of the judgment of the international tribunal can in itself provide important information to the general public and thereby increase its awareness of the criticisms leveled at policies of powerful actors. As Lupu and Voeten show,[28] the reasoning of the case can also be a way of subtly communicating with NCs to persuade or motivate them to withstand domestic pressures.

Finally, an IT can empower NCs to act as its surrogates. As Christina Binder showed,[29] the Inter-American Court of Human Rights (IACHR) interpreted the American Convention on Human Rights (ACHR) as obliging NCs not to apply national norms that were in violation of the ACHR. No doubt, when announcing this doctrine, the IACHR anticipated a positive response on the part of the relevant NCs, given the widespread domestic opposition to amnesty laws.

4.3   The Negative Effects of Fragmentation on Judicial Independence

As discussed in Chapter 2, fragmentation is likely to reduce interstate competition within international organizations. Obviously, ITs would be expected to resolve disputes within the organization, and they may even enjoy wide latitude in developing norms to regulate such disputes. But at no point will courts operating in a fragmented legal space have sufficient freedom to review the actions and policies of those who direct and control the institutions. This is because, for the most part, the composition and mandates of ITs are overseen by a small group of powerful states that enjoy a relatively high level of consensus with respect to the way they perceive the role of the international tribunals.

The five permanent members of the UN Security Council are united in their desire for little more than a perfunctory review of Security Council Resolutions by the ICJ and only limited review of internal administrative

---

[28] *Supra* note 22.
[29] Christina Binder, *The Prohibition of Amnesties by The Inter-American Court of Human Rights*, 12 GERMAN L.J. 1203 (2011).

matters.[30] This same core group of states possesses the capacity and incentive to directly monitor the members of the tribunals. They dominate the process of nomination, define the criteria for renewing the appointments, and approve the court's budget.[31] If conditions warrant, they can also limit the court's independence by disregarding its judgments, threatening to abandon it for a different venue,[32] institutionalizing ways to overcome its interpretations,[33] or simply renegotiating treaty obligations.[34] To the extent that these states can remain united, they can employ these instruments of control both to limit the discretion of ITs and to pressure the ITs into adopting a jurisprudence that will be more conservative in terms of the existing status quo than that of their national court counterparts and the ITs that the states monitor less closely.

In general, the more significant the consequences of a given court are for the interests of dominant states, the more likely it is that those tools limiting that court's independence will be employed. This perspective suggests that the ICJ's practices–"infuriatingly transactional" jurisprudence, "sparse reasoning," and lack of progressivity compared with other ITs[35]–are attributable more to the powerful state scrutiny that the court labors under than to the judicial philosophies of its judges.

ITs serve a variety of functions for the system's principal designers. In addition to settling interstate disputes in ways that broadly reflect the

---

[30] This can be inferred from the decisions of the ICJ in cases like those mentioned in notes 36–38 *infra*.

[31] For an analysis of the methods for controlling international tribunals, see Jacob Katz Cogan, *Competition and Control in International Adjudication*, 48 VIRGINIA J. INT'L L. 412 (2008); Tom Ginsburg, *International Judicial Lawmaking* (2005), *available at* http://papers.ssrn.com/sol3/Delivery.cfm/SSRN_ID693861_code603.pdf?abstractid=693861&mirid=3.

[32] On the effects of the ability of states to pick and choose among international tribunals, see Chapter 2 Section 2.4.4.

[33] Such as the NAFTA Free Trade Commission, composed of representatives of the three member states, which has the authority to overrule interpretations of the NAFTA by arbitrators. See NAFTA Free Trade Commission, Notes of Interpretation of Certain Chapter 11 Provisions, Jul. 31, 2001, *available at* www.international.gc.ca/trade-agreements-accords-commerciaux/disp-diff/nafta-interpr.aspx?lang=en. Similarly, "[t]he [CJEU's] discretion to interpret secondary legislation was curtailed by the move from unanimity to [Qualified Majority Voting] in the [European] Council" (George Tsebelis & Geoffrey Garrett, *The Institutional Foundations of Intergovernmentalism and Supranationalism in the European Union*, 55 INT'L ORG. 357, 359 (2001)).

[34] On the widespread renegotiating of investment treaties, see UNCTAD World Investment Report 2010, 86, *available at* www.unctad.org/Templates/Page.asp?intItemID=1465.

[35] Bruno Simma, *Universality of International Law from the Perspective of a Practitioner*, 20 EUR. J. INT'L L. 265, 288 (2008).

interests of these principals, ITs control their organization's internal agents to whom they delegate day-to-day operational authority. They also expand the obligations that member states have beyond what they had envisioned at the time of concluding the treaty, and thereby serve as vehicles for implementing legal changes in a broader context by altering existing norms or creating new ones in a context that would traditionally have required the consent of all state parties. Specifically, these tribunals enhance the powers of the international organization under which they operate by interpreting widely the institution's powers under the "implied powers" doctrine.[36] Finally, ITs can resist domestic challenges to the international legal order despite the wide appeal of such new norms (for example, curbing the efforts of the Belgian legislature to prosecute incumbent foreign agents for war crimes[37] or quashing the Italian court's challenge to Germany's immunity for damages for crimes committed during World War II).[38] However, judicial review that imposes constraints on the principals of the system is usually not included among the intended functions of ITs. Furthermore, as James Crawford emphasized, the following is "the real problem": since international organizations cannot be sued in contentious cases, member states have no direct avenue to challenge the measures adopted by the institution against them.[39] In general, the ICJ has consistently avoided challenges to the fundamental interests of the P5, as, for example, in its treatment of the request for an advisory opinion on the legality of nuclear weapons[40] or its effort not to rule on the legality of atmospheric nuclear tests.[41] It likewise sought to evade issues over which the P5 were split. For example, its treatment of the various legal issues arising out of the conflict in the former Yugoslavia, including the skirting of the question of the legality of the Kosovo declaration of independence,[42] attests to its

---

[36] Jan Klabbers, AN INTRODUCTION TO INTERNATIONAL ORGANIZATIONS LAW 56–63 (3rd edn., 2015); José E. Alvarez, INTERNATIONAL ORGANIZATIONS AS LAW-MAKERS 92–95 (2005); Eyal Benvenisti, LAW OF GLOBAL GOVERNANCE 115–16 (2014).

[37] Arrest Warrant of 11 April 2000 (Dem. Rep. Congo v. Belg.), 2002 ICJ REP. 3 (Feb. 14).

[38] Jurisdictional Immunities of the State (Ger. v. It.), Judgement, 2008 ICJ REP. 143.

[39] James Crawford, Chance, Order, Change: The Course of International Law, (Collected Courses of the Hague Academy of International Law vo. 365, 2013) at para. 535.

[40] Legality of the Threat or Use of Nuclear Weapons, Advisory Opinion, 1996 I.C.J. Rep. 226 (Jul. 8).

[41] Nuclear Tests (Austl. v. Fr.), Judgment, 1974 I.C.J. Rep. 253 (Dec. 20); Nuclear Tests (N.Z. v. Fr.), Judgment, 1974 I.C.J. Rep. 457 (Dec. 20).

[42] Accordance with International Law of the Unilateral Declaration of Independence in Respect of Kosovo, Advisory Opinion, 2010 I.C.J. Rep. 403 (Jun. 22).

unwillingness to assert claims that would favor one P5 member over others or that might be disregarded.

That said, it should be acknowledged that the ICJ has, on several occasions, departed from its pattern of supporting the position of the P5 and ruled against the United States–criticizing directly its military actions against Nicaragua[43] and Iran,[44] challenging its breaches of the Vienna Convention on Consular Relations,[45] or indirectly rejecting the US interpretation of treaty obligations (for example, in its *Wall* opinion on the applicability of human rights law in the occupied Palestinian territories).[46] While the complicated relationship between the ICJ and the United States is beyond the scope of this chapter, one might speculate that these relatively isolated events arose from the uniqueness of the US position, which ensured that few other powerful states would be affected by the adverse rulings, either because they did not have similar problems (for example, semi-independent subnational units that defy international obligations, such as the consular rights treaty) or because they were not bound by bilateral treaties to litigate before the ICJ. In other words, while the ICJ may be dependent on the P5 with respect to matters of *common* interest of all the P5 members, it can act quite independently when it is able to single out one of the P5 members for more rigorous treatment. In such a case, noncompliance with ICJ rulings does not reflect on the ICJ but only on the losing party. Indeed, an occurrence of interstate competition is not impossible even within the group of the P5.

4.4 Conclusion

In this chapter, we have drawn on the domestic literature on judicial independence for guidance on the assumption that the independence of the judiciary and the political constellations and the perceived legitimacy of judicial lawmaking are closely connected. We suggest that the independence of ITs, which is a precondition for the perceived legitimacy of their jurisprudence, depends on the background political conditions that

---

[43] Military and Paramilitary Activities in and Against Nicaragua (Nicar. v. U.S.), Judgment, 1986 I.C.J. Rep. 14 (Jun. 27).

[44] Oil Platforms (Iran v. U.S.), Judgment, 2003 I.C.J. REP. 161 (Nov. 6).

[45] *See* Avena and Other Mexican Nationals (Mex. v. U.S.), Judgment, 2004 I.C.J. Rep. 12 (Mar. 31); LaGrand (Ger. v. U.S.), Judgment, 2001 I.C.J. Rep. 466 (Jun. 27).

[46] Legal Consequences of the Construction of a Wall in the Occupied Palestinian Territory, Advisory Opinion, 2004 I.C.J. Rep. 136 (Jul. 9).

shape their decisions, especially the extent to which the ITs are believed not to have been unduly influenced by the policy priorities of the great powers. Meeting this test is, of course, only one of many factors that determine the broader legitimacy of the ITs, but there are reasons to believe that it is an important one.

To the extent that the growing political competition between the postwar coalition of powerful developed states and the one composed of developing powers fosters a more independent international court system, the discretion and independence of these tribunals will lead to rulings that less closely reflect the preferences of powerful states. As a result, such ITs should achieve greater legitimacy among politicians from developing countries and the general public than is currently the case. This greater legitimacy, in turn, should enable these bodies to do a better job of containing the level of political conflict in the system so that it does not jeopardize the effectiveness of international institutions in dealing with the growing number of problems that confront them.

Another source of optimism regarding the increasing independence of ITs and their willingness to boldly challenge executive discretion lies in the growing interbranch division at the state level. The newly found willingness of NCs to check executive discretion by global decision-makers promises, as well, to transform the fragmented legal space into a more accountable and therefore a more democratic and inclusive one. This evolution–even revolution–which arguably results from the reactions to the consequences of the fragmented global legal space is analyzed in Chapter 5.

5

The Emergence of Interjudicial Cooperation among National Courts

This chapter describes what we think is key to robust judicial review at the domestic and global levels: the revolutionary new approach of several national courts (NCs) in responding to global regulatory bodies that we believe is a reaction to their perceived loss of authority. The chapter also suggests that this newly found judicial courage is the key to potential coordination with international tribunals (ITs) and their empowerment. The internal dissension between NCs and domestic and global political branches supplies the missing interbranch division that can bolster the independence of ITs and rein in the unruly forces that ride the tide of global fragmentation.

5.1   Introduction

It was not so long ago that the overwhelming majority of courts in democratic countries shared a reluctance to refer to foreign and international law, in conformance with a policy of avoiding any application of foreign sources of law that might clash with the position of their domestic governments. For many jurists, recourse to foreign and international law is inappropriate.[1] But even the supporters of referencing external sources

---

[1] The most passionate debate exists in the United States, most recently triggered by the decision in Roper v. Simmons, 543 U.S. 551 (2005). *See, e.g.,* Melissa A. Waters, *Creeping Monism: The Judicial Trend toward Interpretive Incorporation of Human Rights Treaties,* 107 COLUM. L. REV. 628 (2007); Judith Resnik, *Law's Migration: American Exceptionalism, Silent Dialogues, and Federalism's Multiple Ports of Entry,* 115 YALE L.J. 1564 (2006); Richard A. Posner, *The Supreme Court 2004 Term – Forward: A Political Court,* 119 HARV. L. REV. 32 (2005); Vicki Jackson, *Constitutional Comparisons: Convergence, Resistance, Engagement,* 119 HARV. L. REV. 109 (2005); Jeremy Waldron, *Foreign Laws and the Modern Ius Gentium,* 119 HARV. L. REV. 129 (2005); Ernst A. Young, *Foreign Law and the Denominator Problem,* 119 HARV. L. REV. 148 (2005); Anupam Chander, *Globalization and Distrust,* 114 YALE L.J. 1193 (2005); Roger P. Alford, *Misusing International Sources to Interpret the Constitution,* 98 AM. J. INT'L L. 57 (2004); T. Alexander Aleinkoff, *International Law, Sovereignty, and American Constitutionalism: Reflections on the Customary International Law Debate,* AM. J. INT'L L. 91 (2004), Harold

of law often share the unexplored assumption that reliance on foreign and international law is inevitably in tension with the value of national sovereignty. Hence the scholarly debate is framed along the lines of the well-known broader debate on "the countermajoritarian difficulty."[2] This chapter questions this assumption of tension by arguing that for courts in most democratic countries (even if not for US courts at present) referring to foreign and international law has become an effective instrument *for empowering* the domestic democratic processes by shielding them from external economic, political, and even legal pressures. Citing international law, therefore, can often bolster domestic democratic processes and reclaim national sovereignty from the diverse forces of globalization. Indeed, taking the argument one step further, it is fair to say that most NCs seeking to maintain the vitality of their national political institutions and to safeguard their own domestic status vis-à-vis the political branches cannot afford to ignore foreign and international law.

As a result, in recent years courts in several democracies have begun to engage quite seriously in the interpretation and application of international law and to heed the constitutional jurisprudence of other NCs. A demonstration of this tendency has been the judicial responses to the post-9/11 global counterterrorism effort: NCs have been challenging executive unilateralism in what could become a globally coordinated move. This chapter describes and explains the shift, arguing that the chief motivation of the NCs is not to promote global justice per se, since they continue to regard themselves first and foremost as national agents. Rather, the new jurisprudence is part of a reaction to the forces of globalization that are placing increasing pressure on the different domestic branches of government to conform to global standards. This reaction seeks to expand the space for domestic deliberation, strengthen the ability of national governments to withstand the pressure brought to bear by interest groups and powerful foreign governments, and insulate the NCs from intergovernmental pressures.

For this strategy to succeed, courts need to forge a united judicial front. This entails coordinating their policies with equally positioned courts in other countries and developing shared tools of communication

---

Hongju Koh, *International Law as Part of Our Law*, 98 AM. J. INT'L L. 43 (2004); Gerald L. Neuman, *The Uses of International Law in Constitutional Interpretation*, 98 AM. J. INT'L L. 82 (2004).

[2] *See* Alford, *supra* note 1, at 59 (characterizing an "international contermajoritarian difficulty" that results from "the strategy to utilize international law to interpret the constitution").

consisting of international law and comparative constitutional law. The analysis also explains why the US Supreme Court, which does not need to protect the domestic political or judicial processes from external pressure, is not yet a part of this collective effort.[3] We argue in the next chapter that recourse to foreign and international legal sources is perfectly legitimate from a democratic theory perspective, as it aims to reclaim democracy from the debilitating grip of globalization.

By the end of the Cold War, it was the common practice of NCs across the globe to avoid any application of international law that would clash with the position of their governments. In essence, this guaranteed the latter complete latitude in external affairs.[4] Through an assortment of avoidance doctrines (such as standing, the "political question," and nonjusticiability), the identification or misidentification of customary international law, and the expansive or restrictive interpretation of treaties, NCs managed to align their findings and judgments with the preferences of their governments. Some courts acknowledged their reticence to deviate from the government's position, explaining this as deference to the executive's expertise in negotiating international relations and referring to the necessity for the state "to speak in one voice."[5]

In order for NCs to speak with one voice, however, they must recognize that they are in a classic prisoner's dilemma and find a way to extricate themselves from it. Although this can be difficult, it is not impossible. To the extent states could be assured that courts in other jurisdictions would similarly enforce international law, they may be more willing to cooperate. Indeed, they may be ready to stay their government's hand if they can be reassured that other governments would be similarly restrained. Inter-court cooperation is not easy, but it is worth trying out incrementally and tentatively, since the benefits are substantial and a breached promise is unlikely to be as beneficial for a court as it is for a wealthy investor.[6]

---

[3] For an earlier explanation of this court's retreat from international law during the Cold War era, see Harold Hongju Koh, *Transnational Public Law Litigation*, 100 YALE L.J. 2347, 2360–66 (1991).

[4] See Chapter 3, Section 3; Eyal Benvenisti, *Judicial Misgivings Regarding the Application of International Norms: An Analysis of Attitudes of National Courts*, 4 EUR. J. INT'L L. 159 (1993).

[5] *The Arantzazu Mendi*, [1939] A.C. 256, 264 (H.L.) (appeal taken from Eng.) ("Our State cannot speak with two voices on such a matter, the judiciary saying one thing, the executive another.") *See also* Ralph Steinhardt, *Human Rights Litigation and the "One Voice" Orthodoxy in Foreign Affairs*, in WORLD JUSTICE? U.S. COURTS AND INTERNATIONAL HUMAN RIGHTS 23 (Mark Gibney ed., 1991), Benvenisti, *supra* note 4, at 173–74.

[6] Benvenisti, *supra* note 4, at 175.

The courts' acquiescence specifically in the area of external affairs suggests that international law was not rejected per se in all areas. In matters having no bearing on foreign affairs, several NCs were willing to apply international law. International human rights law, for example, was particularly influential in matters of only domestic consequence;[7] we find that NCs ' reference to one another's decisions on human rights issues has proved a highly effective tool of cross-fertilization.

Anne-Marie Slaughter has suggested that "[c]ourts may well feel a particular common bond with one another in adjudicating human rights case ... because such cases engage a core judicial function in many countries around the world."[8] Some prominent judges actively involved in this interjudicial dialogue on human rights issues shared this outlook.[9] Similarly, in matters of transnational civil litigation that do not raise issues to which governments are usually sensitive–such as giving effect to foreign judgments and laws of recognized states, interpreting the liability of air carriers, according immunity from litigation to foreign states, or more recently raising questions of jurisdiction over Internet service providers–courts have felt comfortable interacting with one another and invoking notions of interjudicial comity.[10]

---

[7] See Anne-Marie Slaughter, *A Typology of Transjudicial Communication*, 29 U. RICH. L. REV. 99, 103–06 (1994). In fact, as Karen Knop has noted, the transjudicial dialogue on human rights has blurred the distinction between comparative constitutional law and international law. Karen Knop, *Here and There: International Law in Domestic Courts*, 32 NYU J. INT'L L. & POL. 501 (2000).

[8] See Anne-Marie Slaughter, *A NEW WORLD ORDER* 79 (2004).

[9] Claire L'Heureux-Dubé, *The Importance of Dialogue: Globalization and the International Impact of the Rhenquist Court*, 34 TULSA L.J. 15 (1998) (describing the increase of cross-pollination and dialogue between courts); Michael Kirby, *International Law –The Impact on National Constitutions*, 99 ASIL PROC. 1, 2 (Seventh Annual Grotius Lecture, 2005) ("[J]udges of municipal courts in this century will assume an important function in making the principles of international law a reality throughout the world.")

[10] See Hilton v. Guyot, 159 U.S. 113, 163 (1895) ("The extent to which the law of one nation ... shall be allowed to operate within the dominion of another nation, depends upon ... 'the comity of nations.'"). For US Supreme Court judgments concerning foreign state's immunity and the interpretation of the Warsaw Convention, see *Permanent Mission of India to the UN v. City of New York*, 127 S.Ct. 2352 (2007), and *Olympic Airways v. Husain*, 540 U.S. 644 (2004). The Supreme Court of Canada invoked "international comity" and "the objectives of order and fairness" in delineating Canada's jurisdiction over internet service providers: Soc'y of Composers, Authors & Music Publishers of Canada v. Canadian Ass'n of Internet Providers, [2004] 2 S.C.R. 427, 456 at para. 60; *see also* August Reinisch, *The International Relations of National Courts: A Discourse on International Law Norms on Jurisdictional and Enforcement Immunity*, in THE LAW OF INTERNATIONAL RELATIONS – LIBER AMICORUM HANSPETER NEUHOLD 289 (August Reinisch & Ursula Kriebaum eds., 2007) (discussing interjudicial dialogue in

With the new millennium, there are early but clear signs of courts venturing to take up issues with their governments even in matters that may restrict governments' freedom in international bargaining and expose them to external pressure. NCs join forces to offer meaningful judicial review of governmental action, even *inter*governmental action. In this quest to restrict executive latitude, international law looms large as a key tool alongside comparative constitutional law. In other words, references to foreign law and international law are being transformed from the shield that protected the government from judicial review to the sword by which the government's (or governments') case is struck down. This chapter describes the transformation and explains its underlying logic.

Below we offer an explanation for the growing interaction among courts that suggests that they are motivated primarily by relatively parochial, even selfish, concerns. They seek to resist what they believe is the threat posed by globalization to their own national democratic processes, as well as to their own recent achievements with respect to bolstering their institutional independence.[11] Hence, when no such threats exist, they are likely to be indifferent to cooperation with other courts.[12] This analysis helps to account for why courts in developing countries, facing immense external pressures, frantically cling to whatever international "soft law" they can cull from international documents, whereas, by contrast, the court of the strongest global power continues to treat international law and comparative constitutional law with puzzlement and even disdain. This explanation offers justification for the practice of the NCs from the perspective of democratic theory: Courts invoke international law not because they defer to other communities' values and interests but because they wish to protect or even reclaim the

the areas of state immunity and the immunities of international organizations); Slaughter, *supra* note 8, 86–91 (discussing the emergence of judicial comity in transnational civil litigation).

[11] On the expansion of judicial power (and judicial autonomy) since the 1980s, see Ran Hirschl, TOWARDS JURISTOCRACY: THE ORIGINS AND CONSEQUENCES OF THE NEW CONSTITUTIONALISM (2004) (explaining this phenomenon as resulting from elites' attempt to secure their dominant positions against challenges of the majority through the political process); Alec Stone Sweet, *The Politics of Constitutional Review in France and Europe*, 5 INT'L J. CONST. L. 69, 80–81 (2007) (explaining the "juridical coup d'état" in France during the 1980s as the result of the frequent alternation of power among the political parties).

[12] For an analysis of noncooperative behavior by courts, see *infra* notes 146–50 and accompanying text. *See also* Antje Wiener & Philip Liste, *Lost without Translation? Cross-Referencing and a New Global Community of Courts*, 21 INDIANA J. GLOB. LEG. STUD. 263 (2014) (emphasizing the instrumental usage of foreign citations rather than a sense of shared normative foundations).

domestic political space that is increasingly dominated by the economic forces of globalization, including the delegation of authority to international institutions. Under contemporary conditions, protecting domestic interests and, in particular, reclaiming domestic democratic processes often require that NCs forge a coordinated cross-boundary judicial resistance to the forces of globalization.

The classic American cases invoking international law–such as *The Paquete Habana*,[13] *Hilton v. Guyot*,[14] and earlier *The Schooner Exchange*[15]–cases that inspired Harold Koh to envision a renaissance of judicial creativity and determination in giving effect in domestic law to international law, cannot be regarded as precursors of the current phenomenon. Those impressive decisions applied international law, even on some occasions against the government, but those courts never engaged in a coordinated and sustained effort to restrain their respective governments, and the latter never tried to preempt such interjudicial coalitions. The phenomenon under consideration in this chapter is novel. It is yet another demonstration of the consequences of the "disaggregated state,"[16] as both the national government and the national court seek foreign allies in their quest to balance each other out.

5.2   The Impact of Globalization on National Decision-Making Processes

We begin here by revisiting the fundamental assumptions that led NCs in the past to defer to their governments against contemporary conditions. The traditional judicial policy of ensuring that the state speak "in one voice," that is, in the voice of the government, rested on three premises.[17]

---

[13] The Paquete Habana, 175 U.S. 677 (1900) (Prize law).

[14] *Hilton, supra* note 10 (enforcement of foreign judgments).

[15] The Schooner Exchange v. M'Faddon, 11 U.S. (7 Cranch) 116 (1812) (foreign sovereign immunity).

[16] Slaughter, *supra* note 8, at 12 (noting "the rising need for and capacity of different domestic government institutions to engage in activities beyond their borders, often with their foreign counterparts.")

[17] Koh, *supra* note 3, at 2383–94, distinguishes between three types of judicial concerns: separation-of-powers concerns, judicial competence concerns, and comity concerns. The more frank judicial statements doubt whether their "engagement in the task of passing on the validity of foreign acts of state may hinder rather than further [their] country's pursuit of goals," Banco Nacional de Cuba v. Sabbatino, 376 U.S. 398, 423 (1964), and mention "[t]he advantage of the diplomatic approach to the resolution of difficulties between two sovereign nations, as opposed to the unilateral action by the courts of one nation," United States v. Alvarez-Machain, 504 U.S. 655, 669 n.16 (1992).

The first was that the world of diplomacy and foreign policy is the province of a nation's chief executive and is inevitably and necessarily detached from the domestic arena, where the rule of law, rather than the executive, should prevail. The second and related assumption was that the government adequately represents the interests of its domestic constituencies in its foreign diplomacy. The third premise was that the government is better able to conduct diplomatic affairs without the interference of the judiciary. Unhappily, none of these assumptions is valid in today's world. The spheres of global regulation increasingly affect the lives of virtually every citizen; governments tend to be more in thrall than ever to narrow domestic interests and, hence, are unable to represent broad constituencies. Last, the contemporary world of diplomacy exposes governments to such extreme pressures that many would actually benefit from domestic legal constraints that would tie their hands in the international bargaining process. NCs are left with only limited opportunities to restrain or slow down the drain of power from domestic institutions. Even more threatening to the courts are measures taken by governments–foreign governments as well as their own–that sap the courts of such opportunities and limit their independence. The newly evolving judicial approach may be interpreted, therefore, as aiming to confront globalization head-on and revitalize the authority of the national institutions.

In the following sections, we address the difficulties with the three basic assumptions of the traditional judicial deference approach and then explain the underlying rationale of the contemporary approach.

5.2.1 Three Contemporary Difficulties with the Traditional Deferential Approach

The first underlying premise of the judicial policy of deference was the lack of connection between domestic politics and world politics. NCs were happy to grant their governments complete leeway in the realm of international politics, on the assumption that it is unrelated in any direct sense to the domestic legal system. This assumption has gradually lost its force over the years, in conjunction with the increasing permeability of the domestic legal system to an ever-increasing number of international regulatory policies that are overseen by international institutions. The formal delegation of authority to these international institutions together with informal intergovernmental coordination has effectively outsourced a substantial portion of what was previously considered domestic policy. Moreover, in many of these areas of regulation—encompassing not only economic activities but also matters of national security and, in recent years, the fight against global terrorism—the issues are ones that can affect everyone in the world.

Many if not most economic matters are determined not by national legislatures but by foreign decision-makers, including powerful foreign governments, international institutions, and even private companies. Coordinated counterterrorism policies cut across the fabric of the domestic regulation of daily life. International organizations and multilateral bodies determine people's levels of health and safety, influence their political freedoms, delineate their privacy, and in general shape their life opportunities.[18] The threat to domestic democratic and legal processes has become tangible and, as a result, is a direct challenge to the very authority of the national court as the guardian of the basic rights of the citizen. Acquiescing to the executive's demand for judicial deference means total abdication of this role. Moreover, the threat is even greater than that, posing as it does a challenge to the very idea of democracy. The ability of citizens to participate in decisions affecting them becomes a mere formality, as domestic political branches increasingly fail to withstand the pressure brought to bear by domestic and foreign interest groups and foreign governments. In all but the strongest of nations,[19] the delegation of authority to international organizations threatens to undermine the effectiveness of the domestic systems of checks and balances.

The growing vulnerability of the domestic legal system to this external influence can be partly attributed to the burgeoning political power of certain interest groups that benefit from the reduced costs of both investment across boundaries and outsourcing. The influence of these groups on governments undermines the second assumption at the base of judicial deference: that governments are the best representatives of

---

[18] Joseph H.H. Weiler, *The Geology of International Law – Governance, Democracy and Legitimacy*, 64 ZEITSCHRIFT FÜR AUSLÄNDISCHES ÖFFENTLICHES RECHT UND VÖLKERRECHT 547 (2004) (describing the emergence of the latest "layer" of international lawmaking—the regulatory layer); Benedict Kingsbury, Nico Krisch & Richard B. Stewart, *The Emergence of Global Administrative Law*, 68 LAW & CONTEMP. PROBS. 15 (2005) (elaborating on the different modalities of global regulation and the challenges they present).

[19] As Curtis Bradley observes, the three branches of the US government have kept the domestic political and legal processes insulated from the direct influence of external policy and law-making through a variety of "non-self-execution filters." Curtis A. Bradley, *International Delegations, the Structural Constitution, and Non-Self-Execution*, 55 STAN. L. REV. 1557, 1587–95 (2003).

national interests abroad. While this premise has always been (or should have been) somewhat suspect, as we saw in Chapter 3, in recent years more evidence has accumulated regarding the exploitation of international politics by small interest groups to advance their narrow interests.[20] Using their economic leverage, they pressure their own governments or foreign governments to accept international agreements that are beneficial to them but detrimental to most other citizens of their countries. The new modalities of global standard setting by private actors have increasingly handed these groups direct authority to shape outcomes.[21] As a consequence, the assumption that the government knows best when it comes to foreign affairs and can be trusted to promote the entire nation's interests can no longer be convincingly asserted.

Finally, the third assumption, that international interaction should be free of legal constraints, has collapsed as well, in the wake of the increased "legalization of world politics"[22] and the dwindling bargaining power of many of the less powerful states. At least until the early 1990s, it was plausible to explain judicial passivity by noting the "advantage of the diplomatic approach to the resolution of difficulties between two sovereign nations, as opposed to the unilateral action by the courts of one nation."[23] Since then, however, the implausibility of the idea of equal sovereignty allowing governments to bargain freely has become increasingly apparent. Most governments lack such freedom. Developing countries can no longer pit one superpower against the other as they did during the Cold War. And their dependence on foreign investment has undercut their bargaining leverage considerably. More and more global standards are being created by coalitions of strong powers–most notably the G8–acting through formal and informal institutions. Governments of powerful states form cartels of actors that set standards that everyone else is forced to follow. Moreover, international institutions govern many areas of interaction between states, as law replaces diplomacy. These institutions and tribunals have created a myriad of norms of general application. This has been the case in particular with regard to the post-9/11 global counterterrorism efforts, which effectively united national

---

[20] *See* Chapter 3; Helen V. Milner, *INTERESTS, INSTITUTIONS, AND INFORMATION* (1997). On the influence exerted by domestic interests in negotiating trade agreements, see George W. Downs & David M. Rocke, *OPTIMAL IMPERFECTION?* (1995).

[21] On the growing power of private actors in transnational regulation, see, *e.g.*, Kingsbury et al., *supra* note 18.

[22] *LEGALIZATION AND WORLD POLITICS* (Judith L. Goldstein et al. eds., 2001).

[23] United States v. Alvarez-Machain, 504 U.S. 655, 669 n.16 (1992).

security agencies in service of a common cause. These agencies act both directly and through a network of international institutions (formal and informal), openly and clandestinely, legally and also illegally (for example, the practices of so-called extraordinary renditions and secret prisons).

Given current conditions, deference to the executive branch's ability to conduct negotiations is a risky policy from the perspective of democracy. For most state executives, and certainly for most legislatures, these trends in policy-making mean greater dependence on external forces, leaving less room and opportunity for meaningful domestic democratic deliberations. They may also mean exposure to outcomes that are detrimental to many if not most citizens.[24] Moreover, while these challenges to domestic decision-making processes and institutions, as well as to the very idea of a right to democratic participation, are significant, it is less clear whether NCs still possess the ability to empower citizens, enhance their government's bargaining power in the international arena, and secure the courts' own independence vis-à-vis intergovernmental institutions. In what follows, we will argue that NCs have begun to explore the possibility of such a role.

5.2.2   The Motivations for Judicial Resistance

Given the economic and political dynamics described above, NCs appear to have come to realize that allowing the government carte blanche to act freely in world politics actually impoverishes the domestic democratic and judicial processes and reduces the opportunity of most citizens to use these processes to shape outcomes. These courts, better insulated from external pressures, seem to have begun to conclude that, by sometimes aggressively restricting their government, they can help to revive their state's domestic democratic processes and, at the same time, strengthen their own autonomy.

---

[24] This is not to suggest that all international delegations result in undesirable consequences from the perspective of democracy. A responsible and effective international institution, such as the European Court of Human Rights, can improve democratic processes and promote individual rights in member states. See, Robert O. Keohane, Stephen Macedo & Andrew Moravcsik, *Democracy-Enhancing Multilateralism*, 63 INT'L ORG. 1 (2009). But as discussed in Chapter 2, such institutions constitute only a small part of the various formal and informal institutions that regulate our lives, and their performance often leaves much to be desired. In the key areas of regulation discussed here, many of the available international institutions have failed to match the national courts' level of scrutiny of intergovernmental cooperation.

The courts may have also concluded that making stricter demands of the government does not necessarily jeopardize its bargaining position vis-à-vis its negotiating partners. In fact, under certain circumstances, a persistent court could actually strengthen its government's hand at the bargaining table. The logic of international negotiations clarifies this point. As mentioned above, the complex interaction between domestic and international politics has been described as a two-level game, namely, a game played simultaneously at the first, international, level between a national government and representatives of a foreign state and at the second, domestic, level among representatives of domestic interest groups. The second-level negotiations are necessary to secure domestic ratification of international agreements negotiated at the first level. This game produces a paradox: All things being equal, the stronger the domestic support for Government A's policies, the weaker government A will find itself at the international level. This is because Government B, its adversary in the negotiations, can play tough and demand additional concessions, knowing that Government A will still have support for them at home.

This leads to negotiating dynamics in which governments often seek to tie their hands domestically to enhance their position at the international level.[25] NCs could prove useful in this regard, while deferential courts would weaken their executives at the international bargaining table. For example, were the court in Country A to intervene, say, by declaring (or hinting at its intention to declare) the negotiated treaty as impinging excessively on citizen rights, then presumably Government B would be prepared to concede in the negotiations so as to ensure ratification and implementation of the agreement by Country A. Thus, pressure from a disapproving court can, in fact, result in greater bargaining leeway for its government, as a constrictive court decision can be used to explain why it is prevented from bowing to the external pressure in the bargaining process. Needless to say, these dynamics rest on the assumption that B would still be interested in the agreement with A under the terms acceptable to the court. If B can find an alternative to A, the leverage facilitated by A's court will be limited.

Not all courts need to be equally assertive in safeguarding the domestic political process. Courts in more powerful countries with relatively robust domestic democratic processes can be expected to show greater

---

[25] Robert D. Putnam, *Diplomacy and Domestic Politics: The Logic of Two-Level Games*, 42 INT'L ORG. 427 (1988); Milner, *supra* note 20.

deference to their governments. Given American dominance in setting global standards, we can anticipate less involvement by the US federal courts in the president's conduct of diplomacy, and in fact, this is precisely what emerges from the rather hesitant jurisprudence of the US Supreme Court in this context.[26]

An assertive court will bolster not only the domestic democratic processes but also its own authority to interpret and apply national and international law. NCs see the new international judicial forums challenging their own authority as interpreters of the law and balancers of competing state interests against rights grounded in constitutional or international law. The most effective way to respond to this challenge is to engage in a dialogue with ITs. There are two reasons for this. As a purely doctrinal matter, NCs are directly and indirectly engaged in the evolution of customary international law: Their decisions that are based on international law are viewed as reflecting customary international law,[27] and their governments' actions in compliance with those decisions will constitute state practice coupled with *opinio juris*. As such, ITs will have to pay heed to the jurisprudence of the NCs. Hence, the more the NCs engage in applying international law, the more their jurisprudence constrains the choices available to the ITs when the latter deal with similar issues.

Moreover, from the perspective of the complex interplay between international and national courts, the ITs are, to a certain extent, dependent on NCs, because they need the latter's cooperation for implementation of their decisions.[28] A national court that engages in a serious application of international law sends a strong signal to international

---

[26] *See supra* note 19, and *infra* notes 74–76, and accompanying text.

[27] *See, e.g.*, Arrest Warrant of 11 April 2000 (Dem. Rep. Congo v. Belg.), 2002 I.C.J. Rep. 3, ¶ 56–58 (Feb. 14) (examining national courts' jurisprudence to assess the extent to which heads of state enjoy immunity in foreign courts).

[28] On the interplay between a supreme court (as the principal) and lower courts (as its agents), see McNollgast, *Conditions for Judicial Independence*, 15 J. CONTEMP. LEGAL ISSUES 105 (2006); McNollgast, *Politics and the Courts: A Positive Theory of Judicial Doctrine and the Rule of Law*, 68 S. CAL. L. REV. 1631 (1995). The dependence of an international tribunal on national courts that are not formally bound by its decisions is even greater. The tense relations that developed between the Court of Justice of the European Union and some of the national courts, in particular the German and Italian courts, confirm this theoretical observation. *See* Juliane Kokkot, *Report on Germany in THE EUROPEAN COURT AND NATIONAL COURTS – DOCTRINE AND JURISPRUDENCE* 77 (Anne-Marie Slaughter, Alec Stone Sweet & J.H.H. Weiler eds., 1998); Bruno de Witte, *Direct Effect, Supremacy, and the Nature of Legal Order*, in *THE EVOLUTION OF EU LAW* 177–213 (Paul Craig & Gráinne de Búrca eds., 1999). See also discussion *infra*, Chapters 6 and 7.

courts that the national court regards itself an equal participant in the transnational lawmaking process and will not automatically accept just any decision rendered by an international tribunal. Since the effectiveness of ITs depends on compliance with their decisions, they must anticipate the reaction of the NCs to those decisions and engage with their jurisprudence. In this sense, assertive NCs invoking international law can effectively limit the autonomy of international tribunals.

But this strategy also requires a crucial additional element for it to be effective: a united, coordinated judicial front. If only one national court were to adopt an assertive policy, it would face the danger of being singled out as a troublemaker whose jurisprudence does not reflect general state practice. Its government could, therefore, be sidestepped when global forces seek out governments that are unconstrained by their courts and, hence, find itself more vulnerable to external pressure. Thus, courts seeking to enhance domestic institutions and processes must try to ensure a common interjudicial stance. The following section explains their cooperation strategy.

5.2.3 The Logic Underlying Interjudicial Cooperation

As noted, a national court that seeks to tie the hands of its government in international negotiations may need to rely on its counterparts, the NCs of other countries, acting similarly. For example, governments in developing countries will not be able to withstand external pressure to maintain low environmental standards for dumping hazardous wastes in their territories unless they coordinate their activities or–if not–benefit from coordinated assertiveness on the part of their respective courts. Likewise, in the context of the fight against terrorism, constraints on counter-terrorism measures imposed by a court in Country A but not by courts in other countries may expose A's citizens to an increased risk of terrorist attacks. A country that refrains from deporting foreign citizens due to concerns regarding torture or a country in which privacy rights are more strictly protected could become (or could be seen as having the potential to become) a haven for terrorists if other countries are less tolerant of migrants or have fewer protections for privacy rights.

Another factor is the international pressure that could be brought to bear on a government to circumvent its court's decisions, or amend the law and thereby force the court into compliance with the international norm, or else risk the loss of peer protection for failing to comply with the group's demands. The optimal response to all these possibilities is coordination among NCs. A transnational united front of the highest domestic courts would ensure that no country would become a dumping ground for imported waste or a terrorist haven; nor would it face collective sanctions. And there would be less peer pressure exerted on governments to ignore the judgments of their own courts.

While this theoretical model suggests that judges would behave in accordance with it even if they were not consciously following its logic, there is in fact evidence that NCs are acutely aware of the need for a coordinated stance.[29] Even the courts of the most powerful nations are concerned that "unilateral action by the courts of one nation"[30] will not produce the desired outcomes. The House of Lords, for example, has stated that "international treaties should, so far as possible, be construed uniformly by the national courts of all states"[31] and has even asserted that "it is not for a national court to 'develop' international law by unilaterally adopting a version of that law which, however desirable, forward-looking and reflective of values it may be, is simply not accepted by other states."[32] In the context of coordinating migration policies, a topic that is explored below,[33] judges from several countries went beyond taking rhetorical positions and actually established an institution to ensure uniformity.[34] Courts need assurances that courts in other jurisdictions will enforce similar rules.

Establishing a higher court to whose decisions NCs must adhere, such as the Court of Justice of the European Union is surely one effective avenue of forging common judicial ground[35] (or, in more sinister scenarios, a means to curtail the authority of NCs). But this is not a prerequisite for

[29] The lack of certainty regarding any such coordination lay at the basis of their earlier policy of deferment. *See supra* note 6 and accompanying text.

[30] Note the quote from the Alvarez-Machain judgment, *supra* note 23, about the "advantage of the diplomatic approach ... as opposed to the *unilateral action* by the courts of one nation" (emphasis added).

[31] Regina v. Bow St. Metro. Stipendiary Magistrate, *ex parte* Pinochet Ugarte (No. 3), [2000] 1 A.C. 147, 244 (H.L.) (appeal taken from Eng.) (per Hope, L.J.); *see also* Regina v. Sec'y of State for the Home Dep't, *ex parte* Adan, [2001] 1 All E.R. 593, 616 (per Hobhouse, L.J.); Regina v. Sec'y of State for the Home Dep't *ex parte* Aitseguer [2001] 1 All E.R. 593, 616.

[32] Jones v. Ministry of Interior (Kingdom of Saudi Arabia), 2006 UKHL 26 para. 63, [2007] 1 A.C. 270 (appeal taken from Eng.) (per Hoffmann, L.J.).

[33] *See infra* text at notes 109–30.

[34] The International Association of Refugee Law Judges (IARLJ), *see* the IARLJ Constitution, as amended Oct. 17, 1998, *available at* www.iarlj.nl/general/. *See also infra* notes 110–13.

[35] For an analysis of the active role played by national courts in strengthening the EU, see Joseph HH Weiler, *A Quiet Revolution: The European Court of Justice and Its Interlocutors* 26 COMP. POL. STUD. 510 (1994).

transnational judicial coordination. Cooperation can also evolve endogenously among courts, even when they seek to promote national interests rather than global justice. Game theory demonstrates that indefinitely iterated prisoner's dilemma games between two players are likely to induce cooperation, even absent external intervention. If the number of iterations is indefinite and the "shadow of the future" is high enough (namely, the players assign a sufficiently high value to the expected payoffs from future iterations of the game), then each player is expected to choose the strategy of conditional cooperation in a "friendly tit for tat." Using the implicit threat of retaliation against defection, the players can elicit cooperation. The same tit-for-tat strategy will also produce cooperation in a game played by groups larger than two players, even when some of the players choose to defect unconditionally. As is often the case, situations that cannot generate cooperation when a game is played only once do generate cooperative equilibriums when they are repeated for an indefinite period of time.

Hence, for courts to succeed in asserting their authority and restraining their governments, they must initiate cooperation with similarly situated courts. The only effective way for courts in developing countries to put a stop to the intensifying levels of pollution, environmental degradation, and imported waste is to take a united stand against external interests shopping for less restrictive jurisdictions. Courts that wish to maintain a higher level of human rights protection within their jurisdiction without turning it into a terrorist haven or diverting the world's asylum seekers to their shores need to forge a united front with their counterparts in other countries. In other words, a commitment to interjudicial cooperation can be the most important strategic choice that can be made by NCs determined to protect their own authority and to reclaim domestic democratic processes.

The optimal way for courts to initiate and maintain cooperation is through the mutual exchange of information. Their judicial reasoning and outcomes convey information about their commitment to cooperating. More specifically, their reliance on the same or similar legal sources facilitates this communication and, to a considerable extent, signals their commitment. Both positive as well as negative messages can be communicated within this framework. Cooperative courts will be cited with approval by their counterparts, whereas courts that step out of line either by refusing to give force to a new standard or by setting a different standard will be criticized, sometimes quite severely.[36] In other words,

---

[36] For example, in the 2004 case Ferrini v. Federal Republic of Germany, the Italian Court of Cassation criticized a decision of the Greek Court of Cassation of 2000, Prefecture of

one court's decisions function as signals to other courts about the former's commitment to cooperation. These signals can embolden the other courts or weaken their resolve in the face of the same dilemmas. At times, specific judgments will present novel or otherwise compelling statements that resonate with courts in other jurisdictions and serve as a model for them. One such example is the landmark *Minors Oposa* judgment rendered by the Philippines Supreme Court, which recognized the stake of future generations in a healthy environment.[37] Yet another case is the Indian Supreme Court setting a standard in the area of environmental protection not only for the Indian subcontinent but also for other places in the developing world.[38]

Courts that wish to signal readiness to cooperate tend to draw upon language other courts understand: comparative law (primarily comparative constitutional law) and international law.[39] The use of comparative analysis signals that courts are willing to learn from one another or are seeking support for their rulings from other jurisdictions, or both. More significantly, they learn from each other's legal systems how best to balance the competing common interests and how to manage the conflicting common risks to their societies. They can compare statutory arrangements, such as, for detaining suspected terrorists or minimizing the infringement on constitutional rights.[40] Even more accessible than specific statutes are the constitutional texts, which often have similar provisions regarding such issues as the right to life, due process, equality,

Voiotia v. Federal Republic of Germany, while the House of Lords criticized the *Ferrini* judgment in Jones, *supra* note 32, paras. 22, 63. *See* Pasquale De Sena & Francesca De Vittor, *State Immunity and Human Rights: The Italian Supreme Court Decision on the Ferrini Case*, 16 EUR. J. INT'L L. 89, 101–02 (2005).

[37] Minors Oposa v. Sec'y of Dep't Env't & Natural Res. (Sup. Ct. 1993), 33 ILM 173 (1994). This celebrated case was cited by the Bangladeshi and Indian courts, and in numerous scholarly articles across the globe. *See, e.g.,* Farooque v. Gov't of Bangladesh, 17 B.L.D. (A.D.) 1 (1997) (App. Div. 1996), *available at* www.elaw.org/resources/printable.asp?id=139; A.P. Pollution Control Bd. (II) v. Nayudu, [2000] INSC 679, [2001] 2 S.C.C. 62 (India Sup. Ct.), *available at* www.commonlii.org/in/cases/INSC/2000/679.html.

[38] *See* text at notes 85–108 *infra*.

[39] Indeed, judgments discussed in the text accompanying notes 146–50 are replete with references to comparative constitutional law and in particular to international law as interpreted by other courts. The discord within the US Supreme Court toward comparative constitutional law and its relative reticence in recent years to cite international law may perhaps be influenced by the relative robustness of the domestic processes in the United States, which currently do not require judicial support. On the debate in the United States on this matter, see *supra* note 1.

[40] See the decisions of the Canadian, New Zealand, and Indian courts, discussed in notes 61, 62, and 64 *infra* and accompanying texts.

and fundamental political rights. And, indeed, courts seeking cooperation often do engage in comparative analysis in their judgments. As will
be shown in Section 5.3, comparative constitutional analysis has taken
center stage in the emerging jurisprudence on counterterrorism and in
court decisions in developing countries concerning the right to a healthy
environment. But even more significantly, international law, the source
of collective standards, has become a most valuable coordination tool for
NCs. The ability of these courts to rely on the same or similar legal norms
(international treaties like the 1951 Geneva Convention Relating to the
Status of Refugees[41] or human rights treaties) facilitates harmonization.
By referring to each other's interpretation of a shared text, they not only
signal their readiness to cooperate but they also to a certain extent
discourage any future retreat by one of them from the shared interpretation. Courts observe one another, and anyone found deviating from the
shared understanding is forced to explain itself to its peers.

Nevertheless, the fact that all are applying the same norm does not
render its implementation unproblematic for a given court. First, the
norm's content may entail disproportionate deference to the national
governments. Second, there is significant variance among jurisdictions
with respect to the status of international law within the domestic legal
hierarchy. Third, the language of the domestic statute that incorporated
the specific international treaty may have modified the specific obligation. But courts that are so inclined have devised ways to overcome these
interpretive hurdles. They can tap into the rich jurisprudence developed
by ITs concerning "effective,"[42] "evolutive,"[43] or "systemic"[44] interpretation of treaties or they can rely on the tribunals' unsystematic ways of
identifying customary norms.[45] Moreover, they interpret domestic

---

[41] Convention Relating to the Status of Refugees, Jul. 28, 1951, 189 UNTS 150, *amended by*
Protocol Relating to the Status of Refugees, Jan. 31, 1967, 19 UST 6223, 606 UNTS 267
[hereinafter 1951 Refugee Convention].

[42] Hersch Lauterpacht, The Development of International Law by the International Court
of Justice 227–28, 267–93 (1958).

[43] *See* Rudolf Bernhardt, *Evolutive Treaty Interpretation, Especially of the European
Convention on Human Rights*, 42 Germ. Y.B. Int'l L. 11 (1999).

[44] C. Maclachlan, *The Principle of Systemic Integration and Article 31(3)(c) of the Vienna
Convention*, 54 Int'l & Comp. L.Q. 279 (2005); D. French, *Treaty Interpretation and the
Incorporation of Extraneous Legal Rules*, 55 Int'l & Comp. L.Q. 281 (2006).

[45] *See, e.g.*, Theodor Meron, *Revival of Customary Humanitarian Law*, 99 Am. J. Int'l L. 817,
819–20 (2005). Meron comments on the ICJ's "complete failure to inquire whether
opinion juris and practice support the crystallization of [the relevant Articles] into
customary law." Meron salutes this "more relaxed approach" and views it as
"essential . . . to the effectiveness of customary law." *Id.*

legislation based on the premise that the legislature does not intend to contravene international obligations. Finally, even domestically unincorporated treaties and customs are often treated as a relevant consideration for the executive when exercising its discretion under domestic authorizing statutes.

5.3 Judicial Cooperation: The Evidence

The strategic uses of foreign and international law characterize interjudicial cooperation that seeks to review and shape government policies. This section argues that this relatively recent phenomenon is most discernible in three areas: the judicial review of global counterterrorism measures, the protection of the environment in developing countries, and the status of asylum seekers in destination countries. These are areas where courts appear to have reacted to governmental responses to external pressures, regarding those responses as either too weak (in the contexts of counterterrorism and the environment) or too strong (against asylum seekers). Additional examples of NCs collectively engaging with ITs will be discussed in Chapter 6.

This section examines the evolution of judicial cooperation as courts seek to serve as a counterbalance to their governments in these three areas. Our aim here is not to provide a comprehensive in-depth analysis of inter-court cooperation but rather to demonstrate the character and likely efficacy of this strategy. The focus here will therefore be more on the means of communications–the increased use of comparative constitutional law and the creative use of international law–than on the specific content of the norms. Further research is necessary to explore these and other areas of judicial cooperation in greater depth.

Note that we are not looking for explicit pronouncements of this strategy, as there are good reasons for judges not to be very explicit about their approach. It is also quite likely that they follow their intuition rather than consciously design their moves.[46] On more than one occasion, judges who read our work have told us that we accurately reflected their reliance on unconscious intuitions.

---

[46] See Gary S. Becker, THE ECONOMIC APPROACH TO HUMAN BEHAVIOR 7 (1976) ("the economic approach does not assume that economic units are necessarily conscious of their efforts to maximize or can verbalize or otherwise describe ... reasons for the systematic pattern of their behavior.")

5.3.1   Reviewing Global Counterterrorism Measures

More than a dozen years into the coordinated global effort against Al-Qaeda and its associated groups, it has become increasingly clear that the persistent attempts by the executive and legislative branches of a number of democracies to curtail judicial review of counterterrorism policies have, by and large, failed. These governments have not succeeded at convincing their courts to withhold judgment and, in fact, have generated a counterreaction on the part of the judiciary. Hesitant at first, the courts have regained their confidence and are increasingly asserting novel claims that are designed to bolster and even expand their judicial authority.

In the wake of the September 11, 2001, terrorist attack, NCs faced a major challenge to their authority. Alarmed over the potentially devastating effects of global terrorism, national governments sought to increase restrictions on rights and liberties that they perceived as potentially facilitating terrorist acts or impeding counterterrorism measures. National executives insisted on broad, exclusive discretion in shaping and implementing these constraints as they saw fit, based on the claim that the executive holds a relative advantage over the other branches of government in assessing the risks of terrorism and in managing those risks. The post-9/11 global counterterrorism effort effectively united national security agencies throughout much of the West. Executive branches began collaborating directly with one another and indirectly through a web of formal and informal international institutions. The central formal collective effort was based on the authority of the UN Security Council;[47] the more informal efforts ranged from the activities of such institutional entities as the Proliferation Security Initiative (PSI)[48] and the Financial Action Task Force (FATF),[49] to government-to-government exchanges, to complicity with illegal practices such as extraordinary renditions and secret prisons.[50]

---

[47] The main UN body set up to curb terrorism is the Counter-Terrorism Committee (CTC). For its mandate and activities, see Counter-Terrorism Committee (2007), *at* www.un.org/sc/ctc/.

[48] See the US government's 2003 PSI, CRS Report for Congress, Proliferation Security Initiative (PSI) (Sept. 14, 2006), *available at* http://fpc.state.gov/documents/organization/74917.pdf.

[49] *See* Financial Action Task Force, 9 Special Recommendations (SR) on Terrorist Financing (TF) (2004), *available at* www.fatf-gafi.org.

[50] *See* Eur. Parl. Ass., Alleged Secret Detentions and Unlawful Inter-state Transfers of Detainees Involving Council of Europe Member States, Doc. No. 10957 (2006), *available at* http://assembly.coe.int/Documents/WorkingDocs/doc06/edoc10957.pdf.

Most legislatures submitted to these measures without demur. Far-reaching legislative changes, hurriedly introduced in most democracies in the weeks and months following the Al-Qaeda attack, sailed through legislatures with little public debate or scrutiny.[51] The immediate shock of 9/11 led many to view the basic principles of due process, which are shaped by the preference of democratic societies to err on the side of liberty, as entailing unacceptable risks. This wave of acquiescence to national political leaders' claims to absolute discretion in acting to guarantee national security swept the courts as well.

In fact, such conformity in times of war and national crisis has tradition-ally been a hallmark of judicial practice.[52] Suffice it to recall the decisions rendered by the highest courts in the United Kingdom and the United States during the two world wars and the early Cold War era, in which they deferred to the executive's discretion, based on the limited authority and institutional capacity of the judiciary to assess and manage the risks of war.[53] And thus, indeed, in the weeks following September 11, the familiar rhetoric of judicial deference was repeated by an alarmed court.[54] The 9/11

---

[51] In some countries, this legislative process was brief and did not encounter any significant opposition. Bills were passed within a few weeks or days (or even hours in the case of Germany) of the September 11 events. On the legislative changes in the various demo-cratic countries, see the comparative studies in TERRORISM AS A CHALLENGE FOR NATIONAL AND INTERNATIONAL LAW: SECURITY VERSUS LIBERTY? (C. Walter et al. eds., 2004); Kent Roach, Sources and Trends in Post 9/11 Anti-terrorism Laws (U. Toronto Legal Stud. Res. Paper 899291, Apr. 2006), available at http://ssrn.com/abstract 899291.

[52] On this wartime jurisprudence, see William Rehnquist, ALL THE LAWS BUT ONE: CIVIL LIBERTIES IN WARTIME (1998), A. W. Brian Simpson, IN THE HIGHEST DEGREE ODIOUS: DETENTION WITHOUT TRIAL IN WARTIME BRITAIN (1994).

[53] As Justice Jackson wrote in dissent in Korematsu v. United States, 323 U.S. 214, 245 (1944): "In the nature of things, military decisions are not susceptible of intelligent judicial appraisal. They do not pretend to rest on evidence, but are made on information that often would not be admissible and on assumptions that could not be proved ... Hence courts can never have real alternative to accepting the mere declaration of the authorities that issued the order that it was reasonably necessary from a military viewpoint."

[54] Lord Hoffmann explained in Secretary of State for the Home Department v. Rehman, UKHL 47, [2001] 3 W.L.R. 877, para. 50 (appeal taken from Eng.), his approval of the secretary of state's decision to deport a Pakistani national based on (disputed) evidence linking him to Islamic terrorist groups operating on the Indian subcontinent:

> [T]he question of whether something is "in the interests" of national security is not a question of law. It is a matter of judgment and policy. Under the constitution of the United Kingdom and most other countries, decisions as to whether something is or is not in the interests of national security are not a matter for judicial decision. They are entrusted to the executive.Lord Slynn, id. para. 26, stated that "the Commission must give

attacks in an all-too-predictable way "proved" more clearly than ever the case for judicial silence.[55]

Three years later, the House of Lords turned to the tragic events and came away with a wholly different lesson. The *Belmarsh Detainees* decision of December 2004, which declared parts of the British Antiterrorism Act to be incompatible with European human rights standards, was described by one of the Law Lords as countering "the public fear whipped up by the governments of the United States and the United Kingdom since 11 September 2001 and their determination to bend established international law to their will and to undermine its essential structures."[56] The transformation in judicial approach evident in this decision was not limited to the United Kingdom. In light of the similar, if not as dramatic, changes in the ways in which NCs have reacted to their executive's security-related claims since September 11, it is now possible to speak of a new phase in the way democracies are addressing the threat of terrorism: executive unilateralism is being challenged by NCs in what could perhaps be a globally coordinated move.

The bold House of Lords decision in 2004 was not the first sign of judicial resistance. This should be credited to the (much criticized)[57] Canadian Supreme Court decision from January 11, 2002.[58] Although the court found that, in principle, there is no prohibition on deportation

> due weight to the assessment and conclusions of the Secretary of State in the light at any particular time of his responsibilities, or of Government policy and the means at his disposal of being informed of and understanding the problems involved. He is undoubtedly in the best position to judge what national security requires even if his decision is open to review. The assessment of what is needed in the light of changing circumstances is primarily for him." Lord Steyn, *id.* para. 29, in turn, asserted: "The dynamics of the role of the Secretary of State, charged with the power and duty to consider deportation on grounds of national security, irresistibly supports this analysis."

[55] As Lord Steyn added in the same judgment, *id.* para. 29, "[T]he tragic events of 11 September 2001 in New York reinforce compellingly that no other approach is possible."

[56] Lord Steyn, *2000–2005: Laying the Foundations of Human Rights Law in the United Kingdom*, 4 EUR. HUM. RTS. L. REV. 349, 350 (2005).

[57] *See, e.g.*, Kent Roach, *Must We Trade Rights for Security? The Choice between Smart, Harsh, or Proportionate Security Strategies in Canada and Britain*, 27 CARDOZO L. REV. 2151, 2194 (2006).

[58] Suresh v. Canada (Minister of Citizenship & Immigration), [2002] 1 S.C.R. 3, [2002] S.C.C. 1. (The Court deliberated on the matter of Suresh, a member of the Tamil Tigers Organization, which was fighting against the Sri Lankan government. In its judgment, the Court approved in principle the decision to deport Suresh to Sri Lanka, despite the possibility that he would be tortured there.)

to a country that may inflict torture on the deportee, the court did, however, require the minister to explain in writing the reasons for deporting a person to a country that is likely to torture him or her. This procedural requirement set the bar high enough to prevent such deportations.[59] The decision of the Canadian Supreme Court in a terrorism-related matter, from February 2007, significantly surpassed its 2002 judgment: The court declared unanimously that the procedures allowing for the deportation of noncitizens suspected of terrorist activities on the basis of confidential information, as well as the denial of a prompt hearing to foreign nationals, are incompatible with the Canadian Charter of Rights and Freedoms.[60] This bold decision was replete with comparative references to foreign and international statutory and case law. The court made specific reference to the British Antiterrorism Act as an example of hearing procedures for suspected terrorists that the Canadian legislature should consider adopting.

This emerging judicial dialogue has not been confined to the British and Canadian courts. It soon included courts from several other jurisdictions, among them France, Germany, Hong Kong, India, Israel, and New Zealand, all in the context of limiting counterterrorism measures.[61] These courts regularly explore the international obligations of their respective states, making references to the texts of treaties on human rights and the laws of armed conflict, as well as to customary international law.[62] The fact that NCs can rely on the same or similar

---

[59] See also the order of October 16, 2006, by Deputy Judge MacKay of the Federal Court of Canada in *Re Jaballah*, [2006] F.C. 1230, 2006 Fed.C.C. LEXIS 1441 (ruling that an Egyptian national who had resided in Canada since May 1996 could be deported, but not to countries where he would face a serious risk of being tortured).

[60] Charkaoui v. Canada (Citizenship & Immigration), [2007] S.C.C. 9, 2007 Can. Sup. Ct. LEXIS 9.

[61] For a review of these decisions, see Eyal Benvenisti, *Inter-Judicial Cooperation to Secure Independent Review of Counter-Terrorism Measures*, in DEMOCRACY, SEPARATIONS OF POWERS AND THE FIGHTS AGAINST TERRORISM 251 (Andrea Bianchi & Alexis Keller eds., 2008).

[62] The prohibition on torture has been the focus of several decisions, including *Suresh*, [2002] 1 S.C.R. 3; A (FC) v. Sec'y of State for the Home Dep't, [2005] UKHL 71; and Zaoui v. Attorney-General (No. 2), [2006] 1 N.Z.L.R. 289 (Sup. Ct.), 2005 NZLR LEXIS 22. The US Supreme Court referred to the Third 1949 Geneva Convention in Hamdan v. Rumsfeld, 126 S.Ct. 2749 (2006), and the Israeli Court has been actively engaged in the interpretation and implementation of the law on armed conflict. On the jurisprudence of the Israeli courts related to counterterrorism, see Yigal Mersel, *Judicial Review of Counter-Terrorism Measures: The Israeli Model for the Role of the Judiciary during the Terror Era*, 38 N.Y.U. J. INT'L L. & POL. 67 (2005); Daphne Barak-Erez, *The International Law of Human Rights and Constitutional Law: A Case Study of an Expanding Dialogue*, 2 INT'L. J. CONST. L. 611 (2004).

legal norms facilitates their productive dialogue.[63] They also learn from each other's constitutional law doctrines.[64] They cite each other extensively in this process of interpretation. For example, in a House of Lords decision concerning the admissibility of evidence obtained through torture by foreign officials, the Law Lords engaged in a comparative analysis of the jurisprudence of foreign courts, including Canadian, Dutch, French, German, and US courts.[65] Moreover, they compare statutory arrangements in different countries in seeking ways to identify measures that minimally impair constitutional rights.[66] They do so, being fully aware of their own role in the global effort to curb terrorism. As the Indian Supreme Court has acknowledged: "Anti-terrorism activities in the global level are mainly carried out through bilateral and multilateral co-operation among nations. It has thus become our international obligation also to pass necessary laws to fight terrorism. [. . .] in the light of global terrorist threats, collective global action is necessary."[67] The Indian court supported this statement with a reference to Lord Woolf's emphasis that "[w]here international terrorists are operating globally . . . a collective approach to terrorism is important."[68]

This accumulation of judicial decisions from various jurisdictions that have collectively resisted their respective executive branches paints a striking picture of an evolving pattern in NCs. This trend stood in clear contrast to the passivity of legislatures toward the executive and to previous judicial trends. NCs are refusing to simply rubber-stamp the actions of the political branches of government. They have unmistakably signaled their intention to constrain counterterrorism measures they

---

[63] *See* Slaughter, *supra* note 8, chapter 2.

[64] The Indian Court, in the case of *People's Union for Civil Liberties* v. *Union of India*, [2004] 1 LRI 1 (Sup. Ct. 2003), *available at* www.commonlii.org/in/cases/INSC/2004/18.html (concerning the constitutionality of the Indian 2002 Prevention of Terrorism Act), refers to the institution of the "independent counsel," appointed in New Zealand and elsewhere.

[65] A (FC) v. Sec'y of State for the Home Dep't, [2005] UKHL 71 (appeal taken from Eng.). See also Lord Carswell's opinion in the *Belmarsh Detainees* decision, A (FC) v. Secretary of State for the Home Department, [2004] UKHL 56, para. 150 (appeal taken from Eng.) (citing former Chief Justice Barak of the Israel High Court of Justice on the need to follow the rule of law when combating terrorism).

[66] In the *Charkaoui* decision, *supra* note 60, the Canadian Supreme Court presented the procedure adopted in the United Kingdom as a model for the Canadian Parliament's consideration when it reenacts the statute. *See id.* para. 86 ("Why the drafters of the legislation did not provide for special counsel to objectively review the material. . . as. . . is presently done in the United Kingdom, has not been explained.").

[67] People's Union for Civil Liberties v. Union of India, *supra* note 64, at para. 10.

[68] A and others v. Sec'y of State for the Home Dep't; X and another v. Sec'y of State for the Home Dep't, [2002] EWCA (Civ) 1502; [2004] QB 335, para. 44.

deem excessive. As reflected in the reasoning in the decisions of many courts, they are seriously monitoring other courts' jurisprudence, and their invocation of international law demonstrates knowledge and sophistication.

As opposed to the jurisprudence of the courts in the context of migration policies discussed below,[69] in the context of counterterrorism there is a discernible effort by the courts to engage their political branches in an ongoing dialogue, rather than expecting to have the final say on the issues under debate. What characterizes many of the decisions on the lawfulness of the counterterrorism measures is their attempt to avoid to the extent possible making a determination on the substance of the specific executive action. Instead they aim to clarify the considerations that the executive must take into account in exercising its discretion[70] or to invite the legislature either to weigh in on the matter or to reconsider a hasty or vague authorization it had granted.[71] While focusing on these institutional levels, the courts have the opportunity to set the bar higher for legislative authorization by invoking the state's international obligations as relevant considerations for the legislature to consider. Direct limitation on the legislature based on constitutional grounds–the ultimate judicial sanction–has been used only sparingly.[72]

---

[69] See text at notes 108–38.

[70] See discussion of Suresh, text at note 58 supra; Zaoui, supra note 62.

[71] In the European Arrest Warrant Act case, the German Constitutional Court examined the European Arrest Warrant Act passed by the German Bundestag to implement the Framework Decision on the European Arrest Warrant, which had been promulgated with a view to facilitating inter-European cooperation in combating crime and terrorism. The Court found the Act to infringe on constitutional rights in a manner beyond what was necessary to meet the goals of the European policy. It thus remanded the matter to the legislature to revise the Act so that the restriction of the fundamental right to freedom from extradition would be proportionate. Bundesverfassungsgericht (Federal Constitutional Court) [BVerfG], 2 BvR 2236/04, Jul. 18, 2005, available at www.bverfg .de/entscheidungen/rs20050718_2bvr223604en.html. In 1996 the French Constitutional Council sent back to the legislature certain measures concerning illegal entrants suspected of being terrorists that criminalized assistance to them and authorized searching them without a judicial warrant. Conseil constitutionnel, [CC] [Constitutional Court] decision No. 96–377 DC, Jul. 16, 1996, translated at www.conseil-constitutionnel.fr/conseil-constitutionnel/root/bank/download/96377DCa96377dc.pdf. See also Charkaoui, supra note 60, which required the Canadian legislature to respond by reshaping the hearing procedures.

[72] The French Constitutional Council found a certain measure unconstitutional because it had retroactive force in overseas territories. Decision no. 96 –377DC, supra note 71. The German Constitutional Court found the Air Security Act of 2005 unconstitutional because it violated, inter alia, the principle of human dignity. BVerfG, Feb. 15, 2006, 115 Entscheidungen des Bundesverfassungsgerichts [BVerfGE] 118, available at www.bverfg

A good example of how carefully courts approach these matters of judicial review is the US Supreme Court's jurisprudence regarding the treatment of post-9/11 detainees in Guantanamo and elsewhere. Referral back to the executive or legislature was the first stage of the Court's involvement in this matter. The *Rasul*[73] and *Hamdi*[74] decisions assert the US court's jurisdiction to review executive action with respect to unlawful combatants held on US territory or territory under US administration and requires the president to clarify his or her authority to act. The second round came two years later with the *Hamdan* decision,[75] which rejected the president's response to the previous judgments. In *Hamdan*, the majority relied on international law as the standard for assessing the legality of the military commissions established by the president to determine the status of Guantanamo detainees. In its judgment, the Court diverged from the executive's position in two important aspects: in asserting, first, that Common Article 3 of the 1949 Geneva Conventions applies to the conflict with Al-Qaeda and, second, that the standards set by that Article are not met by the military commissions.[76] The justices still use the referral technique when they indicate that the executive can seek congressional approval for derogating from those requirements,[77] but four justices hint that the Court may eventually examine the constitutionality of Congress's

---

.de/entscheidungen/rs20060215_1bvr035705.html; *see* Nina Naske & Georg Nolte, *Case Report: "Aerial Security Law,"* in 101 Aм. J. Int'l L. 466 (2007). In 2004 the Indian Supreme Court resorted to implicit constitutional review when it read into the 2002 Prevention of Terrorism Act several additional conditions to some key provisions of the Act, viewing such conditions as constitutionally required. People's Union for Civil Liberties v. Union of India, *supra* note 64.

[73] Rasul v. Bush, 542 U.S. 466 (2004).   [74] Hamdi v. Rumsfeld, 542 U.S. 507 (2004).

[75] Hamdan v. Rumsfeld, 126 Sup.Ct. 2749 (2006).

[76] Justice Stevens, writing for the majority, stated that common Article 3's "requirements are general ones, crafted to accommodate a wide variety of legal systems. But *requirements* they are nonetheless. The commission... convened to try Hamdan does not meet those requirements." *Id.* at 2798.

[77] As Justice Breyer said in concurring in *Hamdan, id.* at 2799:

> The Court's conclusion ultimately rests upon a single ground: Congress has not issued the Executive a "blank check."... Nothing prevents the President from returning to Congress to seek the authority he believes necessary. Where, as here, no emergency prevents consultation with Congress, judicial insistence upon that consultation does not weaken our Nation's ability to deal with danger. To the contrary, that insistence strengthens the Nation's ability to determine–through democratic means– how best to do so. The Constitution places its faith in those democratic means. Our Court today simply does the same.

intervention.[78] The pending petition to the Supreme Court questioning the constitutionality of the Military Commissions Act of 2006[79] would be the ultimate stage of review.

Whereas the US Congress proceeded to deliver "a stinging rebuke to the Supreme Court,"[80] by stripping the courts of jurisdiction over habeas corpus jurisdiction with respect to non-US citizens determined by the executive to be enemy combatants,[81] and immunizing the executive from judicial review based on the 1949 Geneva Conventions,[82] other executive bodies and legislatures have demonstrated a stronger commitment to international standards as interpreted by their courts, despite the fact that they could, if they wanted to, have the last word.[83]

5.3.2 Environmental Protection in Developing Countries

It is not necessary to actually visit India or Pakistan to realize the extent to which their environments are at risk. It is more than sufficient to read the many court decisions rendered in those countries to get a sense of the pervasive health threats due to environmental degradation. The courts in several developing countries[84] are responding to deficient environmental

[78] According to Justice Kennedy (joined by Justices Souter, Ginsburg, and Breyer): "Because Congress has prescribed these limits, Congress can change them, requiring a new analysis *consistent with the Constitution* and other governing laws." *Id.* at *2808 (emphasis added).

[79] Boumediene v. Bush, 127 S.Ct. 1478 (2007), *reh'g granted*, 127 S.Ct. 3078. The Military Commissions Act of 2006 was passed by the U.S. Senate on September 28, and by the U.S. House of Representatives on September 29 of that year in response to the decision in *Hamdi, supra* note 74.

[80] John Yoo, Op-Ed, *Sending a Message: Congress to Courts: Get out of the War on Terror*, WALL ST. J. ONLINE, Oct. 19, 2006, *available at* www.opinionjournal.com/editorial/feature .html?id=110009113.

[81] Military Commissions Act of 2006, Pub. L. No. 109–366, 120 Stat. 2600, §950j(b) (to be codified at 10 U.S.C. §§948a–950w and other sections of titles 10, 18, 28, and 42).

[82] *Id.* 948b(g).

[83] Particularly in the United Kingdom, the courts have only the authority under the Human Rights Act of 1998 to declare a legislative act incompatible with the European Convention on Human Rights without invalidating it.

[84] The list includes the courts in Brazil, Chile, Costa Rica, Ecuador, India, Nepal, Pakistan, Peru, the Philippines, South Africa, Sri Lanka, Tanzania, Turkey, and Uganda. For a review of the practice of these courts, see William Onzivu, *International Environmental Law, the Public's Health, and Domestic Environmental Governance in Developing Countries*, 21 AM. U. INT'L L. REV. 597, 665–72 (2006); Carl Bruch et al., *Constitutional Environmental Law: Giving Force to Fundamental Principles in Africa*, 26 COLUM. J. ENVTL. L. 131, 132–35, 150–88 (2001); Sheetal B. Shah, *Illuminating the Possible in the Developing World: Guaranteeing the Human Right to Health in India*, 32 V AND. J. TRANSNAT'L L. 435 (1999); Vijayashri Sripati, *Toward Fifty Years of Constitutionalism*

laws and institutions, striving as best they can to ameliorate the situation. These courts have transformed themselves into lawmakers by opening up their gates to potential petitioners with lenient standing requirements and by reading into the constitutional right to life a host of environmental obligations on the part of the state. They have even intervened proactively in the executive's sphere of discretion, establishing institutional mechanisms to assess and monitor environmental damage as a form of relief for petitioners.[85] Judge Sabharwal of the Supreme Court of India hinted at this self-assigned role of the Indian courts, when he explained why the Supreme Court must depart from traditional common law doctrines of tort law to address contemporary environmental hazards:

> Law has to grow in order to satisfy the needs of the fast-changing society and keep abreast with the economic developments taking place in the country. Law cannot afford to remain static. The Court cannot allow judicial thinking to be constricted by reference to the law as it prevails in England or in any other foreign country. Though the Court should be [open to enlightenment] from whatever source . . . it has to build up its own jurisprudence. It has to evolve new principles and lay down new norms which would adequately deal with the new problems which arise in a highly industrialized economy.[86]

As this quote implies, aggressive judicial activism is not required in countries, particularly developed ones, where public awareness of environmental issues is translated into effective political action and where modern environmental legislation replaces ancient doctrines of tort law. Where public demand prompts legislators to enact legislation, courts can take a back seat. This may explain the distinction between the Indian Court's activism in the environmental sphere, where existing legislation was viewed as "dysfunctional,"[87] and its passivity in

---

and Fundamental Rights in India: Looking Back to See Ahead (1950–2000), 14 AM. U. INT'L L. REV. 413, 470–71 (1998); Daniel Bodansky & Jutta Brunnée, The Role of National Courts in the Field of International Environmental Law, 7 REV. EUR. COMMUNITY & INT'L ENVTL. L 11 (1998); Michael J. Andersen, International Environmental Law in Indian Courts, 7 REV. EUR. COMMUNITY & INT'L ENVTL. L. 11 (1998).

[85] See Shikhar Ranjan, Legal Controls on the Transboundary Movements of Hazardous Wastes into India – An Evaluation, 41 INDIAN J. INT'L L. 44 (2001) (describing the Indian government's response, primarily by introducing new legislation, as coming only after the courts have acted on public petitions).

[86] Research Found. for Sci. Tech. & Natural Res. Policy v. Union of India, W.P. 657/1995, Jan. 5, 2005 (Supreme Court of India), available at www.judis.nic.in/supremecourt/qrydisp.asp?tfnm 26698.

[87] C. M. Abraham, ENVIRONMENTAL JURISPRUDENCE IN INDIA 62 (1999); see also Shah, supra note 84, at 483–84 (noting that the Indian Court justified its interventions in the

promoting employee rights by its narrow interpretation of statutes intended to improve those rights.[88]

In the absence of specific domestic legislation, courts in environmentally threatened jurisdictions can base their formal authority to expand and enforce environment-related procedures and standards on two sources: their national constitutions and international law. These two sources enable communication with the courts of other nations, through cross-citing of one another's judgments. And in fact, interjudicial communications have proved to be the hallmark of the jurisprudence of these courts, with the Indian Supreme Court leading the way. In 1994 the Pakistani Supreme Court made references to Indian cases.[89] In 1997 Judge Rahman of the Bangladesh Appellate Division presented the Indian jurisprudence as a model for emulation.[90] In 2000 the Sri Lanka Supreme Court referred to an Indian judgment with approval.[91]

environmental sphere by asserting that it is temporarily filling the void created by a lack of strong executive and legislative branches).

[88] In Steel Authority of India Ltd. v. National Union of Waterfront Workers, [2001] 7 S.C.C. 1, *available at* www.commonlii.org/in/cases/INSC/2001/445.html, the Indian Supreme Court refused to give an expansive interpretation of provisions of the Contract Labour (Regulation and Abolition) Act of 1970, finding them to be "clear and explicit." The Court failed to find any flaw in the Act, which, it stated, "was passed to prevent the exploitation of contract labour and also to introduce better conditions of work." Labor unions in India have been successful in securing legislation designed to protect their interests, although ultimately their victories have led to an increase in the informal sector. Timothy Besley & Robin Burgess, *Can Labor Regulation Hinder Economic Performance? Evidence from India*, 119 Q. J. ECON. 91 (2004).

[89] Zia v. WAPDA, (1994) PLD (SC) 693, *available at* www.elaw.org/assets/word/Zia%20v.%20WAPDA.doc.

[90] Farooque v. Gov't of Bangladesh, *supra* note 37. After noting the recent trend of judicial activism of the Supreme Court of India to protect the environment through public litigation, Judge Rahman observed that in Bangladesh "such cases are just knocking at the door of the court for environmental policy making" and that the court was involving itself in them. A global trend toward liberalizing the rules of standing was exemplified by the Indian Supreme Court, which "took the view that when any member of a public or social organization so espouse[d] the cause of the poor and the down-trodden, such member should be permitted to move the Court even by merely writing a letter without incurring expenditure of his own." Furthermore, he added, "The operation of Public Interest Litigation should not be restricted to the violation of the defined fundamental Rights alone. In this modern age of technology, scientific advancement, economic progress and industrial growth the socio-economic rights are under phenomenal change. New rights... call for collective protection and therefore we must act to protect all the constitutional, fundamental and statutory rights as contemplated within the four corners of our Constitution."

[91] Bulankulama v. Sec'y, Ministry of Indus. Dev., [2000] LKSC 18, *available at* www.commonlii.org/lk/cases/LKSC/2000/18/html.

The Indian Supreme Court itself referred to the judgments of courts in the Philippines, Colombia, and South Africa and of the European Court of Human Rights, as well as to a decision of the American Commission on Human Rights, noting, with evident satisfaction, that "the concept of a healthy environment as a part of the fundamental right to life, developed by our Supreme Court, is finding acceptance in various countries side by side with the right to development."[92]

The absence of any explicit text relating to environmental protection in many constitutions has meant that courts must derive such protection from the basic right to life, which is anchored in all constitutions. The Supreme Court of India relied heavily on the constitutional right to life as including the right to enjoy unpolluted water and air.[93] To develop the scope of this right, the Indian court, as well as other courts, looked to international law for its inspiration and even its authority. But recourse to international law also brings with it challenges and impediments. International environmental law is fragmented, with many of its provisions little more than hortatory declarations. The status of these norms in the internal domestic legal order often presents an additional obstacle to their judicial invocation. But faced with impending environmental disasters, courts in several countries have waived all doctrinal concerns and embraced whatever guidance they can derive from the stock of diverse international documents dealing with the environment. The Supreme Court of India has taken the lead in tapping these international legal sources. Its decisions refer to the Declaration of the 1972 Stockholm Conference on Human Environment as the "Magna Carta of our environment"[94] and import into domestic law concepts and principles such as "sustainable development,"[95] "the pollution pays" principle,[96] and

---

[92] A.P. Pollution Control Bd. (II) v. Nayudu, *supra* note 37.

[93] Kumar v. State of Bihar, [1991] S.C.C. 598, *available at* www.commonlii.org/in/cases/INSC/1991/3.html; Narmada Bachao Andolan v. Union of India, [2000] 10 S.C.C. 664, *available at* http://judis.nic.in/supremecourt/qrydisp.asp?tfnm17165 (approving the displacement of indigenous and tribal populations due to the construction of a dam on the Narmada River, with the court considering, inter alia, ILO Convention No. 107, the Indigenous and Tribal Peoples Convention of 1957, and principles of international environmental law).

[94] Essar Oil Ltd. v. Halar Utkarsh Samiti, [2004] 2 S.C.C. 392, *available at* www.commonlii.org/in/cases/INSC/2004/31.html.

[95] Vellore Citizens' Welfare Forum v. Union of India, [1996] 5 S.C.C. 647, *available at* www.commonlii.org/in/cases/INSC/1996/1027.html.

[96] Indian Council for Enviro-Legal Action v. Union of India, [1996] A.I.R. SC 1446, *available at* www.commonlii.org/in/cases/INSC/1996/244.html.

the "precautionary principle,"[97] all mentioned in international "soft law" instruments.[98] The court often does not explain the legal significance of these international documents; for instance, it refers at times to declarations such as the 1992 Rio Declaration on Environment and Development as simply "agreements" that were "enacted."[99] The multiplicity of such non-binding documents and the fact that they have been endorsed by a great number of governments at high-profile gatherings have apparently been the basis for the court's reference to them as having been transformed into "customary international law though [their] salient features have yet to be finalized by the international law jurists."[100] The Indian court has grounded its decisions on standards set in unincorporated international agreements based on the premise that these conventions "elucidate and go to effectuate the fundamental rights guaranteed by our Constitution [and therefore] can be relied upon by Courts as facets of those fundamental rights and hence enforceable as such."[101] Other courts in the region (in Pakistan,[102] Sri

---

[97] *Vellore Citizens' Welfare Forum, supra* note 95; Mehta v. Union of India, [1997] 2 S.C.R. 353, *rep. in* www.commonlii.org/in/cases/INSC/1997/769.html.

[98] *See generally* Karnataka Indus. Areas Dev. Bd. v. Kenchappa, [2006] A.I.R. SC2546, *available at* www.elaw.org/resources/printable.asp?id=3133. *See also* Narmada Bachao Andolan, *supra* note 93.

[99] *Karnataka Indus. Areas, supra* note 98, para. 54 (emphasis added): "The Earth Summit held in Rio de Janeiro in 1992 altered the discourses of environmentalism in significant ways. Sustainability, introduced in the 1987 Brundtland Report–Our Common Future–and *enacted* Rio *agreements*, became a new and accepted code word for development" (emphasis added).

[100] *Vellore Citizens' Welfare Forum, supra* note 95 (referring to the concept of sustainable development). The Kerala High Court viewed the other principles as part of customary international law based on the Indian Supreme Court's reasoning in Soman v. Geologist, [2004] 3 K.L.T. 577, para. 15, *available at* www.elaw.org/resources/printable.asp?id=2680.

[101] Research Found. for Sci. Tech. & Natural Res. Policy v. Union of India, *supra* note 86, para. 33.

[102] Zia, *supra* note 89, para. 9. Despite the fact that the international documents do not have the force of binding law, the Court observed, "the fact remains that they have a persuasive value and command respect. The Rio Declaration is the product of hectic discussion among the leaders of the nations of the world and it was after negotiations between the developed and the developing countries that an almost consensus declaration had been sorted out. Environment is an international problem having no frontiers creating transboundary effects. In this field every nation has to cooperate and contribute and for this reason the Rio Declaration would serve as a great binding force and to create discipline among the nations while dealing with environmental problems. Coming back to the present subject, it would not be out of place to mention that Principle No. 15 envisages rule of precaution and prudence."

Lanka,[103] Nepal,[104] and Bangladesh)[105] have concurred with the juris-prudence of the Indian Supreme Court, by invoking these principles in a similar fashion in their own judgments concerning the environment.

Clearly, these courts are fully aware of the potentially adverse economic implications of their pro-environment jurisprudence.[106] Interjudicial cooperation must therefore be seen as a way to mitigate those adverse consequences. In fact, given the grave environmental threat hovering over the Indian subcontinent, these NCs may have pushed for reform just as doggedly even without the backing of their counterparts in neighboring nations. But absent such cooperation, they might have been much less resistant to pressures brought to bear by domestic and foreign industry groups for which lower environmental standards mean greater economic gain. Even now these courts are far from being all-powerful in their quest to restrain the economic forces of globalization.[107]

5.3.3 Coordinating the Migration into Destination Countries

Waves of asylum seekers from strife-riven and poverty-stricken regions, especially since the early 1990s, have prompted developed countries to modify their migration policies by restricting considerably the access of refugees and limiting their rights.[108] Such restrictions increased the

---

[103] Bulankulama v. Sec'y, Ministry of Indus. Dev., *supra* note 91 (Sri Lanka, referring to the international declarations as "[i]nternational standard setting instruments").

[104] Surya Prasad Sharma Dhungel v. Godavari Marble Indus., 4 INT'L ENVTL. L. REP. 321 (2004) (Nepal Sup. Ct. 1995) (en banc), available at www.elaw.org/resources/printable .asp?id=2287 (referring to the principle of sustainable development).

[105] Farooque v. Gov't of Bangladesh, *supra* note 37, (referring to the Rio Declaration on Environment and Development as a source of inspiration).

[106] Harish Salve, *Justice between Generations: Environment and Social Justice, in* SUPREME BUT NOT INFALLIBLE: ESSAYS IN HONOUR OF THE SUPREME COURT OF INDIA 360, 372 (B. N. Kirpal et al. eds., 2000) (suggesting that in Centre for Environment Law, WWF I v. Union of India, [1999] 1 S.C.C. 263, the Indian Supreme Court ordered the closing of tanneries despite the fact that those tanneries were "a major foreign exchange earner for the country as leaders in the export of leather goods").

[107] A prominent commentator has accused the Indian Supreme Court of "licit and illicit complicity with global capitalism." Upendra Baxi, *"A Known but an Indifferent Judge": Situating Ronald Dworkin in Contemporary Indian Jurisprudence,* 1 I-CON 557, 569 (2003).

[108] On the modifications introduced by destination states since the early 1990s, see Jane McAdam, COMPLEMENTARY PROTECTION IN INTERNATIONAL REFUGEE LAW (2007); James C. Hathaway, *Harmonizing for Whom? The Devaluation of Refugee Protection in the Era of European Economic Integration,* 26 CORNELL INT'L L.J. 719 (1993); Gerald L. Neuman, *Buffer Zones against Refugees: Dublin, Schengen, and the German Asylum Amendment,* 33 VA. J. INT'L L. 503 (1993); Karin Oellers-Frahm & Andreas Zimmermann, *France's and*

importance of better defining the minimal obligations states owed to refugees under international law. The courts in these destination countries have played an important role in shaping the policies toward the various asylum seekers subject to *refoulement* or deportation. Because the migration policy adopted by one state had immediate effects on other states, the coordination of migration policies was of the essence for many states. The examination of the ways NCs in destination countries have interpreted and applied the international law on migration is therefore a key test to the thesis presented in this chapter.

Compared with the two areas of judicial creativity discussed earlier in this section, the formulation of national migration policies has been high on the political agenda of many of the destination countries. In the sphere of migration policies, the courts were expected by their political branches to respect their domestic political processes and uphold the results of sustained deliberations and popular support. The possible cost of defying the popular will by abiding by the demands of international law was not only the heavy criticism. A court that "cooperated" with the strict requirements of international law while other courts "defected" by interpreting international law toward refugees less generously would potentially channel a larger and more politically controversial number of refugees its way.

By and large, courts could not immediately reflect the transformation of national policies. The jurisprudence related to *refoulement* and expulsion to countries where torture could be committed against the expellee was too clear to be waived. The direct contact with the individual refugee and her or his painful life story, together with judges' confidence that they could distinguish genuine from bogus claims, probably also moved judges to adopt a critical stance toward new executive and legislative policies. Decisions of courts in the majority of destination jurisdictions reflect this sentiment.

Interjudicial cooperation is necessary in this area in order to stand up to the domestic political process without incurring the "costs" of increasing the numbers of refugees. The stakes, however, were high, and it was ineffective, even irresponsible, for judges to rely only on the old practice of comparing decisions and intermittent exchanges. Such sentiments

Germany's Constitutional Changes and Their Impact on Migration Law: Policy and Practice, 38 GER. Y.B. INT'L L. 249 (1995); Liza Schuster, *A Comparative Analysis of the Asylum Policy of Seven European Governments*, 13 J. REFUGEE STUD. 118 (2000). See also the special issue of volume 13 of the *Journal of Refugee Studies*, No. 1, Mar. 2000, devoted to the policies of European countries.

may have been behind the establishment in 1995 of the International Association of Refugee Law Judges (IARLJ). Dr. Hugo Storey, then a vice president of the UK Immigration Appeal Tribunal and a member of the IARLJ Council, explained in 2003 the raison d'être of this association:

> [One] of IARLJ's principal objectives is the development of consistent and coherent refugee jurisprudence. Ideally a person who claims to be a refugee under the 1951 Convention should receive the same judicial assessment of his case whether he is in Germany, the USA, Japan or South Africa.[109]

The constitution of IARLJ reflects this ambitious program and two of its preambles set forth the extent of the challenge:

> Whereas the numbers of persons seeking protection outside of their countries of origin are significant and pose challenges that transcend national boundaries;
>
> Whereas judges and quasi-judicial decision makers in all regions of the world have a special role to play in ensuring that persons seeking protection outside their country of origin find the 1951 Convention and its 1967 Protocol as well as other international and regional instruments applied fairly, consistently, and in accordance with the rule of law. . ..[110]

This constitution also asserts that one of its objectives is "[t]o foster judicial independence and to facilitate the development within national legal systems of independent institutions applying judicial principles to refugee law issues."[111] Membership in the IARLJ is open to judges or "quasi-judicial decision makers," of which there were in August 2007 332 members from 52 countries. Members can access an online database of court decisions in asylum law. A leading expert in refugee law, James Hathaway, praised the association, viewing it as an alternative to the "more vigorously collaborative and formalised models" of international enforcement mechanisms known in other areas of international human rights law, including international tribunals.[112]

During the 1990s, NCs dealing with asylum seekers began citing each other's interpretation of the 1951 Convention Relating to the Status of Refugees, in particular its key provision regarding the definition of

---

[109] Hugo Storey, *The Advanced Refugee Law Workshop Experience: An IARLJ Perspective*, 15 INT'L J. REFUGEE L. 422 (2003).

[110] IARLJ Constitution, *supra* note 34.   [111] *Id.* Art. 2(2).

[112] James C. Hathaway, *A Forum for the Transnational Development of Refugee Law: The IARLJ's Advanced Refugee Law Workshop*, 15 INT'L J. REFUGEE L. 418, 419 (2003).

a "refugee."[113] This convention provided a basis for coordinating a shared judicial position that often enabled these courts to strike down restrictive governmental policies without risking an influx of immigrants. This is not to suggest that the courts were always unanimous on all aspects of the elaborate qualifications of a "refugee." But what becomes clear from several key decisions of the highest courts of the majority of the destination states is their effort to offer a contemporary meaning to the 1951 Convention–one that expands the definition of a "refugee" beyond the one envisioned in 1951, and despite the concerns of contemporary governments. This effort is captured in the following statement by Lord Carswell:

> The persecution of minorities and the migration of people seeking refuge from persecution have been unhappily enduring features, which did not end with the conclusion of the Second World War. [. . .] The vehicle [for balancing the states' international obligations against their concerns] has been the [1951 Geneva Convention], which was the subject of agreement between states over 50 years ago, when the problems of the time inevitably differed in many respects from those prevailing today. That a means of reaching an accommodation suitable to cater for modern conditions has been achieved is a tribute to the wisdom and humanity of those who have had to construe the terms of the Convention and apply them to multifarious individual cases.[114]

In their wisdom, the courts turned to construe the terms of the Convention collectively. This judicial dialogue can be traced to the early 1990s, when a 1993 judgment of the Canadian Supreme Court[115] cites a 1985 decision of the United States Board of Immigration,[116] to be later cited by

---

[113] In particular, the qualification for refugee status was discussed. *See* 1951 Refugee Convention, *supra* note 41, Art. 1A(2): "For the purposes of the present Convention, the term 'refugee' shall apply to any person who. . . (2). . . owing to well-founded fear of being persecuted for reasons of race, religion, nationality, membership of a particular social group or political opinion, is outside the country of his nationality and is unable or, owing to such fear, is unwilling to avail himself of the protection of that country. . . ."

[114] Januzi (FC) v. Sec'y of State for the Home Dep't, [2006] UKHL 5, [2006] 2 A.C. 426, para. 62 (appeal taken from Eng.).

[115] Canada (Attorney Gen.) v. Ward, [1993] 2 S.C.R. 689.

[116] *In re* Acosta, 19 I. & N. Dec. 211 (1985), BIA LEXIS 2. It is noteworthy that the decision takes into account "various international interpretations" of the term "refugee" in the Convention, explaining that "[s]ince Congress intended the definition of a refugee in [the implementing legislation] to conform to the [Convention], it is appropriate for us to consider various international interpretations of that agreement. However, these interpretations are not binding upon us in construing the elements created by [the implementing legislation], for the determination of who should be considered a refugee is ultimately left [. . .] to each state in whose territory a refugee finds himself. [. . .] While we

the High Court of Australia (1997),[117] the New Zealand Refugee Status Authority (1998),[118] and the House of Lords (1999).[119] In that 1999 judgment, the House of Lords commends the New Zealand Refugee Status Authority for its "impressive judgment" that draws on "the case law and practice in Germany, The Netherlands, Sweden, Denmark, Canada, Australia and the USA."[120] In 2000, the United States Court of Appeals for the Ninth Circuit retreated from its prior interpretation,[121] which these other courts refused to follow, and endorsed the evolving common position, acknowledging that this is also the position of the neighboring Canadian court.[122] This interjudicial exchange necessarily also involves disagreements on particular aspects of the definition,[123] but this dialogue is conducted with utmost respect and careful attention.[124] As evidenced by the Ninth Circuit's 2000 judgment,[125] this deliberation is ultimately capable of yielding general agreement.

> do not consider the [Office of the United Nations High Commissioner for Refugees'] Handbook to be controlling, the Handbook nevertheless is a useful tool to the extent that it provides us with one internationally recognized interpretation of the [Convention]." *Id.* at 220–21

[117] A v. Minister for Immigration & Ethnic Affairs, (1997) 190 CLR 225; *see also* Al-Kateb v. Godwin, (2004) 219 CLR 562; Minister for Immigration & Multicultural Affairs v. Khawar, (2002) 210 CLR 1; S v. Minister for Immigration & Multicultural Affairs, (2004) 217 CLR 387; Minister for Immigration & Multicultural Affairs v. Applicant Z, (2001) 116 FCR 36 (Fed. Ct. Austl.); Applicant S v. Minister for Immigration & Multicultural Affairs, (2001) FCA 1411 (Fed. Ct. Austl.).

[118] *In re GJ*, Refugee Appeal No. 1312/93, [1995] 1 NLR 387.

[119] Islam (A.P.) v. Secretary of State for the Home Department, Regina v. Immigration Appeal Tribunal, *ex parte* Shah, [1999] 2 A.C. 629, 643 (H.L.) (appeal taken from Eng.).

[120] *Id.* at 643 (Steyn, L.J.).

[121] Sanchez-Trujillo v. INS, 801 F.2d 1571, 1576 (9th Cir. 1986).

[122] Hernandez-Montiel v. INS, 225 F.3d 1084, 1093 (9th Cir. 2000).

[123] For example, the House of Lords in *Januzi, supra* note 114, prefers the English and Canadian approach to that supported by some courts in New Zealand and Australia.

[124] The US Supreme Court decision in Sale v. Haitian Ctrs. Council, Inc., 509 U.S. 155, 183 (1993), is an example of narrow interpretation. On the basis of a textual reading of the 1951 Convention in light of its *travaux pré-paratoires*, the Court concluded that the *non-refoulement* obligation did not apply to individuals situated outside the territorial jurisdiction of the state. For criticism of this interpretation, see Harold Hongju Koh, *The "Haiti Paradigm" in United States Human Rights Policy*, 103 YALE L.J. 2391 (1994). This interpretation, however, was endorsed by the House of Lords in Regina v. Immigration Officer at Prague Airport, *ex parte European Roma Rights Centre*, [2004] UKHL 55, para. 17 (appeal taken from Eng.), and by the Australian High Court in *Khawar, supra* note 117, para. 42. Lord Bingham of Cornhill emphasized that "[t]he House was referred to no judicial authority to contrary effect." *Ex parte* Eur. Roma Rights Ctr., *supra* note 124, para. 17.

[125] Hernandez-Montiel, *supra* note 122.

In 2001 the House of Lords openly addressed the role of NCs in preventing "gross distortions" in the implementation of the 1951 Geneva Refugees Convention through "a uniformity of approach to the refugee problem."[126] Lord Steyn insisted on a joint judicial effort designed to look beyond national peculiarities when interpreting a shared text:

> In principle therefore there can only be one true interpretation of a treaty. If there is disagreement on the meaning of the Geneva Convention, it can be resolved by the International Court of Justice (art 38 of the Geneva Convention). It has, however, never been asked to make such a ruling. The prospect of a reference to the International Court of Justice is remote. In practice it is left to national courts, faced with a material disagreement on an issue of interpretation, to resolve it. But in doing so it must search, untrammelled by notions of its national legal culture, for the true autonomous and international meaning of the treaty. And there can only be one true meaning.[127]

But this very decision also demonstrated the limits of judicial independence, as well as the limited ability of the written word to withstand domestic political pressures. Some courts, most notably in France and Germany, operated since the early 1990s in a political environment increasingly concerned with the influx of refugees. Restrictive policies were adopted in both countries by constitutional amendment.[128] During the 1990s, many if not most refugees were fleeing countries affected by civil wars and intercommunal strife, and European courts were called upon to decide whether "persecution" in the sense of the 1951 Geneva Convention could be effected also by nonstate agents. While the majority of courts, including the courts in the United Kingdom, recognized that nonstate agents could also be deemed "persecutors," some other courts, including those of Germany and France, refused to follow

---

[126] Regina v. Sec'y of State for the Home Dep't, *ex parte Adan*, *supra* note 31, at 616 (Hobhouse, L.J.):

The scheme of the Geneva Convention is that any such differences should be referred to and resolved by the International Court of Justice under art 38 of that convention. However, there is no prospect that the presently relevant difference (which has existed now for many years) will be resolved in that way.

So long as such differences continue to exist, the intention of the Geneva Convention to provide a uniformity of approach to the refugee problem will be frustrated and the scheme of the international response will remain grossly distorted.

[127] *Id.* at 617.

[128] *See* Oellers-Frahm & Zimmermann, *supra* note 108, at 260–63 (noting that the constitutional amendment in France was designed to circumvent the outcome of a previous decision of the *Conseil Constitutionnel*).

suit.[129] As a result, German courts would not recognize as "refugees" asylum seekers from countries such as Afghanistan, Bosnia, Sri Lanka, or Somalia who suffered at the hands of nonstate actors. French courts would similarly reject the applications of Algerians persecuted by militias, lacking evidence that the Algerian state either encouraged or tolerated the persecution.[130] The lesser protection afforded to such refugees in these two countries prompted the House of Lords to quash the decision to send refugees from Somalia and Algeria to Germany and France, respectively, out of concern that they might be deported and face persecution.[131]

The judicial "defections"[132] by the French and the German courts were based on traditional justifications: These courts gave precedence to the peculiarities of their national constitutions and interpreted the international obligations narrowly, invoking governmental practice rather than the jurisprudence of the foreign and international courts. The French Constitutional Council and the German Federal Constitutional Court examined domestic legislation in light of their recently amended constitutions.[133] The German Federal Administrative Court gave precedence to a domestic act that incorporated the international obligation to protect refugees, interpreting that act in light of the German Basic Law.[134] The same court acknowledged the different interpretation of

---

[129] On the differences of interpretations see Catherine Phuong, *Persecution by Non-state Agents: Comparative Judicial Interpretations of the 1951 Refugee Convention*, 4 EUR. J. MIGRATION & L. 521 (2002). The EU Qualification Directive of 2004 (Council Directive 2004/83/EC of 29 April 2004 on Minimum Standards for the Qualification and Status of Third Country Nationals or Stateless Persons as Refugees or as Persons Who Otherwise Need International Protection and the Content of the Protection Granted, 2004 O.J. (L 304) 12) resolved these differences, by recognizing non-state actors as potential persecutors. *See* Guy S. Goodwin-Gill & Jane McAdam, THE REFUGEE IN INTERNATIONAL LAW 98–100 (3rd edn., 2007). On the "long battle" in Germany over legislation that, inter alia, would adopt this interpretation, see Marion Schmid-Drüner, *Germany's New Immigration Law: A Paradigm Shift?*, 8 EUR. J. MIGRATION & L. 191 (2006).

[130] Adan, *supra* note 31, at 600.

[131] Adan, *supra* note 31. The Canadian Federal court, following the approach of the House of Lords, refused to allow the return of a Colombian asylum seeker to the United States. Canadian Council for Refugees v. The Queen, [2007] F.C. 1262, *available at* www.canlii .org/en/ca/fct/doc/2007/2007fc1262/2007fc1262.pdf.

[132] "Defection" in the sense of failing to adopt the position of the majority of courts, which, as Goodwin-Gill and McAdams suggest, seems to be the more plausible interpretation of the text. Goodwin-Gill & McAdam, *supra* note 129, at 98–100.

[133] *See* Oellers-Frahm & Zimmermann, *supra* note 108.

[134] Bundesverwaltungsgericht [Federal Administrative Court] [BVerwG], 95 Entscheidungen des Bundesverwaltungsgerichts, Jan. 18, 1994 [BVerwGE] 42. Article

other courts that had recognized the refugee status of those persecuted by nonstate agents (referring to jurisprudence in the United States, the United Kingdom, France, Canada, and Australia). It even asserted that the interpretation of the same treaty by other courts usually carries "special weight" for the interpreting court, but not when the intention of the national legislator was as clear as it was in this case. In a subsequent decision, this court added that its understanding of international law also reflected the understanding of most of the *governments* of the state parties of the Convention.[135] The court refused, however, to accept an "expansive" and "creative" conflicting interpretation, noting:

> It is not the task of the courts to expand the boundaries of the member-states ability and willingness to absorb [refugees] through creative interpretation of treaties and thereby to disregard the constitutionally protected sovereignty of the national lawmaker and constitution-maker.[136]

The German Federal Constitutional Court, when reviewing the constitutionality of decisions of the Federal Administrative Court, expanded somewhat the opportunities of asylum seekers who fled nonstate persecution. However, it did not refer to international law in its interpretation of the relevant provisions in the German law.[137]

16a(1) of the Basic Law provides: "Persons persecuted *on political grounds* shall have the right of asylum" (emphasis added). The German legislation, according to this court, was in line with the 1951 Convention, since the convention too insisted on state-sponsored persecution as a condition for "refugeeness." This interpretation was based, according to established rules of treaty interpretation, on the ordinary meaning of the text, in light of its object and purpose. The convention, recalled the court, was drafted in 1951 with the persecutions by regimes such as Nazi Germany or the Soviet Union in mind. *See* Berthold Huber, *The Application of Human Rights Standards by German Courts to Asylum-Seekers, Refugees and other Migrants*, 3 Eur. J. Migration & L. 171, 174 (2001).

[135] BVerwG, 104 BVerwGE 254, Apr. 15, 1997. The German court ruled further that the obligation under the European Convention on Human Rights not to expel individuals to jurisdictions where they might face inhumane treatment was also confined to situations where such treatment was expected from the ruling state authority or, exceptionally, the quasi-state authority. *Id.* at 269.

[136] BVerwG, Apr. 15, 1997, 104 BVerwGE 265, 272 (referring to Ahmed v. Austria, 1996–VI Eur. Ct. H.R. 2195). Another explanation given for disregarding the European Court's ruling was that it was obiter dictum. BVerwG, Sept. 2, 1997, 105 BVerwGE 187, 189; *see* Huber, *supra* note 134, at 176.

[137] Bundesverfassungsgericht (Federal Constitutional Court) [BVerfG], 2 BvR 260/98 Aug. 10, 2000, *available at* www.bundesverfassungsgericht.de/entscheidungen/ rk20000810_2bvr026098.html. Note that according to the prevailing German law at the time, if an asylum seeker was neither recognized as entitled to asylum under Article 16a(1) of the Basic Law nor granted the status of a refugee under section 51 of the Aliens Act, then he or she might still enjoy so-called subsidiary protection. The latter satisfied the requirements of the European Convention on Human Rights, *see*

The coalition of courts determined to develop a consistent interpreta-tion of the 1951 Convention and the opposition which consists of those other courts that preferred a different outcome are two sides of the same coin, the coin being the use of international law as a strategic tool by NCs. For courts that seek to establish a common front, a shared text is a desirable asset to be cultivated. At the same time, however, this story suggests that international law may also be important for those courts that seek to protect their domestic political process from external pres-sures. The German Federal Administrative Court offers an example of a court that uses the language of international law to explain why the common standard should not apply in Germany.

Note that a common judicial front may not always be beneficial to asylum seekers. As Gerald Neuman noted, a common position privileges the status quo, since changes require consensus and careful coordination, and asylum seekers could benefit from divergence between national policies defining their status and rights.[138] But in the trade-off between the common position of the governments and that of the courts, the latter has so far proved more beneficial for the refugees.

5.4 Assessment: The Potential and Limits to Further Cooperation

The picture that emerges from reviewing the way courts employ foreign and international law is complex, but it indicates that recourse to foreign and international law has become an effective tool for interjudicial coordination. It indicates as well that courts tend to resort to such tools either to protect the independence of their domestic political branches from external pressures or to protect their own independence (from encroachment by their respective governments). What is significant is that the courts have identified international law as a tool that no longer governs only the relations between states. Rather, they see it as a tool that can regulate the intrastate relations between governments and courts, one to be used, even manipulated, by both sides for their common or diverging purposes. As we will see in Chapter 6, also potentially of far-

---

T. I. v. United Kingdom, 2000–III Eur. Ct. H.R. 435, and the House of Lords, which approved the removal of Tamil refugees from the United Kingdom to Germany, see Regina v. Sec'y of State for the Home Dep't, ex parte Thangarasa, [2002] UKHL 36, [2003] 1 A.C. 920 (appeal taken from Eng.).

[138] See Neuman, supra note 108 (referring to the potentially adverse consequences of convergence in Europe in the early 1990s).

reaching consequences are judicial alliances that involve coordination with international tribunals.

In theory, we can expect cooperation in other spheres where judicial alliances are necessary to withstand external pressure by foreign actors that seek to preempt the domestic political processes or to pressure them into compliance.[139] Cooperation among courts of developing countries can, for example, develop in the area of trade law, in reaction to pressures from foreign companies to enforce trade or trade-related norms through decisions of international institutions or pressure on governments. Resisting courts could invoke other international norms, such as human rights or environmental law or constitutional principles such as the right to life, to counter claims based on general trade law or specific treaties. The prime example for this prospect is the 2013 judgment of the Supreme Court of India in *Novartis v. India*.[140] At stake was access to Gleevec, a lifesaving drug for leukemia patients, and the continued supply of the much cheaper generic version by Indian companies to patients in India and other developing countries.[141] The court rejected Novartis's claims that the Indian patent law violated India's obligations under the Trade-Related Aspects of Intellectual Property Rights (TRIPS) Agreement by rendering a narrow interpretation of the TRIPS agreement's scope of protections for intellectual property. The judgment exhibited the potential for offsetting the clout of the big multinationals by using state institutions,[142] and it "caused a stir, almost in the form of a 'tsunami' among intellectual property practitioners, both nationally

---

[139] Currently, interjudicial cooperation cannot be traced in the sphere of labor law. National courts do cite international standards, including ILO conventions, but not each other. For a compendium of national judgments referring to international labor law, see Use of International Law by Domestic Courts, *available at* http://training.itcilo.it/ils/CD_Use_Int_Law_web/Additional/English/default.htm.

[140] Novartis AG v. Union of India (Aug. 6, 2007, High Ct. Madras), *available at* www.commonlii/in/cases/INTNHC/2007/2604.html.

[141] This decision follows an aborted attempt of international pharmaceutical corporations to sue against South African legislation that authorized the compulsory licensing of life-saving drugs, claiming that this was a violation of South Africa's TRIPS-based obligations. The case was dropped in 2001 after the court allowed NGOs to present affidavits. Pharm. Mfrs. Ass'n of S. Afr. v. South Africa, No. 4138/98 (High Ct., withdrawn Apr. 17, 2001). On this litigation, see David Barnard, *In the High Court of South Africa, Case No. 4138/98: The Global Politics of Access to Low-Cost AIDS Drugs in Poor Countries*, 12 Kennedy Inst. Ethics J. 159 (2002). On the question of access to drugs in developing countries see Eyal Benvenisti & George W. Downs, *Distributive Politics and International Institutions: The Case of Drugs*, 36 Case W. Res. J. Int'l L. 21 (2004).

[142] Gupakumar G. Nair, Andreya Fernandes & Karthika Nair, *Landmark Pharma Patent Jurisprudence in India*, 19 J. Intel. Prop. Rts. 79 (2014).

and internationally."[143] Moreover, it provided a model for other NCs to emulate. In fact, a decade earlier the Supreme Court of Sri Lanka concluded that a bill that would have precluded compulsory licensing and parallel importing (important tools to ensure affordable access to pharmaceutical drugs) required a special majority in parliament because it infringed the principle of equality enshrined in the constitution.[144]

But the logic of interjudicial cooperation has its limits. Courts remain sensitive to the national interest. Interjudicial cooperation will be confined, therefore, to those areas where the courts deem that from a nationalist perspective the benefits of interjudicial cooperation outweigh the costs. For example, despite an initial willingness to adjudicate suits against foreign officials for alleged war crimes or crimes against humanity–exemplified in the *Pinochet* case[145]–many courts ultimately concluded that the costs outweighed the benefits and so deferred to their governments: While trials of fallen dictators like Pinochet may not incur excessive risks for the forum state, it is far riskier for most economies–again, not perhaps for the United States[146]–to allow suits against incumbent heads of state or senior government officials of affluent states who had invested heavily in the forum state.[147]

Courts are also unlikely to cooperate when foreigners are suing their government for war crimes. An example of a judicial conflict is the confrontation between the Greek and Italian Supreme Courts, on the one hand, and the German Supreme Court, on the other, regarding suits

---

[143] *Id.* at 80.

[144] Case of S.C. Special Determination on the Intellectual Property Bill, No. 14/2003 *available at* www.elaw.org/system/files/
Sri±Lanka±SC±Determination±on±Intellectual±Property±Bill.doc.

[145] House of Lords judgment in the *Pinochet* case, *supra* note 31.

[146] In this respect, the US courts again stood out, at least for a while: Inasmuch as they are not particularly anxious to protect their domestic processes from external influence, *see* text at notes 3 and 26, they have been, until recently, the least perturbed by the potential adverse consequences of rendering judgments against foreign violators of international law. Sosa v. Alvarez-Machain, 542 U.S. 692 (2004).

[147] *Compare* the *Pinochet* decision, *supra* note 31 (no immunity for former heads of state against prosecution for acts of torture), *with* its judgment in Jones, *supra* note 32 (immunity against prosecution for acts of torture for incumbent officials of a foreign state, Saudi Arabia), *and* the *Qaddafi* case, *as analyzed in* Salvatore Zappalà, *Do Heads of State in Office Enjoy Immunity from Jurisdiction for International Crimes? The* Ghaddafi *Case before the French Cour de Cassation*, 12 Eur. J. Int'l L. 595 (2002) (the French court relied on customary law to suggest vaguely that Qaddafi enjoyed immunity, but without explaining which type of immunity and whether it would expire when he is no longer in power).

for damages for German war crimes in World War II.[148] Reading these cases reminds one of the jurisprudence of the earlier generation, when courts ingeniously interpreted international law to uphold their government's position.[149] Indeed these decisions are standing proof that interjudicial cooperation is a strategy of choice, pursued for purely parochial ends. And when these ends change, we should expect the cooperation to end with them.

Finally, it is possible to envision state executives (and the interest groups behind them) pressing to nip in the bud the emergence of transjudicial cooperation in key spheres. The 2013 *Novartis* judgment was one of the triggers for redoubled efforts to sidestep NCs altogether. Pharmaceutical companies, keen to prevent the *Novartis* precedent from spreading around the developing world, lobbied for a new trade regime that would offer privatized mechanisms of dispute resolution as an alternative to NCs.[150] These are the so-called mega-regional agreements. The Trans-Pacific Partnership (TPP) between the United States and eleven other Pacific Rim states[151] includes such provisions, and in the Transatlantic Trade and Investment Partnership (TTIP), currently being negotiated between the United States and the EU, this issue is under debate, but both sides have agreed to keep NCs out of the business of interpreting the new trade rules.[152]

---

[148] The Greek Supreme Court rendered a default judgment against Germany for war crimes during World War II, awarding damages. Prefecture of Voiotia v. Fed. Republic of Germany, Areios Pagos [Supreme Court], 11/2000; *see* Maria Gavouneli & Ilias Bantekas, *Case Report: Prefecture of Voiotia v. Federal Republic of Germany*, 95 AM. J. INT'L L. 198 (2001). The German Supreme Court refused to recognize the Greek judgment. Bundesgerichtshof [BGH] [Federal Court of Justice], Jun. 26, 2003, III ZR 245/98 (*Distomo Massacre* case), *translated in* 42 INT'L LEGAL MATERIALS 1030 (2003). The Italian Court of Cassation reached a conclusion similar to that reached by the Greek court in a suit brought by Italian citizens against Germany. Ferrini v. Fed. Republic of Germany, cass., sez. un., Mar. 11, 2004, 87 RIVISTA DI DIRITTO INTERNAZIONALE 539 (2004); *see* Andrea Bianchi, *Case Report: Ferrini v. Federal Republic of Germany*, in 99 AM. J. INT'L L. 242 (2005). But in a parallel decision, the same court refused to consider a suit brought by Serbian citizens against Italy for war crimes during the 1999 NATO Kosovo campaign. President of Council of the Minister v. Markovic, cass., sez. un., Jun. 5, 2002, No. 8157, *translated in* 128 INT'L L. REP. 652; *see also* Markovic v. Italy, App. No. 1398/03, Eur. Ct. H.R. (2006) (Grand Chamber), *available at* www.echr.coe. int.

[149] *See supra* notes 4–10 and corresponding text.

[150] Amy Kapczynski, *Engineered in India – Patent Law 2.0*, 369 N. ENGL. J. MED. 497 (2013).

[151] Asia Pacific region states include Australia, Brunei, Canada, Chile, Japan, Malaysia, Mexico, New Zealand, Peru, Singapore, the United States, and Vietnam.

[152] *See* Eyal Benvenisti, *Democracy Captured: The Mega-Regional Agreements and the Future of Global Public Law*, 23 CONSTELLATIONS 58 (2016).

5.5 Conclusion

In this chapter we have argued that the judicial aspiration to "speak in one voice" has characterized the efforts of a growing number of NCs across the globe. But unlike the situation that prevailed until the end of the Cold War, this time it was no longer the wish of these courts to speak in the voice of their executive branches. Rather, they sought to sound their own judicial voice, one they shared with other NCs. Comparative constitutional law and international law have proved to be useful tools for effecting this strategy. We explain this strategy as a reaction to the delegation of governmental authority to formal or informal international institutions and the mounting economic pressures on governments and courts to conform to global standards. This judicial reaction, in turn, can resist the depletion of the domestic democratic space and ensure adequate room for deliberation while simultaneously securing the national governments' ability to withstand pressure brought to bear by interest groups and powerful foreign governments. As we will demonstrate in Chapter 6, when this reaction also entails cooperation with international tribunals, it has the potential to correct at least some of the harmful aspects of fragmentation. Therefore, as will be further elaborated in Chapter 7, we believe that such motivation for transjurisdictional coordination is fully justified under democratic theories that conceive of the court as a facilitator of democratic deliberation.

As discussed, the coordination strategy is primarily limited to situations in which courts observe that their government, their legislature, or they themselves have succumbed to or are threatened by economic or political powers that operate to stifle the democratic process through coordinated supranational standards, whether formal (in treaties) or informal. This suggests that courts might not be equally adamant when there are only local dimensions to a given dispute, as would be the case, for example, in disputes over conditions for detaining local criminals or over the displacement of indigenous inhabitants due to dam construction.

It is too early to assess the success of this emerging trend. Every collective action depends on a sufficient number of contributors to the effort. Changes in the domestic rules protecting judicial independence could put a damper on the willingness of the courts in the relevant countries to take on an assertive role. Governments may also be pressured to submit to intergovernmental efforts seeking to deprive courts of the authority or opportunity to act, as the new mega-regional trade agreements seek to do. But given the analysis presented in this chapter, it seems safe to assume that courts will not sit idly by while their authority to review the actions of the political branches is eroded. In an era when governments are opting for alternatives to formal internal or international lawmaking, it is the NCs that are turning very seriously to comparative constitutional law and international law. This is a surprising mirror image of the state of affairs that existed until the beginning of the twenty-first century.

6

Interjudicial Cooperation and the Potential for Democratization of the Global Regulatory Sphere

6.1 Introduction

It is widely appreciated that under contemporary conditions of global interdependence, described and analyzed in Chapters 2 and 3, domestic democratic institutions have grown increasingly unresponsive to the preferences of many of their traditional domestic stakeholders. International organizations (IOs) and other global regulatory bodies are failing to consider in any systematic way the interests of diffuse stakeholders who are increasingly affected by them. These bodies–in all their multiplicity–are poorly designed to address the resulting democratic deficits at the global and national levels, because they tend to be dominated by the internal politics of a handful of powerful states. In this chapter we argue that democratic failures at both the national and international levels can be best addressed through greater interaction and coordination between national courts (NCs) and international tribunals (ITs). These emerging interactions between relatively assertive NCs (as elaborated in Chapter 5) and the relatively more timid ITs (whose constraints are discussed in Chapter 4) potentially bolster both and especially the latter. Collectively, this thickening web of judicial bodies is in a position to enhance the demand for and increase the supply of accountability from global regulators. NC-IT coordination can promote democracy at both the domestic and international levels by helping to ensure that the interests of a greater proportion of relevant stakeholders (both within rich democratic countries and within poorer countries) are taken into account by decision-makers and that the resulting outcomes are more informed and balanced. We further argue that "democracy" in this context must be understood as providing a voice to those stakeholders who are all too often silenced in domestic and global decision-making processes.

Historically, NCs have been instrumental in strengthening domestic democratic mechanisms and developing legal tools that address the ongoing challenges posed by asymmetric information in democracies. Increasingly, this remedial judicial role has become more and more crucial, as in most democratic societies the policy-making processes at the global level have become more complex and opaque than those at the domestic level. This new environment is not one in which NCs can continue to give their states' executives a free hand to fashion global regulatory policies as they see fit. Left unchecked, such power will impoverish both domestic democratic processes and judicial processes. And it will dramatically reduce the opportunities for citizens to effectively promote their own priorities.

These concerns may have inspired, for example, the German Federal Constitutional Court in its judgment concerning the constitutionality of Germany's accession to the Maastricht Treaty. In that judgment the court asserted its authority, under German law, to review the actions of the European institutions:

> [I]f European institutions or agencies were to treat or to develop the Union Treaty in a way that was no longer covered by the Treaty in the form that is the basis for the [German parliament's] Act of Accession, the resultant legislative instruments would not be legally binding within the sphere of German sovereignty. The German state organs would be prevented for constitutional reasons from applying them in Germany. Accordingly the [German] Federal constitutional Court will review legal instruments of European institutions and agencies to see whether they remain within the limits of the sovereign rights conferred on them or transgress them.[1]

It seems likely that NCs seeking to protect the integrity of their domestic legal system and their autonomous space will increasingly engage themselves in reviewing the expanding powers of IOs. Their activism will be an opportunity also for ITs.

6.2   Responding to the Democratic Challenges via National and International Court Coordination

Our analysis suggests that the most likely solution to the democratic challenges just described rests with the emerging symbiotic cooperation between national and international courts. Through conditional

---

[1] Brunner v. The European Union Treaty, German Federal Constitutional Court Judgment of Oct. 12, 1993 (trans. in [1994] 57 COMMON MKT. L. REP.), 89 (Part C(c)). For similar positions of the Polish and Spanish courts see Adam Łazowski, *Poland. Constitutional Tribunal on Conformity of the Accession Treaty with the Polish Constitution. Decision of 11 May 2005*, 3 EUR. CONST. L. REV. 148 (2007).

cooperation they have been able to begin to address and occasionally overcome some of the key difficulties with democratic participation at both the national and the international levels. This section demonstrates and evaluates this phenomenon. It explains the necessary and sufficient conditions that enable courts to curtail executive discretion when they review the policies of either a member state or an IO. Based on these insights, Chapter 7 explains how such judicial review promotes democracy at the national level, as well as at the level of the IOs.

As discussed in Chapter 5, NCs within the dominant coalition of powerful democratic states are aware of the challenges that the international regulatory structure poses for their domestic democratic processes, and they have begun to develop tools to respond to them. In particular, they have exhibited a newfound willingness to intervene in policymaking at the global level and to curb the domestic enforcement of such policies, a trend that holds out the promise of curbing excessive executive discretion, reducing pressure from private companies, and improving domestic accountability. In addition, NCs have shown some tentative willingness to exploit their considerable independence from their respective executive branches to review deficits at the international level and determine which of the often conflicting international legal standards can be applied within their own jurisdictions.

If NCs continue to review a steady flow of cases and experience a willingness on the part of other NCs to reciprocate in the process of norm creation, it is likely that they will increasingly preempt IOs by insisting on their own right to participate in international lawmaking. As a purely doctrinal matter, NCs are directly and indirectly engaged in the evolution of customary international law. Their decisions that are based on international law are viewed by ITs as reflecting customary international law, and their governments' actions that are in compliance with their decisions will constitute state practice coupled with *opinio juris*. As a result, ITs will increasingly find themselves having to pay heed to the jurisprudence of NCs. It follows that the more NCs engage in applying international law and the more united they are with respect to their arguments, the more their jurisprudence will constrain the choices available to ITs when the latter deal with similar issues.

There are, of course, limits to what NCs can do. In particular, concerted executive effort or unfavorable public opinion can undermine their resistance. As mentioned in Chapter 5, there are already signs that executive branches orchestrate collective intergovernmental responses aimed at preempting or restraining NCs. As will be illustrated below, the establishment of the UN Counter-Terrorism Committee is an example of one such attempt to preempt NC review.[2] In the sphere of migration policy, there is also evidence of European governments bypassing their courts by resorting to the apparatus of the European Union.[3] The trends toward informal lawmaking and a reliance on private regulation and private arbitration also seem likely to further constrain the range of cases subject to judicial monitoring and review.[4]

In contrast to NCs, to date, ITs have had only modest success in reviewing global regulation or regulating IO decision-making. Some ITs have sometimes been able to impose some restrictions on IOs, by exploiting differences between state parties to the extent that states were unable to unite to modify a given treaty in accordance with the interpretation rendered by the IT or to credibly threaten to exit the IO. For reasons explained in previous chapters, only in such circumstances can ITs promote policies that diverge from the executive's initial under-standings. Unfortunately, as the ITs lack independence from the powerful states–the system's chief architects–that appointed them, more often than not both conditions are absent. This state of affairs is consistent with the literature on domestic judicial review that suggests that courts are likely to remain dependent and faithfully impose the

---

[2] *See infra* text accompanying notes 9–25.

[3] *See* Directive 2004/83/EC of the Counsel of the European Union of 29 April 2004 on Minimum Standards for the Qualification and Status of Third Country Nationals or Stateless Persons as Refugees or as Persons Who Otherwise Need International Protection and the Content of the Protection Granted, 2004 O.J. (L 304) 12 (calling for a common policy on asylum across the European Union); Directive 2001/55/EC of the Counsel of the European Union on 20 July 2001 on Minimum Standards for Giving Temporary Protection in the Event of a Mass Influx of Displaced Persons and on Measures Promoting a Balance of Efforts Between Member States in Receiving Such Persons and Bearing the Consequences Thereof, 2001 O.J. (L 212) 12, *available at* www.ecre.org /eu_developments/temporary%20protection/tpdir.pdf; Scott Reynolds, *European Council Directive 2001/55/EC: Toward a Common European Asylum System*, 8 Colum. J. Eur. L. 359 (2002) (stating the European Commission's desire to afford immediate protection and rights to displaced persons and to balance domestic efforts to address the issue). For a similar measure at an earlier stage, see James C. Hathaway, *Harmonizing for Whom? The Devaluation of Refugee Protection in the Era of European Economic Integration*, 26 Cornell Int'l L.J. 719 (1993).

[4] On "informal international law," Eyal Benvenisti, *"Coalitions of the Willing" and the Evolution of Informal International Law in* Coalitions Of The Willing – Avantgarde Or Threat? (C. Calliess, C. Nolte & G. Stoll eds., 2008); Informal International Lawmaking (Joost Pauwelyn, Ramses Wessel & Jan Wouters eds., 2012).

principals' policies, as long as the principals remain capable of effective oversight and are united enough to collectively sanction them.[5]

However, improved cooperation between NCs and ITs can potentially help both types of institutions strengthen their positions vis-à-vis their domestic and international executives. Such a symbiotic relationship is likely based on two factors: on the one hand, on the relatively greater independence of NCs from the pressures generated by coalitions of powerful states and the stronger domestic public support for NCs, and, on the other hand, on the greater capacity of ITs to effectively monitor the policy compliance of any particular state. Taken together, the relatively greater independence and domestic legitimacy of NCs can indirectly and inadvertently contribute to the strengthening of IT review capacity in the international sphere, as ITs find support in NC activism. NCs, in turn, also benefit from strong ITs whenever found. This is particularly true when the two share an interest in curbing the growth of executive power (for example, the Inter-American Court of Human Rights).

ITs also bring resources to the table that under certain circumstances can prove to be invaluable to NCs. ITs can facilitate coordination between NCs by endorsing, or at least not opposing, their shared interpretation of the law. In addition, ITs' endorsement of NC jurisprudence by, for example, regarding it as reflecting customary law, can lend added legitimacy to the NC decision and help pressure recalcitrant courts in other states to comply with that NC ruling. Such endorsement can also operate to preempt the possibility of any government threatening to "appeal" a national court decision before an IT. David Kosař and Lucas Lixinski have recently shown how the European and inter-American human rights courts were instrumental in bolstering the independence of NCs domestically by insisting on the individual's right of access to the courts and to due process. As they suggested, by empowering domestic judiciaries, these regional courts have indirectly also empowered themselves.[6]

---

[5] On the political preconditions for judicial independence, see Mark C. Stephenson, *"When the Devil Turns . . . ": The Political Foundations of Independent Judicial Review*, 32 J. LEGAL STUD. 59 (2003); Tom Ginsburg, JUDICIAL REVIEW IN NEW DEMOCRACIES: CONSTITUTIONAL COURTS IN ASIAN CASES 21–33 (2003); John Ferejohn, *Judicializing Politics, Politicizing Law*, 65 LAW & CONTEMP. PROBS. 41, 57 (2002); Robert D. Cooter, THE STRATEGIC CONSTITUTION 225 (2000); McNollgast, *Politics and the Courts: A Positive Theory of Judicial Doctrine and the Rule of Law*, 68 S. CAL. L. REV. 1631 (1995); Mark J. Ramseyer, *The Puzzling (In)dependence of Courts: A Comparative Approach*, 23 J. LEGAL STUD. 721 (1994). *See also* Chapter 4.

[6] David Kosař & Lucas Lixinski, *Domestic Judicial Design by International Human Rights Courts*, 109 AM. J. INT'L L. 713 (2015).

While a measure of mutual dependence and vulnerability between NCs and ITs can occasionally cause friction, it can also serve as the basis for productive dialogue and cooperation. Defragmentation–if carefully coordinated between NCs and Its–can benefit both in this regard.[7] NCs are likely to welcome the efforts of ITs to defragment the international legal system and to broaden their authority when these actions reduce the extent to which executive branches can employ IOs to escape domestic accountability and traditional constitutional constraints.

Similarly, ITs are likely to tolerate increased NC review if it also provides a measure of cover for ITs and increases the likelihood that they will escape retribution if they deviate from the outcome preferred by the executives of powerful states. If NCs are expected to rule against them, executives may be more inclined to tolerate the ruling of ITs. As we will see below, there is reason to believe that the effects of regulatory fragmentation on ITs and NCs are quite different but also have the potential to be strategically complementary.

In sum, while serious areas of potential disagreement exist between NCs and ITs and are likely to persist, if intermittently, both will generally be better off if they coordinate their actions. Acting independently will only perpetuate judicial marginalization and facilitate the further expansion of executive discretion.

6.3   Examples of Budding Cooperation

The benefits of such symbiotic dynamics were recently exemplified in the evolution of the targeted sanctions regime of the UN Security Council. This example is particularly significant and worth exploring because it demonstrates both the determination of the five permanent members of the UN Security Council to evade review of their policies and their reluctant acquiescence to the unexpected intervention by NCs and ITs.[8]

---

[7] In saying this, we do not mean to suggest that the judges share similar motivations, only that the expansion of the role of judiciary and judicial discretion are phenomena that benefit judges irrespective of the microfoundations of their individual decision-making.

[8] On this litigation *see also* Lisa Ginsborg & Martin Scheinin, *Judicial Powers, Due Process and Evidence in the Security Council 1267 Terrorist Sanctions Regime: The Kadi II Conundrum* (Eur. U. Inst., EUI Working Paper RSCAS 2011/44, 2011), *available at* http://cadmus.eui.eu/handle/1814/18238; Katalin Tünde Huber & Alejandro Rodiles, *An Ombudsperson in the United Nations Security Council: A Paradigm Shift?* 10 ANUARIO MEXICANO DE DERECHO INTERNACIONAL 107 (2012); Peter Hipold, *UN Sanctions before the ECJ: The Kadi Case, in* CHALLENGING ACTS OF INTERNATIONAL ORGANIZATIONAL BEFORE NATIONAL COURTS 18 (August Reinisch ed., 2010).

Beginning with Resolution 1267 (1999), a series of Chapter VII Security Council Resolutions mandated that states impose asset freezes and travel bans on persons determined by Security Council (SC) committees to be associated with the Taliban or specific terrorist networks. These "targeted sanctions" have gradually come under challenge because of a growing perception that they lack proper procedural safeguards and judicial remedies. While it has generally been the case in the post-9/11 era that both executive and legislative branches in democracies have tolerated counterterrorism-related measures without demur, the NCs in several countries have resolved to review such measures. In spite of, or perhaps because of, the pervasive public fear that they see in their societies, they have by and large refused to deviate from their traditional stance in support of individual rights and have thereby signaled their unwillingness to relinquish indefinitely their hard-won authority to protect individuals from governmental abuse of power.

Traditionally, NCs have shied away from legal challenges to Security Council Resolutions, and when they have chosen to engage–as in the case of the first direct challenges to the authority of the Security Council to set up ad hoc international criminal tribunals–they have done so with considerable hesitancy.[9] However, in the post-9/11 era several prominent NCs appear to have realized that Security Council Resolutions related to counterterrorism pose a potential threat to their own standing as institutions that are constitutionally empowered to determine the balance between security and liberty.[10] As a result, they have responded by asserting their authority to interpret Security Council Resolutions narrowly, in line with the principles of their national constitutions.

In 2006, the French Court of Cassation declared that in France Security Council Resolutions had no direct effect until incorporated into national law by domestic measures that would be subject to judicial review.[11] In 2007, the House of Lords was faced with the

---

[9] On the challenges in NCs to the authority of the ICTY and the ICTR see Jean d'Aspremont & Catherine Brölmann, *Challenging International Criminal Tribunals before Domestic Courts, in* CHALLENGING ACTS OF INTERNATIONAL ORGANIZATIONS BEFORE NATIONAL COURTS 111 (August Reinisch ed., 2010); Erika de Wet & André Nollkaemper, *Review of Security Council Decisions by National Courts*, 45 GERMAN Y.B. INT'L L. 166 (2002).

[10] *See* Chapter 5 Section 5.3.

[11] Iraqi State v. Corporation Dumez GTM (SA), Appeal (cassation) judgment, Cour d'appel [CA][regional court of appeal] Paris, 1e civ, Apr. 25, 2006, ILDC 771 (Fr.).

claim that a Security Council Resolution limited its authority to review the implementation of the European Convention on Human Rights (ECHR).[12] Like the French court, the British court, too, interpreted the Security Council Resolution narrowly and subjected compliance with it to a proportionality analysis. It found that the Security Council Resolution qualified but did not displace the obligation of UK forces to comply with the ECHR unless it was "necessary for imperative reasons of security" to deviate from it.[13] To these judgments one could add the "Solange"-type of judgments of courts in Europe that have kept European institutions mindful of their dependence on domestic implementation.[14] More specifically, a few NCs have upheld indirect challenges to the "targeted sanctions" regime.[15]

It is quite likely that those judgments had an impact on the Grand Chamber of the CJEU in *Kadi*.[16] On appeal, the court's advocate general, Miguel Maduro, outlined a way for the court to overcome the apparent obligatory compliance with Security Council Resolutions, which the court endorsed. It appears that Maduro's suggestion to the court, in particular, was determinative–that NCs had both the authority and the inclination to step in if the CJEU would not and that it was "very unlikely that national measures for the implementation of [Security Council Resolutions] would enjoy immunity from [national] judicial review."[17] The CJEU's *Kadi* judgment could, in turn, have reinforced the resolve of NCs to limit the scope and authority of Security Council Resolutions.

---

[12] R. v. Secretary of State for Defence, [2007] UKHL 58.

[13] *See* A, K, M, Q & G v. HM Treasury, [2008] EWHC 869 (Admin).

[14] In a series of judgments, the German Federal Constitutional Court said that it would comply with decisions and judgments of European institutions "as long as" these decisions are compatible with the values of the German Basic Law: Juliane Kokkot, *Report on Germany, in* THE EUROPEAN COURT AND NATIONAL COURTS – DOCTRINE AND JURISPRUDENCE 77 (Anne-Marie Slaughter, Alec Stone Sweet & J.H.H. Weiler eds., 1998). This act was followed by several other courts in the EU. *See* Wojciech Sadurski, '*Solange, chapter 3': Constitutional Courts in Central Europe–Democracy–European Union*, 14 EUR. L.J. 1, 1–35 (2008); Bruno de Witte, *Direct Effect, Supremacy, and the Nature of Legal Order, in* THE EVOLUTION OF EU LAW (Paul Craig & Grainne de Burca eds., Oxford University Press, 1999).

[15] For a review of these and other NC judgments, see Antonios Tzanakopoulos, *Domestic Court Reactions to UN Security Council Sanctions, in* CHALLENGING ACTS OF INTERNATIONAL ORGANIZATIONS BEFORE NATIONAL COURTS 54 (August Reinisch ed., 2010).

[16] Joined Cases C-402/05 P & C-415/05 P, Kadi & Al Barakaat v. Council of the European Union, 2008 E.C.R.I-6351.

[17] Opinion of Advocate General Poiares Maduro, Case C-402/05 P, delivered on 16 Jan. 2008, *available at* http://blogeuropa.eu/wp-content/2008/02/cnc_c_402_05_kadi_def.pdf, at 12, footnote 34.

In 2009, the Canadian Federal Court held that Canada had violated the constitutional rights of Abousfian Abdelrazik, a dual citizen of Canada and Sudan despite the fact that the Canadian government was implementing the sanctions regime pursuant to Resolution 1267.[18] The court found that the sanctions regime was "untenable under principles of international human rights"[19] and that its interpretation and implementation by the Canadian authorities was a violation of its Charter obligations. It interpreted the relevant Security Council Resolutions narrowly to explain why ordering the government to respect Mr. Abdelrazik's Charter rights did not violate the Security Council Resolutions. Later in 2009, in other cases, the English High Court,[20] and on appeal the newly established Supreme Court,[21] refused to give effect to domestic executive measures promulgated to implement sanctions based on Security Council Resolution 1267. Both courts regarded these measures as ultra vires the United Kingdom's United Nations Act 1946 (which empowers the executive to issue provisions that are "necessary or expedient" for implementing Security Council Resolutions). The Supreme Court, citing the above-mentioned judgments, interpreted the Security Council Resolution as not requiring state action based merely on a permissive test of "reasonable suspicion" and therefore found that "[i]t was not necessary to introduce the reasonable suspicion test in order to reproduce what the Security Council Resolution requires."[22] This interpretation was supported by constitutional concerns for the separation of powers ("Is it acceptable that the exercise of judgment in matters of this kind should be left exclusively, without any form of Parliamentary scrutiny, to the executive?")[23] and for the fundamental rights of UK citizens.[24]

It was not only the (mainly) European courts that put pressure on the Security Council to amend its ways. Several European and other governments also tried to get the Security Council to modify its procedures.[25] However, it seems clear that it was the judicial proceedings and judgments that played a crucial framing function both in terms of sharpening the legal question and in terms of suggesting that the

---

[18] Abdelrazik v. Minister of Foreign Affairs & Attorney General of Canada, [2009] F.C. 580 (Can.).
[19] Id. at para. 51.   [20] Hay v. HM Treasury, [2009] EWHC 1677 (Admin) (QB).
[21] Ahmed and others v. HM Treasury, [2010] UKSC 2, [47].   [22] Id. at [58] (Lord Hope).
[23] Id.   [24] Id. at [77]–[82].
[25] Ian Johnstone, *Legislation and Adjudication in the UN Security Council: Bringing Down the Deliberative Deficit*, 102 AM. J. INT'L L. 275, 295–97 (2008).

sanctions regime could face effective resistance. As a result, the Security Council amended its listing and delisting procedures.

After the Court of First Instance (CFI) rendered its *Kadi* judgment (2005), the president of the SC mentioned that "[i]nternational, national and regional courts must review Security Council Resolutions to ensure that they comply fully with internationally recognized human rights norms and the principles and purposes of the United Nations Charter."[26] The chair of the Sanctions Committee admitted that "[o]ne cannot ignore the international context... [the Security Council] sanctions regimes find themselves increasingly under pressure and have recently been questioned, especially in light of the need for fair and clear procedures for listing, de-listing and the granting of humanitarian exemptions."[27] Indeed, it was "European pressure" that in 2008 compelled the SC committee to "identify formal guidelines or evidentiary standards for states to follow in proposing names, and to incorporate humanitarian exceptions and a de-listing procedure."[28] By that time the *Kadi* case was already in appeal before the Court of Justice of the European Union, and the SC Sanctions Committee had expressly stated its concern that the Court would undermine the targeted sanctions regime by holding the implementation regulation invalid and warned that "it would trigger similar challenges that could quickly erode enforcement."[29] As a result, "[t]he Committee has made a series of incremental improvements to its procedures."[30] After adopting Security Council Resolution 1904 (Dec. 2009),[31] Ambassador Susan Rice of the United States explained the measure as "address[ing] concerns that have been expressed by some European courts."[32] However, these new measures were deemed insufficient by the EU General Court (the successor of

---

[26] U.N. SCOR, 61st Sess., 5599th mtg. at 3, U.N. Doc. S/PV.5599 (Dec. 19 2006), *available at* www.un.org/ga/search/view_doc.asp?symbol=S/PV.5599.

[27] U.N. SCOR, 63rd Sess., 6043rd mtg. at 9, U.N. Doc. S/PV.6043 (Dec. 15, 2008).

[28] José E. Alvarez, *Contemporary International Law: An "Empire of Law" or the "Law of Empire"?* 24 Am. U. Int'l L. Rev. 811, 830 (2009).

[29] Letter dated May 13, 2008 from the Chairman of the Security Council Committee to the President of the Security Council, ¶ 40, U.N.Doc. S/2008/324 (May 14, 2008), *available at* www.un.org/ga/search/view_doc.asp?symbol=S/2008/324.

[30] *Id.* at ¶ 41.

[31] S.C. Res. 1904, U.N. Doc. S/RES/1904 (Dec. 17, 2009), *available at* www.un.org/ga/ search/view_doc.asp?symbol=S/RES/1904(2009).

[32] Ambassador Susan E. Rice, U.S. Permanent Representative to the U.N., Remarks on S.C. Res. 1904 (Dec. 17, 2009), *available at* http://usun.state.gov/briefing/statements/2009/ 133836.htm.

the CFI),[33] and so the struggle to shape the policies of the Security Council's targeted sanctions regime continues, with NCs and the EU courts both playing a crucial role. [34]

Another, less prominent but not less telling example relates to the imposition of labor standards within international organizations. Although initially several international organizations sought to insulate themselves from judicial supervision of their employment conditions, shielding themselves from the scrutiny of NCs by the absolute immunity they had under international law, they eventually had to heed the pressure brought to bear by NCs. The World Bank established its Administrative Tribunal only after it became clear that the Bank's employment policies could be subjected to challenges in NCs.[35] In Europe, both European NCs and the European Court on Human Rights incrementally expressed their authority and their willingness to condition the immunity from suit that the Bank and other IOs had enjoyed (according to the then prevailing norm of international law)[36] on the adoption by the international organizations of equivalent protection of labor rights. After initial remarks by the French Court of Cassation in 1995 that raised the concern that such immunity could amount to a denial of justice, a French appellate court in 1997 rejected UNESCO's plea of immunity by directly invoking the ECtHR.[37] In 1999, the ECtHR endorsed this view by suggesting that decisions of domestic courts respecting immunity of international organizations in labor disputes were subject to scrutiny to determine their compliance with European human rights law. According to this court, respect for the immunity of international organizations would be conditional on their providing a reasonable alternative means for securing the rights of their

---

[33] Case T-85/09, Kadi v. Comm'n, 2010 EUR-Lex LEXIS 825 (Sept. 30, 2010).

[34] The most recent modifications to the procedures of the U.N. Sanctions Committee were introduced by S.C. Res. 1989, U.N. Doc. S/RES/1989 (Jun. 17, 2011) *available at* www.un .org/ga/search/view_doc.asp?symbol=S/RES/1989(2011).

[35] On the events leading up to the establishment of the WBAT *see* Theodor Meron & Betty Elder, *The New Administrative Tribunal of the World Bank*, 14 N.Y.U. J. INT'L L. & POL. 1 (1981); C.F. Amerasinghe, *The World Bank Administrative Tribunal*, 31 INT'L & COMP. L.Q. 748 (1982).

[36] On this "functional immunity" and its rationales see Jan Klabbers, AN INTRODUCTION TO INTERNATIONAL ORGANIZATIONS LAW 131–39 (3rd edn., 2015); Hazel Fox, THE LAW OF STATE IMMUNITY 724–34 (2nd edn., 2008).

[37] August Reinisch, *The Immunity of International Organizations and the Jurisdiction of Their Administrative Tribunals*, 7 CHINESE J. INT'L L. 285, 297 (2008).

employees.[38] As August Reinisch demonstrates, this attitude adopted by the ECtHR subsequently "inspired"[39] various NCs in Europe to scrutinize the treatment of employees by international organizations situated within their own territory. Obviously, these national demands enhance the independence of the administrative tribunals established by the international institutions. [40]

A third and more fruitful example of NC-IT cooperation in opposition to the interests of the executive branches of at least some key governments relates to the issue of reparations for individual victims in connection with violations of humanitarian law. NCs have been debating the question of whether individuals have a right to international legal recourse against foreign governments. Some courts, notably in Germany, subscribe to the traditional doctrine, according to which only states of the affected citizens could invoke such a right against the violating government, but others have disagreed. In 2004, the ICJ's Wall opinion was worded in such a way that it appeared to give implicit recognition to individual rights. Subsequent decisions of NCs have explicitly recognized such a right.

A fourth example that was unfolding at the time of writing involved the legal proceedings instituted by the international sporting federations such as FIFA and the International Skating Union against athletes who had failed drug tests. These proceedings are brought to arbitration under the auspices of the Court of Arbitration for Sports (CAS). Athletes have leveled serious allegations concerning potential conflict of interest by arbitrators who are appointed by the sporting federations. Petitions brought in domestic courts, and which were partially successful,[41] have

---

[38] Beer v. Austria, App. No. 30428/96, Eur. Ct. H.R. (2001); Waite & Kennedy v. Germany, App. No. 26083/94, Eur. Ct. H.R. ¶ 67 (1999) ("The Court is of the opinion that where States establish international organisations in order to pursue or strengthen their cooperation in certain fields of activities, and where they attribute to these organisations certain competences and accord them immunities, there may be implications as to the protection of fundamental rights. It would be incompatible with the purpose and object of the Convention, however, if the Contracting States were thereby absolved from their responsibility under the Convention in relation to the field of activity covered by such attribution.").

[39] Reinisch, *supra* note 37, at 295.

[40] See Eyal Benvenisti, THE LAW OF GLOBAL GOVERNANCE 245 (2014).

[41] *Compare* the Pechstein decision, Oberlandesgericht (OLG) München, Az. U 1110/14 Kart., Jan. 15, 2015, *available at* https://openjur.de/u/756385.html (accepting jurisdiction against CAS proceedings), *with* the negative judgment of the German Federal Administrative Court (Urteil des Kartellsenats, KZR 6/15, Jun. 7, 2016, *available at* http://juris.bundesgerichtshof.de/cgi-bin/rechtsprechung/document.py?Gericht=bgh&Art=en&client=12&nr=75021&pos=0&anz=1&Blank=1.pdf). *See also*

led to reforms in CAS procedures.[42] The questions remain whether these reforms are sufficient and whether domestic courts would dare to challenge the global regime of sports. It is quite likely that when one of these disputes reaches an IT such as the ECtHR, the IT will have sufficient resolve to protect the athletes from a regime that has little interest in protecting the athletes' individual rights.[43]

Another example that illustrates the potential challenges as well as the promise of NC-IT coordination involves the litigation concerning immunities granted to foreign heads of states and other foreign state officials in NCs. In recent years, several NCs have grappled with the question of whether international law should recognize an exception to this immunity for alleged acts of torture or genocide. The call for recognizing such an exception to immunity was founded on the alleged supremacy of the prohibition on *jus cogens* violations such as torture. In 1996, the British Court of Appeals refused to recognize such an exception in the context of an alleged case of torture by Kuwaiti officials.[44] But in 1999, in the famous *Pinochet* decision, the House of Lords accepted this claim with respect to former heads of state (while using language and logic that would also support the rejection of such immunity for *incumbent* officials).[45] In 2001, the Belgian courts also

John G. Ruggie, *"For the Game. For the World." FIFA and Human Rights,* (Harvard Kennedy School, Corporate Responsibility Initiative Report No. 68., 2016) *available at:* www.hks.harvard.edu/centers/mrcbg/programs/cri/research/reports/report68.

[42] *See, e.g.,* CAS's own admission: "the CAS will continue to listen and analyze the requests and suggestions of its users, as well as of judges and legal experts in order to continue its development, to improve and evolve with changes in international sport and best practices in international arbitration law with appropriate reforms. For example, since 2009 and the resolution of the case Pechstein/ISU, a procedure for legal aid has been implemented to assist athletes without sufficient financial means to access to CAS arbitration. A real diversity in the composition of ICAS has also been achieved with a majority of members not linked to sports organizations and an equal representation of men and women" (Statement of the Court of Arbitration for Sport (CAS) on the Decision Made by the German Federal Tribunal (Bundesgerichtshof) in the Case between Claudia Pechstein and the International Skating Union (ISU) 7 June 2016, *available at* www.tas-cas.org/fileadmin/user_upload/ Media_Release_Pechstein_07.06.16_English_.pdf.

[43] In the case of David Meca-Medina and Igor Majcen v. Commission of the European Communities, the CJEU insisted on the applicability of EU law and particularly standards concerning individual rights to sporting institutions (Case C-519/04, Meca-Medina v. Comm'n, 2006 E.C.R. I-6991).

[44] Al-Adsani v. Government of Kuwait, 107 I.L.R. 536 (1996).

[45] R v. Bow St. Metro. Stipendiary Magistrate & Others, *ex parte* Pinochet Ugarte (No. 3), [2000] 1 A.C. 147, 244 (H.L.).

rejected such immunity in connection with the incumbent Congolese foreign minister.[46]

Both the 1996 British decision and the 2001 Belgian decision were "appealed" to ITs, the ECtHR (2001) and the ICJ (2002), respectively.[47] Each of the tribunals refused to recognize an exception to incumbent foreign state officials' immunity. Rather than basing their decisions on a jurisprudential analysis of the hierarchical relationship between the different norms (whether in principle violations of *jus cogens* have doctrinal superiority over rules concerning immunity of foreign officials and therefore create exceptions to those rules), the courts instead carefully examined the decisions of the various NCs in cases dealing with immunity. They then concluded that they were "unable to deduce from this practice that there exists under customary international law any form of exception to the rule according immunity."[48]

This response is notable in two respects. First, the fact that the two ITs looked to NC opinions for guidance in the shaping of the exception to immunity[49] suggests that they believe that the latter are better positioned to challenge a norm that most executives of powerful states are likely to support. Second, we suspect that the ITs' reference to the fact that they were currently unable to deduce a clear pattern with respect to exceptions to immunity indicates an openness on their part to join with NCs in embracing a common standard–if the NCs themselves were able to achieve a common consensus and send them a coherent signal concerning a series of cases.

6.4   Appraisal

Evidently, a risk associated with this strategy of deference to NCs is that the latter may interpret it as indicating dissension on the part of the ITs themselves. Were this the case, NCs would likely conclude that they could not rely on IT support in their efforts to alter an existing standard.

---

[46] The Belgian courts' jurisprudence is described in the Arrest Warrant judgment, Arrest Warrant of 11 April 2000 (Dem. Rep. Congo v. Belg.), 2002 ICJ REP. 3 (Feb. 14).

[47] Al-Adsani v. United Kingdom, App. No. 35763/97 (2001) (Grand Chamber), 34 E.H.R.R. 273; Arrest Warrant *supra* note 46.

[48] Arrest Warrant, *supra* note 46, at para. 58.

[49] In Al-Adsani (2001), *supra* note 47, at para. 62, the European Court of Human Rights refers to the ILC working group that "itself acknowledged, while national courts had in some cases shown some sympathy for the argument that States were not entitled to plead immunity where there had been a violation of human rights norms with the character of *jus cogens*, in most cases. . . the plea of sovereign immunity had succeeded."

In fact, this appears to be what happened in this example. When the issue of immunity for foreign state officials returned to the British courts in 2006, in a case involving claimants who had accused Saudi officials of having tortured them, the House of Lords concluded that the ICJ ruling on this matter was so authoritative that the NCs were "obliged to accept."[50] Nevertheless, despite such instances of miscommunication, it is difficult not to be impressed with such IT efforts to promote coordination among NCs by signaling their receptivity to such collective action, and it is reasonable to assume that the success rate associated with such efforts will increase over time.

A major source of friction between ITs and NCs that is not likely to disappear anytime soon is the amount of independence NCs have in implementing the judgments of ITs. Whereas ITs usually expect NCs to comply fully with their decisions, NCs insist on preserving their right to exercise discretion. From their perspective as guardians of the domestic constitutions, NCs believe that renouncing that right would be to further incentivize their executives to short-circuit the domestic democratic process and delegate greater authority to the relatively more compliant international body.

This NC concern was apparent in the decision of the US Supreme Court in the case of Medellín v. Texas,[51] in which the court refused to give effect to the ICJ ruling in domestic US law, despite the US president's endorsement of that ruling. The court determined that the president did not have the constitutional authority to demand that US courts comply with ICJ judgments. The justices (including those dissenting) shared the concern that the US president, acting alone or with the advice and consent of the Senate, would deprive state and federal courts of the authority to determine the domestic effects of US international obligations.[52]

Another example of friction is the judgment of the Italian Constitutional Court,[53] which refused to accept the consequences of

[50] Jones v. Ministry of Interior Al-Mamlaka Al-Arabiya as Saudiya (the Kingdom of Saudi Arabia) [2006] UKHL 26 (appeal taken from Eng.).

[51] Medellín v. Texas, 128 S.Ct. 1346 (2008).

[52] Id. at 1385 ("ICJ decisions... must be domestically legally binding, and enforceable in domestic courts *at least sometimes*.") (emphasis added).

[53] Simoncioni v. Repubblica Federale di Germania, Corte Cost., Cass., sez. un., 22 ottobre 2014, n. 238, Gazzetta Ufficiale [G.U.] (ser. spec.) n. 45, 29 ottobre 2014, I, 1, *available at* www.cortecostituzionale.it/documenti/download/doc/recent_judgments/S238_2013_en .pdf.

the judgment of the International Court of Justice that had found Italian courts in violation of international law.[54] While the Italian court recognized that "at the international law level, the interpretation by the ICJ of the customary law . . . is particularly qualified and does not allow further examination by national governments and/or judicial authorities, including this Court," it was the Italian court's responsibility "to exercise the constitutional review, in order to preserve the inviolability of fundamental principles of the domestic legal order, or at least to minimize their sacrifice."[55]

While this source of friction is likely to persist far into the future, it is hoped that the damage it creates will decline as NCs and ITs acquire more experience in dealing with each other. Interaction may not reliably result in mutual affection, but it should lead to the development of more nuanced "terms of engagements," greater mutual respect that goes beyond the binary dual/monist formal divide between the national and the international legal systems,[56] fewer jurisdictional confrontations,[57] and perhaps even a more well defined division of labor between the two types of courts.

---

[54] Jurisdictional Immunities of the State (Ger. v. It.: *Greece intervening*), Judgement, 2012 I.C.J. Rep. 99 (Feb. 3).

[55] *Supra* note 53, at para. 3.1.

[56] In this vein see Matthias Kumm, *Democratic Constitutionalism Encounters International Law. Terms of Engagement*, in The Migration of Constitutional Ideas 256 (Sujit Choudhry ed., 2007).

[57] *See* Yuval Shany, Regulating Jurisdictional Relations between National and International Courts (2007) (suggesting comity and other doctrines that would diffuse jurisdictional conflicts between NCs and ITs).

How Global Judicial "Countermajoritarianism" Can Enhance Democracy and Inclusion

7.1   Introduction

In this chapter we assess both the negative and positive political externalities that could potentially arise as a result of increased judicial activism and the expansion of judicial review on the part of International Tribunals (ITs) and National Courts (NCs). We first examine the possibility that expansive judicial review, while seemingly improving accountability and transparency, might gradually replace executive discretion with a countermajoritarian judiciary that may operate to stifle deliberations and silence voters. While we acknowledge that this is a possibility, we suspect that the likelihood of it occurring is relatively remote. As we argue below, traditional democratic worries about countermajoritarianism are exaggerated and the positive externalities of increased judicial review of policies of global regulatory bodies and their decision-making procedures are likely to substantially outweigh any negative effects. By contrast, we suggest that judicial review is likely to enhance rather than impede democratic deliberation at the domestic and international levels by more systematically ensuring that the interests of larger groups of stakeholders are taken into account by decision-makers and that the outcomes are appropriately informed and balanced.

We believe that this goal will be easier to achieve than many imagine. Even on those occasions when courts represent the will of their domestic constituents less well than do their executives, the controversy between these institutions frequently generates useful information to which voters would otherwise not have access. Such information is necessary in order to keep political actors accountable to diverse stakeholders and to compensate for the fact that citizens are generally poorly informed both about policy-making at the level of international organizations (IOs) and about the extent to which their interests are being reliably represented. Greater transparency and deliberation are virtues independent of the representativeness or purity of the motivations of the institutions promoting them.

More broadly, as in the case of the desirability of domestic review of administrative action, the virtues of judicial activism are largely situational.[1] It must be evaluated in the harsh light of contemporary conditions that include the uncertain and sometimes negative consequences of rapid globalization for people's lives and opportunities, the highly skewed distribution of geopolitical and economic power among states, the current fragmented character of the international legal system, and the scarcity of IO review at the international level. All of these factors threaten to increase executive power and the influence of special interests, as well as further marginalizing both the voice of voters and the effectiveness of domestic judicial review.

It is in such an environment that expanded and coordinated judicial review of IO policies is likely to produce positive externalities that are most effective in terms of increasing transparency and deliberation and in curbing preventing predatory policies against weak states. Progress in these areas further increases the quality of both domestic and global public decision-making by providing a badly needed check on the growth of executive power. While judicial review cannot and should not play the same central role in global government as it does domestically, it still has an important role to play under current conditions.

To provide a comprehensive normative assessment of the role of judicial review, we need to take into account different venues of democratic deliberation, the first being the domestic one. The question in this context is the extent to which judicial review by NCs or ITs of domestic or international norms advances or harms the domestic democratic process, already subject to the challenges described in Chapter 3. Another question concerns the extent to which such review advances or harms democratic processes in other venues of democratic deliberations, such as in global bodies (to the extent that they provide room for such deliberations) or foreign countries. We posit that an assessment of the positive and negative aspects of judicial review at the global level must weigh the consequences of such review while taking into account the interests of "all affected stakeholders," whether they are domestic voters whose voices are silenced by the pressures of globalization or foreigners who are not entitled to vote but are nonetheless significantly affected by

---

[1] Jerry Mashaw, *Public Law and Public Choice: Critique and Rapprochement, in* RESEARCH HANDBOOK ON PUBLIC CHOICE AND PUBLIC LAW (Daniel A. Farber & Anne J. O'Connell eds., 2010).

the consequences of such voting.[2] We believe that courts are uniquely capable of protecting the voices of all these different sets of silenced voters and thereby contributing to ameliorating the democratic losses associated with globalization.

We begin by identifying two different types of effects that judicial review has had on democratic decision-making. The first type, which we examine in Section 7.1, enhances the domestic democratic processes that result from globalization by providing diffuse stakeholders with information that can benefit them but to which they otherwise would not have access. The second type of contribution, discussed in Section 7.2, takes into account the interests of those who have no opportunity to participate in decisions that affect them because they are not citizens. We argue that such intervention also enhances democratic outcomes when viewed from a global perspective that endorses the rights of all to take part in decisions that affect their lives, including those normally excluded because of their foreign status. Courts are justified in protecting and promoting the interests of stakeholders who are not represented in the democratic processes because of their foreign status. Finally, in Section 7.3 we discuss the potential costs of judicial intervention in terms of the harms–specifically to their legitimacy and functionality–that IOs may suffer, as well as the possible countermeasures that may be employed by executive branch officials who have been reviewed by these institutions and who are searching for ways to neutralize and limit their courts' jurisdiction.

7.2 Inter-Court Coordination and the Facilitation of Democratic Deliberation at the Domestic Level

Judicial review of international organizations by courts is no panacea for the accountability problems that international organizations present. The general debate concerning the legitimacy of judicial review of political decision-making and the justification of judicial preemption of politics is relevant to this case. The fundamental difficulty with the

---

[2] There is a growing literature that attempts to determine the sphere of the affected stakeholders. *See, e.g.,* Nancy Fraser, SCALES OF JUSTICE: REIMAGING POLITICAL SPACE IN A GLOBALIZING WORLD 65–66 (2009) (suggesting the "all subjected principle," which includes all those subjected to a structure of governance that sets the ground rules that govern their interaction); Robert E. Goodin, *Enfranchising All Affected Interests, and Its Alternatives,* 35 PHIL. & PUB. AFF. 40 (2007) (arguing for the "all possibly affected principle," "affected" including "anything that might possibly happen as a result of the decision").

growing prowess of NCs from the perspective of democracy is obviously the traditional concern with the proper balance between the court and the elected branches, between law and politics. Many defenders of the democratic process have pointed out the concern that judicial review tends to preempt politics. Against such a backdrop, our advocacy of inter-court coordination may sound even more alarming, especially since it entails both the occasional judicial preemption of elected officials and the collusion of judges in different countries. Many have used Bickel's term "the countermajoritarian difficulty"[3] to characterize this tension between the courts and the political branches. The "countermajoritarian difficulty" assumes that there is a zero-sum game between the court and the political branches and that, without the court's interference, the popular vote will have its way. We do not wish to engage in the debate that starts off from these premises, because we believe that given the conditions for policy-making explored in Chapters 2 and 3, in the current international context IO–driven policies pose more severe countermajoritarian concerns than judicial review. It is this assumption that drives our conclusion that at this juncture judicial review by national and international courts is more likely to enhance democracy than to curtail it.

In general, courts, in the course of their proceedings, generate information and make it widely available to a broad range of political actors, as well as to the public, thereby promoting better accountability and more effective deliberation. This function is acutely important in facilitating public deliberations. In most discussions of the countermajoritarian difficulty in the domestic sphere, both opponents and proponents of judicial review tend to focus on the most salient part of the judicial action, namely, the ultimate approval or disapproval of the policy in question. This is especially true in connection with controversial issues such as the legality of abortion or same-sex marriage. In such cases the judges cannot claim that their decisions are necessarily definitive. As a consequence of the saliency associated with these "yes or no" moments, observers and analysts often ignore the many subtle, indirect, and yet significant contributions that courts make to the political system and public deliberation. In the age of global governance, the real

---

[3] Alexander Bickel, THE LEAST DANGEROUS BRANCH (1962). Karen Alter argues that the countermajoritarian difficulty is less pronounced for international tribunals because they seek to co-opt the support of domestic interlocutors to secure compliance with their judgments: Karen J. Alter, THE NEW TERRAIN OF INTERNATIONAL LAW, chapter 9 (2015).

countermajoritarian difficulty lies in what are too often impoverished domestic democratic deliberations and the continued domination of most IOs and ITs by a handful of powerful state executives.[4] In such circumstances, judicial intervention–particularly in its collective or coordinated form–has a critical democratic role to play. While judges are not trained to be expert policy-makers, they are trained to be expert fact finders. This expertise in employing fact-finding procedures also enables them to credibly monitor the decision-making procedures of administrative agencies. The relative insulation of judges from executive domination and from the influence of special interests often lends relatively more credibility to the information that courts generate.[5]

A major part of a national court's contribution to the information in the public domain consists of monitoring its state's system of checks and balances in order to prevent any branch from overstepping its limits and disturbing the political equilibrium of the system. This is not only consistent with its role as the constitutionally prescribed guardian of the legal system but it also helps prevent the emergence of a concentration of political power that might potentially threaten the court's independence.[6] In parliamentary systems, courts provide structural rather than substantive support to the opposition vis-à-vis the reigning coalition by requiring that the executive obtain prior parliamentary approval for his or her plans: The debate that ensues in Parliament provides information to the public concerning government policies.[7] In general, the more independent the actors involved in policy-making and the more contestation there is among them, the greater the amount and quality of information the political process will generate.[8] By bolstering the independence and stature of opposition parties, experts within the bureaucracy, and local governments (and state authorities in

---

[4] *See supra* discussions in Chapters 2 and 3.

[5] *See* Patrick A. Luff, *Captured Legislatures and Public-Interested Courts*, 2013 UTAH L. REV. 519, 533–36 (2012); Jonathan R. Macey, *Promoting Public-Regarding Legislation through Statutory Interpretation*, 86 COLUM. L. REV. 223, 225 (1986) (judicial review and activist interpretation is justified by the need to mitigate the harmful effects of interest group domination of the political process).

[6] On the perception of NCs as the guardians of their national legal system see *infra* notes 16–29 and accompanying text.

[7] On the democratizing effects of political contestation between political actors see THE FEDERALIST No. 51 (James Madison).

[8] Eyal Benvenisti, *Judicial Review and Democratic Failures: Minimizing Asymmetric Information through Adjudication*, 32 IYUNEI MISHPAT (*Tel-Aviv U. L. Rev.*) 277 (2010) (Isr.) (Hebrew).

federal systems) vis-à-vis the national executives, courts help ensure that public debate about policies will be adequately informed.

Beyond maintaining checks and balances between and within the political branches, courts have developed principles of administrative law that require officials to ensure the transparency of and public participation in executive decision-making processes. In addition, judicially protected constitutional guarantees for political rights–such as the freedoms of speech, association, and information–foster the generation of publicly available information.

The litigation process itself, as well as the eventual outcome, is also information generating. The courts serve as venues for public deliberation where conflicting claims are examined in structured proceedings. In reviewing administrative and legislative acts for compatibility with the constitution (or, where relevant, for compatibility with international law), courts require that the relevant decision-makers provide public justifications for their acts and afford litigants and *amici* opportunities to contest those reasons. Perhaps surprisingly, the cost of triggering the review of a given public policy is often relatively low: A single individual can take the executive or the legislature to task if he or she has standing to seek judicial review. Briefs by *amici*, in jurisdictions where they are accepted, shed light on various considerations that are pertinent to the questions at hand. The structured and transparent deliberations in court are closely watched by the public, and for the most part the court's reasoned decisions are carefully scrutinized by legal experts who elaborate on the judgments.

From the various occasions when information is the only thing that the court provides, it is clear just how important, often crucial, is the generation of information by the judiciary. For example, the UK Supreme Court can declare legislation incompatible with the UK 1998 Human Rights Act, but this declaration by itself would not render the legislation invalid.[9] The assumption is that the court's declaration would make the public aware of the incompatibility, which in turn would put pressure on the legislature to amend the law. Besides compensation, which is negligible in most cases when governments are involved, the main remedy that the ECtHR offers is a declaration of incompatibility with the European Convention of Human Rights.[10] The only remedy

---

[9] Human Rights Act, 1998, c.42 § 4(1) & (6) (U.K.).

[10] *See* Convention for the Protection of Fundamental Human Rights and Freedoms art. 50, Nov. 4, 1950, 213 U.N.T.S. 221 ("If the Court finds that a decision or a measure taken by a legal authority or any other authority of a High Contracting Party, is completely or

available to other ITs is their ability to provide authoritative information regarding the compliance of domestic actors. While the effectiveness of such information as a sanctioning mechanism is highly variable, the track records of success compiled by such agencies as the World Bank Inspection Panel,[11] the Aarhus Compliance Commission,[12] the Human Rights Committee,[13] or the UNESCO World Heritage Committee[14] suggest that judicially generated information can often be effective when executives are expected to demonstrate a good reputation for compliance in the face of either internal or external political pressure.[15] Indeed, given the reluctance of judges to assume responsibility for annulling acts and their preference for less intrusive and politically less costly remedies, one could argue that information as a remedy plays a more important cumulative role in the long run than does the more radical act of invalidation.

When courts declare a given policy to be incompatible with a certain norm, they always invite deliberation, often leaving the ultimate decision in the hands of the political branches, which have the discretion to uphold the criticized decision. Even strong courts choose their battles carefully. They often prefer to engage in "weak"[16] or "soft" forms of judicial review in order to promote public deliberation and heightened public scrutiny in the event that the political branches ignore the decision without offering an adequate explanation. Over time, most courts have developed a graduated ladder of potential responses and they tend to

---

partially in conflict with the obligations arising from the present convention, and if the internal law of the said Party allows only partial reparation to be made for the consequences of this decision or measure, the decision of the Court shall, if necessary, afford just satisfaction to the injured party.").

[11] International Bank for Reconstruction and Development, Resolution IBRD 93–10, International Development Agency, Resolution IDA 93–6, Sept. 22, 1993, *available at* http://siteresources.worldbank.org/EXTINSPECTIONPANEL/Resources/ResolutionMar ch2005.pdf.

[12] The Aarhus Convention: Convention on Access to Information, Public Participation in Decision-making and Access to Justice in Environmental Matters art. 15, *opened for signature* June 25, 1998, 2161 U.N.T.S. 447.

[13] International Covenant on Civil and Political Rights art. 28, *opened for signature* Dec. 16, 1966, 999 U.N.T.S. 171.

[14] Convention Concerning the Protection of the World Cultural and Natural Heritage art. 8, *adopted* Nov. 16, 1972, 1037 U.N.T.S. 151.

[15] *See* George W. Downs & Michael A. Jones, *Reputation, Compliance and International Law*, 31 J. LEGAL STUD. 595 (2002).

[16] On "weak" versus "strong" forms of judicial review see Mark Tushnet, WEAK COURTS, STRONG RIGHTS: JUDICIAL REVIEW AND SOCIAL WELFARE RIGHTS IN COMPARATIVE CONSTITUTIONAL LAW (2009).

climb it one step at a time, prompting the legislature to respond to its rulings, rather than to preempt them altogether. This graduated approach allows courts to apply pressure on the executive branch in a way that encourages the executive to make an informed and publicly accountable decision via a reasoned administrative act or to seek explicit statutory authorization from the legislature, which now has the opportunity to weigh in on the matter at hand. As mentioned in Chapter 5 Section 3.1, the example provided by the US Supreme Court's treatment of the petitions of the Guantanamo detainees is a prominent case in point,[17] and there are many other examples from around the world.[18]

As we shift our sights to inter-court coordination and examine the effects of courts' review of an IO on domestic democratic processes, we notice similar outcomes. When NCs directly or indirectly decline to implement an IO demand, they increase public awareness about the demand and raise the stakes for the IO or the national executive branch. But in most instances they do not preempt public deliberation. For example, an NC that requires specific statutory authorization for freezing the assets of suspected terrorists, notwithstanding the demands of the UN Security Council,[19] invites the legislature to weigh in on the matter while at the same time publicly pressing the Security Council to improve its procedures.

An additional benefit of inter-court coordination is the strategic gain it provides to subsets of relatively weak countries that are imprisoned in their respective sovereignty "cells" and are subjected to the predatory policies of powerful states or economic actors who exploit divisions among them in order to extort concessions, much to the dissatisfaction of their citizens.[20] Given their shared legal vocabulary, their commitment to following their own precedents, their relative immunity to pressure from special interests, and their mutual knowledge of each other's preferences as revealed by their formal opinions, developing state NCs

---

[17] Rasul v. Bush, 542 U.S. 466 (2004); Hamdi v. Rumsfeld, 542 U.S. 507 (2004); Hamdan v. Rumsfeld, 548 U.S. 557 (2006); Boumediene v. Bush, 553 U.S. 723 (2008).
[18] Suresh v. Canada (Minister of Citizenship & Immigration), [2002] 1 S.C.R. 3 (Can.) (considering whether a member of the Tamil Tigers, who were fighting against the Sri Lankan government, could be deported to Sri Lanka, despite the possibility that he would be tortured there); A (FC) v. Sec'y of State, [2005] UKHL 71, [2005] 2 A.C. 68 (H.L.) (appeal taken from Eng.) (House of Lords declaring parts of the British Anti-terrorism Act incompatible with European human rights standards). See generally Chapter 5.
[19] See, e.g., Ahmed and others v. HM Treasury, [2010] UKSC 2 (U.K.). For more on this see Chapter 6, Section 3.
[20] On the "sovereignty trap" see Chapter 3, Section 4.

often have a very refined prior knowledge about which of their peers are likely to support a given policy position and what position is likely to garner the greatest degree of support.

This information can then serve as a focal point for NCs in the developing world. In turn, these NCs can help overcome the uncertainty and distrust that typically characterize the relations among their political branches, with the result that better choices are made. For example, developing countries would have served as the dumping ground for hazardous wastes produced in the rich North if not for the successful common resistance of Southern NCs led by the Indian court.[21] NCs in Europe took an active part in demanding that IOs improve their internal labor standards and joined forces to reduce the IOs' immunity from their jurisdiction.[22]

Inter-court coordination does not require courts to abandon their primary responsibility to their respective communities. To date, NC review of IOs, even when it requires coordination with other NCs, has not led them to neglect their primary roles as the guardians of their domestic legal systems and the protectors of the interests of their domestic constituencies. They are well aware that they need public support to fulfill their constitutional role in a democracy[23] and that those NCs that lose public support will jeopardize their ability to constrain government in a host of matters apart from those related to global governance. While NCs have increasingly turned their attention to how other courts deal with global problems that their states also face, the interests that NCs have in cooperating with each other is more tactical than strategic. Thus, they continue to regard themselves first and foremost as national agents, and their chief motivation remains to protect the domestic rule of law, rather than overseeing the global governance regime or promoting global justice. Moreover, their primary sensitivity to the national interest is

---

[21] *See* Chapter 5, Section 5.3.2.

[22] Waite & Kennedy v. Germany, App. No. 26083/94, Eur. Ct. H.R. (1999); Beer & Regan v. Germany, App. No. 28934/95, Eur. Ct. H.R. (1999). In *Waite & Kennedy*, para. 67, the court asserts that it would be incompatible with the purpose and object of the European Convention on Human Rights if the State parties were absolved from their responsibility under the Convention by delegating competences to international organizations, hinting that the states are expected to make sure that the organizations provide comparable protection of the human rights of their employees). *See also* August Reinisch, *The Immunity of International Organizations and the Jurisdiction of Their Administrative Tribunals* 7 CHINESE J. INT'L L. 285, 305–06 (2008) (on the role of the European courts in imposing labor standards in international organizations).

[23] On this need see Chapter 4, Section 2.

reflected in any number of traditional and predictable ways. Thus, they may refuse to constrain their executives and other local actors when such constraints might harm their economies–for example, by imposing international trade law obligations on their executives,[24] implementing anti-bribery provisions against domestic companies that export to corrupt regimes,[25] or disregarding the immunity granted by international law to acting officials of foreign states.[26] In the face of constitutional amendments and public pressure, as in the case of immigration laws that ran counter to the 1951 Refugee Convention,[27] NCs have found ways to wiggle out of the international obligation and to defect from what had initially been a shared understanding of the treaty.[28] In short, inter-court coordination can and does enable and enhance domestic democratic processes.

Finally, ITs can also enhance domestic democratic processes, in three principal ways. First, ITs often operate as the external protector of internal "discrete and insular minorities" and of diffuse majorities whose voices are stifled in a captured political system.[29] Second, ITs can provide backing for domestic courts vis-à-vis their respective political branches. The Inter-American Court for Human Rights has

---

[24] Joined Cases C-120/06 & C-121/06, Fabbrica Italiana Accumulatori Motocarri Montecchio SpA (FLAMM) et al. v. Comm'n, 2008 E.C.R. I 6513, *available at* http://eur-lex.europa.eu/LexUriServ/LexUriServ.do?uri=CEL EX:62006J0120:EN:HTML.

[25] R (on the application of Corner House Research and others) v. Dir. of the Serious Fraud Office (Appellant), [2008] UKHL 60, [2009] 1 A.C. 756 (H.L.) (appeal taken from Eng.).

[26] Jones v. Ministry of Interior (Kingdom of Saudi Arabia), [2006] UKHL 26, [2007] 1 A.C. 270 (1 All E.R. 113) (H.L.) (appeal taken from Eng.).

[27] Geneva Convention Relating to the Status of Refugees, Jul. 28, 1951, 189 U.N.T.S. 150, amended by Protocol Relating to the Status of Refugees, Jan. 31, 1967, 19 U.S.T. 6223, 606 U.N.T.S. 267.

[28] For example, the French and German courts reacted to constitutional amendments that limited the extent to which refugees were granted asylum by reinterpreting the definition of "refugee" under the Refugee Convention. *See* Karin Oellers-Frahm & Andreas Zimmermann, *France's and Germany's Constitutional Changes and Their Impact on Migration Law: Policy and Practice*, 38 GERMAN Y.B. INT'L L. 249 (1995); James C. Hathaway, *Harmonizing for Whom? The Devaluation of Refugee Protection in the Era of European Economic Integration*, 26 CORNELL INT'L L.J. 719 (1993); Gerald L. Neuman, *Buffer Zones against Refugees: Dublin, Schengen, and the German Asylum Amendment*, 33 VA. J. INT'L L. 503 (1993).

[29] *See, e.g.,* Laurence R. Helfer & Erik Voeten, *International Courts as Agents of Legal Change: Evidence from LGBT Rights in Europe*, 68 INT'L ORG. 77, 106 (2014). This is the logic of the *Carolene Products* footnote (United States v. Carolene Products Co., 304 U.S. 144, 152–53 n.4 (1938)), John Hart Ely, DEMOCRACY AND DISTRUST: A THEORY OF JUDICIAL REVIEW (1980), and also Robert O. Keohane, Stephen Macedo & Andrew Moravcsik, *Democracy-Enhancing Multilateralism*, 63 INT'L ORG. 1 (2009).

been very active in supporting the constitutional courts of Latin American member states.[30] Third, ITs can resolve collective action problems in states that are unable to overcome the "sovereignty trap," by rebuffing a demand by a powerful state or a multinational company that the weaker states comply with their demands. The European courts, in particular, have been quite successful in this context, by resisting international institutions that sought immunity from national labor laws[31] or by imposing European legal standards on sporting associations that sought insulation from public law obligations.[32]

7.3   Judicial Review and the Global Dimension of the Democratic Deficit

Of course, courts do more than provide information by their decisions and the doctrines they promote. At times they also render judgments that preempt political challenges: NCs may determine that certain policies are precluded by the national constitution, or ITs may find a national law incompatible with a treaty obligation. Can these actions also be justified as democracy promoting? This question requires us to revisit the countermajoritarian difficulty[33] from a global perspective that takes account of the unique failures of the domestic democratic processes that result from globalization.

We offer two answers to this question. The first answer minimizes the potentially negative effects of judicial intervention relative to the mostly unchecked power of the executive branches of powerful states, because the intervention of courts holds out potentially greater benefits for

---

[30] David Kosař & Lucas Lixinski, *Domestic Judicial Design by International Human Rights Courts*, 109 AM. J. INT'L L. 713 (2015); Cabrera García and Montiel Flores v. Mexico, Inter-Am. Ct. H.R. (ser. C) No. 220 (Nov. 26, 2010), *available at* www.corteidh.or.cr/docs/casos/articulos/seriec_220_ing.pdf (requiring national courts to "exercise ex officio a form of 'conventionality control' between domestic legal provisions and the American Convention"). *See* Ariel E. Dulitzky, *An Inter-American Constitutional Court? The Invention of the Conventionality Control by the Inter-American Court of Human Rights*, 50 TEXAS INT'L L.J. 46 (2015); Christina Binder, *The Prohibition of Amnesties by The Inter-American Court of Human Rights*, 12 GERMAN L.J. 1203 (2011).

[31] See *supra* note 22 and accompanying text.

[32] Case C-519/04 P, David Meca-Medina and Igor Majcen v. Comm'n of Eur. Cmtys., 2006 ECR I-06991; Case C-415/93, Union Royale Belge des Sociétés de Football Ass'n ASBL v. Jean-Marc Bosman, 1995 ECR I-04921.

[33] Bickel, *supra* note 3. On this framing of the debate in US constitutional scholarship, see Barry Friedman, *The Birth of an Academic Obsession: The History of the Countermajoritarian Difficulty, Part Five*, 112 YALE L.J. 153 (2002).

disenfranchised stakeholders. The second answer emphasizes the normative obligations that democracies have toward each other. These obligations legitimate the attention of both NCs and ITs to the interests of affected stakeholders who are foreigners and have no voice in the domestic democratic process.

7.3.1   National Courts and the Interests of Weaker States

A source of concern associated with any court coordination is that the courts of powerful democratic states will dominate any inter-court interaction just as their executives do within international organizations. The NCs of powerful democratic states tend to enjoy a first-mover advantage over other NCs both because the scale of their economies ensures them a steady stream of cases and because they characteristically enjoy more independence than do the courts of many weaker states. Given the fact that the judges care first and foremost for their own domestic constituency, their tendency is to generate information that is relevant to their particular states and to remain relatively oblivious to the perspectives and considerations of other states.

As in the case of the "domestic" countermajoritarian difficulty discussed above, our point of departure in evaluating the merits of this concern is to question the implicit assumption that the executive-driven treaty has historically been adequately reflective of diverse national constituencies. Certainly, the assumption seems implausible in the contemporary global context. The less democratic the country is, the less likely it is that its executive will internalize its citizens' interests when it negotiates treaties. The weaker the country is, the less likely it is that its executive will be able to promote its citizens' interests in global negotiations. But even strong democratic countries often represent narrow interests in treaty negotiations and in decision-making by international institutions.

We believe that, in general, strong courts are more likely than strong executive branches to promote the interests of the weak states and diffuse voters.[34] The reason for this lies in their very different modes of operation. Executives tend to employ complicated fragmentation

---

[34] For a similar observation with respect to courts in the United States, see Luff, *Captured Legislatures, supra* note 5 (courts generally act in the public interest because they receive different information than the legislature and they process the information they receive differently than legislators or administrative agents, and because they are not captured by interest-groups as legislators); Reginald S. Sheehan, William Mishler & Donald R. Songer, *Ideology, Status, and the Differential Success of Parties Before the Supreme Court*, 86 AM. POL.

strategies that operate to isolate and obscure their actions. As explained in Chapter 2, this is typically done to increase the oversight costs that rival branches of government and weaker states must pay to question their actions. Courts, by contrast, generally employ what are essentially "defragmentation strategies,"[35] in the sense that they attempt to weave disparate executive-created policy fragments into webs of coherent legal obligations that are transparent, well reasoned, and accessible to all actors. These judicial efforts to generalize and rationalize the international legal landscape provide weaker states with a stable and interconnected hierarchy of claims–for example, linking trade obligations with human rights concerns–that they can then employ in a variety of venues, and it increases the likelihood that a victory in a particular venue will have wide-ranging implications.

Increased collective action on the part of prominent NCs and their willingness to cooperate with ITs, as mentioned in Chapter 6, holds out the promise that under the right political and social conditions they can create constellations of linked obligations that are more dense, more coherent, and more equitable than those that currently exist. The leadership role of NCs is crucial, however, because the powerful state executives that have leverage over many of the ITs may otherwise be reluctant to allow the ITs to curtail their freedom to resort to divide-and-rule tactics.[36]

Besides defragmenting the legal space, judicial coordination also generates information that has practical political benefits for diffuse constituencies. The litigation in the South African court concerning access to lifesaving drugs, for example, helped reframe the public discourse about the costs of compliance with the Trade-Related Aspects of Intellectual Property Rights (TRIPS) agreement to the populations in developing countries.[37] The Novartis judgment of 2013 by the Indian Supreme Court, discussed in Chapter 5, endorsed the Indian Parliament's authority to weigh in on the same issue (that is, the proper balance between the right to life and the protection of intellectual

---

Sci. Rev. 464, 469 (1992) (only a negligible correlation between the financial and other resources that litigants have and actual outcome of the litigation in the US Supreme Court).

[35] *Supra* text accompanying note 7 in Chapter 6.

[36] For these tactics see *supra* Chapter 2.

[37] In 2001, several international pharmaceutical corporations dropped their suit that made a similar claim against a South African Act after the South African court allowed NGOs to present affidavits (Case No. 4138/98, High Court of South Africa). On this litigation see David Barnard, *In the High Court of South Africa, Case No. 4138/98: The Global Politics of Access to Low-Cost AIDS Drugs in Poor Countries*, 12 J. Kennedy Inst. Ethics 159 (2002).

property rights of Northern pharmaceutical companies).[38] Courts in Bangladesh, India, and Pakistan prevented the importation of contaminated food and blocked advertising campaigns of foreign tobacco companies.[39] NGOs committed to promoting the interests of constituencies in weaker states then use such information to raise global consciousness about the effects of IO policies in developing countries and among those that are less well represented within developed economies.[40] The resulting public awareness can prove politically significant not only in weak autocracies but also in strong democracies whose civil societies are sensitive to such concerns. As we mentioned above,[41] the intervention of a handful of NCs of powerful states can generate a process of information dissemination that often yields significant positive externalities for constituencies that do not even have independent courts.

Finally and most important, as mentioned above,[42] judicial cooperation holds out the promise of overcoming the predatory policies of powerful states or economic actors who exploit divisions among relatively weak states in order to extort concessions. Unable to overcome their political barriers, wary of being exploited, and unsure whether they are involved in a repeated game, the weak states, trapped as prisoners in their respective sovereignty cells, find themselves competing against their peers to satisfy the demands of the powerful external actor, to the discontent of many of their constituencies. As we saw earlier, ITs are particularly well situated to respond to predatory policies by private companies. As discussed earlier, NCs can also resist the pressure of powerful external actors. Their shared legal vocabulary, commitment to following their own precedents, relative immunity to pressure from special interests, and their mutual knowledge of each other's preferences as revealed by their formal opinions, provide NCs with effective tools to communicate with their peers and negotiate common positions that will

---

[38] *See* note 139 in Chapter 5 and accompanying text.

[39] *See* Farooque v. Bangladesh, 48 DLR (1996) 438 (Ban.), Vincent v. Union of India, A.I.R. 1987 S.C. 990 (India), Islam v. Bangladesh, 52 DLR (2000) 413 (Ban.); ILDC 477 (BD 2000) (Ban.) (referring to the similar decisions of the Indian court in Bamakrishna v. State of Kerala, 1992 (2) KLT 725 (Ker.), and Pakistan in Pakistan Chest Foundation v. Pakistan, (1997) CLC 1379 (Pak.)).

[40] Keck and Sikkinik emphasize the role of "framing" in mobilizing global public opinion. *See* Margaret E. Keck & Kathryn Sikkinik, ACTIVISTS BEYOND BORDERS 16–18 (1998).

[41] *See supra* notes 5, 19, 33 and note 8 in Chapter 1, and accompanying text. On the conditions for judicial independence of international tribunals, see Chapter 4.

[42] *Supra* notes 21–22, 32.

serve to withstand external pressures that stifle domestic voices. Inter-court coordination can thereby overcome the uncertainty and distrust that typically characterize relations among the political branches. As mentioned above, such cooperation has functioned to enable developing countries to protect themselves from becoming the dumping grounds of hazardous wastes produced in the rich North due to the successful common resistance of Southern NCs led by Indian courts.[43] NCs in Europe took the initiative to demand that IOs improve their internal labor standards and joined forces to limit the IOs' immunity from their jurisdiction.[44]

To conclude, at least at this juncture in the evolution of the global regulatory regime, evidence suggests that IO-driven policies pose more severe countermajoritarian concerns than does judicial review by NCs. On the whole, the latter are more likely to enhance domestic democracy than to curtail it.

7.3.2   Democracy (and Hence Courts) and the Interests of Strangers

The countermajoritarian debate reflects the concern that the deliberative process should be open to all relevant stakeholders. The countermajoritarian concern is exacerbated by decision-making by international institutions and tribunals, since they do not act "in the name of all the individuals whose lives they affect; and they do not ask for the kind of authorization by individuals that carries with it a responsibility to treat all those individuals in some sense equally."[45]

However, the premise that underlies the countermajoritarian concern in both the domestic and global settings is outdated and no longer reflects contemporary conditions.[46] In particular, our observations about the democratic deficits that globalization often fosters suggest that this premise is based on assumptions that do not reflect the present reality of global interdependence. If one takes seriously the democratic impulse and adapts it to contemporary conditions, it is difficult to escape the

---

[43] *See* Chapter 5.   [44] See *supra* note 33 and accompanying text.

[45] See Thomas Nagel, *The Problem of Global Justice*, 33 PHIL. & PUB. AFF. 113, 138 (2005). Although Nagel clearly assumes that such conditions obtain within states and only within states, it is difficult to see how any democracy today fulfills these conditions without ensuring voice to affected foreigners.

[46] Criticisms of the countermajoritarian difficulty in the domestic scene abound: Christopher F. Zurn, DELIBERATIVE DEMOCRACY AND THE INSTITUTIONS OF JUDICIAL REVIEW (2007); Louis Michael Seidman, OUR UNSETTLED CONSTITUTION 55 (2001).

conclusion that "democracy" cannot be confined to the sovereign state as an insulated entity. Instead, every democracy must take the interests of others into account even though the latter have no legal right to take part in the decision-making process.[47] This can be explained on utilitarian-reciprocal grounds or on moral grounds. In either case, what is required is the understanding that judicial interference in decision-making for the purpose of including the voice of the globally disregarded[48]–far from being a violation of democratic and egalitarian concerns–may well be compatible with and in fact mandated by them.[49]

Both ITs and NCs can function to correct this myopic failure of domestic legislative bodies that tend to focus only on domestic issues. ITs have had opportunities in recent years to limit the discretion of sovereigns while balancing their interests against those of foreign stakeholders. Several of them, most notably in the areas of trade and foreign investment, have increased the demands on states to take into account global interests when forming their regulatory policies. As described in Chapter 5, a similar interactive process has taken place among NCs.

As will be illustrated below, this inter-court coordination has functioned to limit the discretion of states and international bodies. The Appellate Body of the World Trade Organization as well as other ITs, have developed jurisprudence that incrementally increased the demands on states to take the interests of foreign stakeholders into account when formulating their regulatory policies. NCs have also become involved in the review of global standard setting in such disparate areas as migration, environment protection, and counterterrorism.[50]

---

[47] Eyal Benvenisti, *Sovereigns as Trustees of Humanity: On the Accountability of States to Foreign Stakeholders*, 107 AM. J. INT'L L. 295, 314 (2013).

[48] Richard B. Stewart, *Remedying Disregard in Global Regulatory Governance: Accountability, Participation, and Responsiveness*, 108 AM. J. INT'L L. 211 (2014).

[49] The literature on global justice is vast. Some of the leading books include Charles Beitz, THE IDEA OF HUMAN RIGHTS (2009); David Miller, NATIONAL RESPONSIBILITY AND GLOBAL JUSTICE (2008); Thomas Pogge, WORLD POVERTY AND HUMAN RIGHTS: COSMOPOLITAN RESPONSIBILITIES AND REFORMS (2nd edn., 2008); James Bohman, DEMOCRACY ACROSS BORDERS: FROM DĒMOS TO DĒMOI (2007); Seyla Benhabib, THE RIGHTS OF OTHERS: ALIENS, RESIDENTS AND CITIZENS (2004); Allen Buchanan, JUSTICE, LEGITIMACY, AND SELF-DETERMINATION: MORAL FOUNDATION FOR INTERNATIONAL LAW (2004).

[50] *See* Chapter 5.

Although state parties seek to retain their right to be the ultimate arbiter of the delicate balance between national interests and collective goals such as free trade or environmental protection,[51] several ITs have intervened and subjected this discretion to an external assessment that gives weight, if not precedence, to global welfare considerations. As Alan Sykes has observed in the area of trade law, "a serious tension indeed arises, and the goals of open trade and respect for national sovereignty can be irreconcilably at odds to the point that one must give way."[52]

Famously, in its report on *Korea–Various Measures on Beef*,[53] the Appellate Body (AB) of the WTO stated that "[i]t is not open to doubt that Members of the WTO have the right to determine for themselves the level of enforcement of their WTO-consistent laws and regulations."[54] But at the same time it asserted that "the determination of 'necessary'. . . involves in every case a process of weighing and balancing a series of factors which prominently include the contribution made by the compliance measure to the enforcement of the law or regulation at issue, the importance of the common interests or values protected by that law or regulation, and the accompanying impact of the law or regulation on imports or exports."[55] Even more telling is its subsequent report in the case of *United States–Measures Affecting the Cross-Border Supply of Gambling and Betting Services*,[56] where the AB identifies the factors that determine "necessary" to include "the restrictive impact of the measure on international commerce."[57]

The logic of IT intervention in national regulation can often be justified by the narrow and idiosyncratic design of domestic regulatory

---

[51] Robert Howse, *Adjudicative Legitimacy and Treaty Interpretation in International Trade Law*, in THE EU, THE WTO AND THE NAFTA: TOWARDS A COMMON LAW OF INTERNATIONAL TRADE? 35 (Joseph H. H. Weiler ed., 2000); Steven P. Croley & John H. Jackson, *WTO Dispute Procedures, Standard of Review and Deference to National Governments*, 90 AM. J. INT'L L. 193 (1996).

[52] Alan O. Sykes, *Domestic Regulation, Sovereignty, and Scientific Evidence Requirements: A Pessimistic View*, 3 CHI. J. INT'L L. 353, 368 (2002). See also John H. Jackson, WORLD TRADE AND THE LAW OF GATT 788 (1969): "The perpetual puzzle. . . of international economic institution is . . . to give measured scope of legitimate national policy goals while preventing the use of these goals to promote particular interests at the expense of the greater common welfare."

[53] Appellate Body Report, Korea–*Measures Affecting Imports of Fresh, Chilled and Frozen Beef*, WT/DS/161/AB/R (Dec. 11, 2000).

[54] *Id.* ¶ 176.   [55] *Id.* ¶ 164.

[56] Appellate Body Report, *United States–Measures Affecting the Cross-Border Supply of Gambling and Betting Services*, WT/DS285/AB/R (Apr. 7, 2005).

[57] Id. ¶ 306.

measures. Looking from the outside into the domestic democratic processes, the immediate concern is that these regulations are designed to disadvantage outsiders who have no direct voice or influence on the outcomes.[58] The same concern that has led federal courts such as the US Supreme Court,[59] the Court of Justice of the European Union[60] and the European Court on Human Rights[61] to scrutinize domestic regulation for potential disregard of outsiders' interests plays out, as it should, at the IT level. Arbitrators of foreign investment disputes invoked the normative requirement of protecting expectations of foreign investors as the key to their scrutiny of national decisions.[62] As a result,

---

[58] *See* James v. United Kingdom, App. No. 8793/79, Eur. Ct. H.R., ¶ 63 (1986) (noting that "non-nationals are more vulnerable to domes- tic legislation" than nationals, and that "there may well be legitimate reason for requiring nationals to bear a greater burden in the public interest than non-nationals."); Tecnicas Medioambientales Tecmed S.A. v. Mexico, ICSID Case No. ARB(AF)/00/2, Award, ¶ 122, (May 29, 2003) ("[I]t should be also considered that the foreign investor has a reduced or nil participation in the taking of the decisions that affect it, partly because the investors are not entitled to exercise political rights reserved to the nationals of the State, such as voting for the authorities that will issue the decisions that affect such investors."). *But see* David Schneiderman, *Investing in Democracy? Political Process and International Investment Law*, 60 U. TORONTO L.J. 909, 931–40 (2010) (presenting and assessing evidence that foreign corporate actors are as effective as nationally based corporate actors and hence do not need special judicial protection).

[59] The doctrine of the "Dormant Commerce Clause" was developed by the US Supreme Court to discipline state regulation that affects out-of-state interests by subjecting it to a demanding judicial examination of the compelling state interest and the narrow tailoring of the measure. The justification for this rigorous examination is, according to Laurence Tribe, not only to ensure economic efficiency through open interstate commerce, but also to "ensure national solidarity" as the democratic processes within states tend to give precedence to local interests. Lawrence H. Tribe, AMERICAN CONSTITUTIONAL LAW 1057 (3rd edn., 2000) (discussing Baldwin v. G.A.F. Seelig, Inc., 294 U.S. 511, 522–23 (1935)).

[60] The Court of Justice of the European Union invoked the principle of the free movement of goods between member states as the "fundamental principle" from which it derived a similar burden on national regulation by EU members, under the proportionality test. Case C-41/02 Comm'n v. Neth., 2004 E.C.R I-11375 ¶ 47; Case 302/86 Comm'n v. Den., 1988 E.C.R 4607 ¶ 10. On this matter see Simona Morettini, *Community Principles Affecting the Exercise of Discretionary Power by National Authorities in the Service Sector*, in GLOBAL AND EUROPEAN CONSTRAINTS UPON NATIONAL RIGHT TO REGULATE: THE SERVICES SECTOR 106, 118 (Stefano Battini & Giulio Vesperini eds., 2008) (noting that the court gives greater deference to states in matters of public health and safety, areas considered "closely related to national sovereignty," as opposed to other areas such as consumer protection, an area of Community competence where there is broad agreement as to the appropriate level of protection).

[61] *See* James v. United Kingdom, *supra* note 58.

[62] *See, e.g., Tecnicas Medioambientales Tecmed, supra* note 58.

when it comes to weighing the interests of outsiders, the traditional deference to the domestic democratic processes increasingly reveals its limitations.

For similar reasons, it is not necessarily countermajoritarian for ITs to ensure that stakeholders from developing countries have effective opportunities to influence the democratic deliberative processes within developed countries. The WTO's Appellate Body seems to be especially fastidious in this context. It insisted that the United States provide an effective right of hearing before issuing import restrictions.[63] It also interpreted the treaty language in a way that strengthens the hand of developing states. In *European Communities–Conditions for the Granting of Tariff Preferences to Developing Countries*,[64] the AB interpreted the text of the GATT agreement as "intended to provide developing countries with increasing returns from their growing exports, which returns are critical for those countries' economic development."[65] The General Court of the European Union had found that before adopting a 2010 EU-Morocco Agreement (on agricultural, processed agricultural, and fisheries products), the EU Council "must examine carefully and impartially all the relevant elements to ensure that products production for export activities are not conducted at the expense of the population of the territory in question or imply violations of their fundamental rights [under the [EU] Charter of Fundamental Rights]."[66]

7.4 Coordination among National and International Courts and the Functionality of Global Governance Structures

Three other potential costs of judicial intervention remain. The first relates to the functionality of IOs. Unless judicial review is employed with discretion and balance, it could easily undermine the effectiveness of IOs by creating gridlock that would make reform and adaptation to new

---

[63] Appellate Body Report, *United States–Import Prohibition of Certain Shrimp and Shrimp Products*, WT/DS58/AB/R (Oct. 12, 1998) (*Shrimp/Turtle*); *United States–Measures concerning the Importation, Marketing and Sale of Tuna and Tuna Products*, WT/DS381/AB/R (May 16, 2012) (*Tuna/Dolphin II*).

[64] Appellate Body Report, *European Communities–Conditions for the Granting of Tariff Preferences to Developing Countries*, WT/DS246/AB/R (Apr. 7, 2004).

[65] *Id.* ¶ 106.

[66] Case T-512/12 *Front populaire pour la libération de la saguia-el-hamra et du rio de oro* (Front Polisario) v. Council of the E.U., Judgment of 10 December 2015 (not yet published).

circumstances even more difficult. The second problem relates to the legitimacy of the reviewed IOs being challenged by courts. And the third problem concerns the possible reactions of the executives of powerful states to court coordination. The latter may well turn out to pose the greatest challenge. History suggests that executive branch officials will search for ways to neutralize and limit their courts' jurisdiction, just as they have adjusted to the increased scrutiny of IOs by creating a variety of informal and privatized decision-making venues that enable them to evade IO oversight. This could potentially lead to further fragmentation of international law and undermine the efforts of generations of internationally oriented lawyers and judges to create a coherent international legal system.

7.4.1   The Functionality of IOs

As with the rise of judicial review of domestic administrative agencies and administrative tribunals, coordinated judicial review of IOs promises mixed results. The review process will slow the administrative process and encumber it with procedural and substantive requirements, but at the same time such interventions are likely to promote better informed and more equitable policies. The interplay between efficiency on the one hand and deliberative transparency on the other is constantly shifting, and the process must be carefully managed to maintain a satisfactory balance between the two.[67] Review by internal bodies within IOs and peer review may be helpful, but as we have noted, they are generally no substitute for rigorous scrutiny of IOs by NCs.

NC intervention in IT jurisprudence provides informational benefits that are similar to those provided by courts when they intervene in the domestic administrative review. IOs are no less (if not more) prone to capture by special interests than are national executives, and to the extent that ITs are unwilling or unable to restrain special interests, NCs could step in. Judicial review functions can be effective in developing norms concerning the decision-making processes within IOs–Global Administrative Law norms[68]–to ensure accountability and attention to

---

[67] Jerry Mashaw, *Public Law and Public Choice: Critique and Rapprochement, in* RESEARCH HANDBOOK ON PUBLIC CHOICE AND PUBLIC LAW (Daniel A. Farber & Anne J. O'Connell eds., 2010). A contemporary example is the ongoing debate concerning the appropriate procedures for listing and de-listing individuals suspected of financing global terrorism (discussed in Chapter 6, Section 3.).

[68] Benedict Kingsbury, Nico Krisch & Richard B. Stewart, *The Emergence of Global Administrative Law,* 68 L. & CONTEMP. PROB. 15 (2005).

all affected stakeholders. This is also why we think that judicial activism is more likely to enhance, rather than undermine, the evolution of a more egalitarian and coherent international legal system. Indirectly, by exercising their review authority collectively, even a relatively small group of NCs motivated by a shared desire to safeguard their domestic democratic processes can promote what is arguably a global public good in the form of the increased accountability of international decision-makers to more diverse groups of stakeholders around the globe.[69]

The likelihood that courts will become too activist is limited by (1) the need to cooperate in some areas with other courts; (2) the unwillingness of states and IOs to comply; and (3) the court's dependency on public opinion, which may oppose the outcome. In any case, the fragmented systems of review–especially the interaction between ITs and NCs–encourage robust dialogue, which produces information (for public monitoring) and necessitates compromises between competing decision-makers. Relatively speaking, this is the optimal outcome.

7.4.2 Legitimacy Losses?

It is possible, of course, that the information generated by judicial review of IO policies and decisions could at least in the short run harm the reputation of the IOs and undermine their legitimacy in the eyes of civil society. In the longer run, however, the most likely outcome is just the opposite. Anticipating NC review, IOs can be expected to adhere to court demands by offering more opportunities for the participation of affected stakeholders and improving the accountability of their internal decision-making processes. The several examples of NC review of IOs, discussed in Chapter 6, indicate such a trend among reviewed IOs: Those that seem to have relatively transparent and accountable mechanisms are likely to enjoy greater legitimacy among diffuse stakeholders.

7.4.3 Executive Flight from IOs

It is also possible, of course, that growing interjudicial coordination will prompt the executives of major states to seek out different ways to preempt or evade judicial monitoring, just as they have periodically resorted to serial bilateralism to avoid the political transaction costs

---

[69] Eyal Benvenisti & George W. Downs, *Court Cooperation, Executive Accountability and Global Governance*, 41 N.Y.U. J. INT'L. L. & POL. 931 (2009).

associated with multilateral agreements. To a certain extent, they have already tried to preempt judicial review by adopting treaty amendments or working through the UN Security Council to issue resolutions that are binding on the member states.[70] However, as we have seen in the *Kadi* saga,[71] such efforts have had only limited success.

To some extent, an alternative route to escape review–by resorting to more protective regimes, informal regulation, and even privatization–is already under way. We have discussed these possibilities throughout the book. This escape route has generally operated to expand the de facto authority of the executive branch in comparison with other branches of government and thereby to reduce the likelihood of accountability and deliberation generally.[72] The further proliferation of this strategy raises the prospect that the international regulatory system could become even more fragmented and more subject to executive discretion than is currently the case.

Although the greater fragmentation, informality, and reduced transparency that might accompany greater judicial scrutiny are obviously not desirable, experience at the domestic level suggests that this is a price worth paying in order to curb executive excesses and that such efforts are often successful. In part, this is because over time courts have developed a variety of tactics for minimizing the costs of executive reactions. For example, as mentioned in Chapter 2,[73] courts have restricted the delegation of public authority to private actors by imposing legal obligations on private actors who exercise public functions. There is every reason to expect that courts will be able to develop similar tactics for use at the global level.

It is also important not to exaggerate the risks associated with more stringent review. For example, while outsourcing on the part of executive branches to informal and privatized venues has its own virtues in terms of flexibility and low transaction costs, such venues also have a host of

---

[70] *See, e.g.*, Directive 2004/83/EC of the Counsel of the European Union of 29 April 2004 on Minimum Standards for the Qualification and Status of Third Country Nationals or Stateless Persons as Refugees or as Persons Who Otherwise Need International Protection and the Content of the Protection Granted, 2004 O.J. (L 304) 12 (calling for a common policy on asylum across the European Union); Directive 2001/55/EC of the Counsel of the European Union on 20 July 2001 on Minimum Standards for Giving Temporary Protection in the Event of a Mass Influx of Displaced Persons and on Measures Promoting a Balance of Efforts Between Member States in Receiving Such Persons and Bearing the Consequences Thereof, 2001 O.J. (L 212) 12, *available at* www.ecre.org/eu_developments/temporary%20protection/tpdir.pdf.
[71] *Supra* note 9 in Chapter 6.   [72] *See supra* note 4.   [73] *See* Section 2.4.

disadvantages with respect to representativeness, enforceability, perceived legitimacy, and stability–disadvantages that render them second-best substitutes for IOs in many situations. This is likely to be especially true from the perspective of powerful states whose dominance of the treaty-making system enables them to lock other states into regimes that are beneficial to themselves. Just as one is likely to prefer a formal constitution to an unwritten, informal one if one is fortunate enough to be one of its designers, so it is with treaties. Had this not been the case, it is unlikely that powerful states would have bothered to negotiate elaborate formal agreements in the first place.

7.5   Case Study: The Rise of Judicial Governance in the EU

In its *Van Gend en Loos* judgment,[74] the CJEU gave a teleological justification for its view that Community law not only "imposes obligations on individuals but is also intended to confer upon them rights which become part of their legal heritage"[75]–rights that can be invoked before national and Community courts. The court was concerned that a different outcome "would remove all direct legal protection" of the individual rights of the Community's nationals: "There is the risk that recourse to the procedure under these Articles would be ineffective if it were to occur after the implementation of a national decision taken contrary to the provisions of the Treaty."[76]

Since "this Treaty is more than an agreement which merely creates mutual obligations between the contracting states," and in light of the need to protect the rights of individuals and ensure the effective implementation of the treaty, it makes little sense to rely solely on the states or, more accurately, on state executives who represent their respective states in the international arena. Instead, the CJEU lifts the veil of sovereignty and observes two important actors: the individual citizen and the national court. The judgment assigns to citizens directly enforceable rights vis-à-vis their respective state executives, and it assigns the NCs the obligation to protect those rights: "according to the spirit, the general scheme and the wording of the Treaty, Article 12 must be interpreted as producing direct effects and creating individual rights which national courts must protect."[77]

---

[74] Case 26/62, NV Algemene Transporten Expeditie Onderneming van Gend en Loos v Nederlandse Administratis der Belastingen [1963] ECR 1.
[75] *Id.* at 12.   [76] *Id.* at 13.   [77] *Id.*

What explains the court's suspicion of state executives as the sole actors to implement Community law (acting directly or through the Commission)[78] and its confidence in the central role of NCs moved to action by the complaints of individuals?

The very same case provides an initial answer: the three states that appeared before the CJEU–the Netherlands, Belgium, and Germany–tried to convince the court to defer to their discretion. They did not want to be legally accountable to their citizens or to share responsibility for the implementation of the treaty with their own courts. They made this argument despite the fact that two of them (Belgium and the Netherlands) had been responsible for the infringement that *Van Gend en Loos* was complaining about by their signing of a Protocol that was incompatible with the EC Treaty. The Commission did not react to this breach–most likely because it was not aware of a relatively minor infringement, the imposition of a higher import duty by a local customs agency.

This, then, is one premise that informs the court: To ensure that an IO is effective and accountable to the citizens, it is not enough to leave matters in the hands of state executives and the bureaucracy of the organization.

A second premise is implied: NCs can effectively function as reviewing bodies of the policies of state executives and thereby take part in protecting individuals and implementing the treaty. The courts are independent both from state executives and from the interest groups that support them. Their independence is guaranteed by the EC treaty

---

[78] Articles 169 and 170 (respectively) of the Treaty of Rome (Treaty Establishing the European Economic Community, 1957) allowed the Commission or a member state to refer to the CJEU complaints against member states for non-compliance. In the early decades of the EEC, the Commission's use of its power of reference to the court was limited, and the court actually "reprimanded the Commission for having been inactive although [the Commission] knew that several of the Member States were deliberately sidestepping the fulfillment of their obligations." (Hjalte Rasmussen, ON LAW AND POLICY IN THE EUROPEAN COURT OF JUSTICE 238 (1986). On the dependence of the Commission on Member States see Stefanie Bailer, *The European Commission and Its Legislative Activity – Not as Integrationist and Autonomous as Believed*, Center for Cooperative and International Studies Working Paper No. 24, at p. 15 (2006), *available at* https://www .files.ethz.ch/isn/24126/WP_24_Bailer_EuropeanCommission.pdf ("the success of the Commission hinges on the willingness of the member states and the ability of the Commission to predict the member states' preferences"). Bailer discusses the internal power structure in the commission and the influence exerted by the member states through "their" commissioners, noting that "In several instances, it has been known that EU member states have tried to influence EU policies via their Commissioners or that Commissioners have been defending national interests."

itself, which resolves various collective action problems that the courts would otherwise face.[79] As a result, such a law-based order is generally less susceptible to power and manipulation. Yet while this premise may have informed the court, we believe that it is not crucial to explaining the court's reliance on NCs as a check on state executives.

We suspect that there is a third premise operating in the background of the judgment, one that is never fully articulated but that is ultimately more influential: that the cooperation of NCs among themselves and with the guidance and backing of the CJEU will help protect citizens of the relatively weaker countries in the organization–the Benelux countries in this case, developing countries in the global context–from the predatory policies of the more powerful states. While smaller member states stood to benefit relatively more than the larger members from the opening of the markets in the EC, their executives could have remained subjected to pressures by the stronger ones. Indeed, given the interest of the smaller Common Market countries in openness, it was surprising to see the Belgian and Dutch governments joining Germany in objecting to the direct effect rule of the court. The court may well have taken notice of this same inconsistency and inferred that smaller governments were under external pressure to argue against their interests and that, unless protected, they would continue to be subjected to similar pressures.

That the three smaller members of the EEC were keen to embrace the EC Treaty and give it legal effect was already reflected in their national law. The Dutch Constitution of 1953 provided for the supremacy of international treaties over domestic statutes.[80] The Luxemburg Court of Cassation (in 1950) and its Conseil d'État (in 1951) acknowledged the supremacy of treaty obligations over local laws.[81] In Belgium "the van Gend en Loos decision, though revolutionary, created hardly a ripple at

---

[79] On these challenges, see Eyal Benvenisti, *Judicial Misgivings Regarding the Application of International Norms: An Analysis of Attitudes of National Courts*, 4 EUR. J. INT'L L. 159, Chapter 5 (1993).

[80] The Dutch constitution of 1953 was designed to provide supremacy to EC law (including CJEU decisions). As Daniel Halberstam observed, the reference in the Van Gend case came from the Netherlands, which already had adopted monism (Daniel Halberstam, *Constitutionalism and Pluralism in Marbury and Van Gend*, in THE PAST AND THE FUTURE OF EU LAW: REVISITING THE CLASSICS ON THE 50TH ANNIVERSARY OF THE ROME TREATY, (M.P. Maduro & L. Azoulai eds., 2008)).

[81] As the Luxemburg Court of Cassation later explained in its Pagani judgment of July 14, 1954, "a treaty is a law of a superior nature [essence] having a superior origin than the will of an internal [national] organ." (quoted, together with the other cases, in J. Polakiewicz & V. Jacob-Foltzer, *The European Human Rights Convention in Domestic Law*, 12 HUM. RTS. L.J. 65 (Part I), 125 (Part II), (1991), at 126.

the time,"[82] given the prointegration attitude of the "most outstanding" members of the Belgian judiciary.[83] The Belgian Procureur General, Ganshof van der Meersch, stated that the Rome Treaty created a common legal order whose subjects are not only states but also their citizens.[84] The celebrated judgment of the Belgian Court of Cassation in its 1971 *Le Ski* decision,[85] which endorsed monism and accepted the primacy of EEC law, was considered a "logical and easy"[86] application of the principle of direct effect. These three small states fully grasped the benefits of international cooperation and understood that arguing in favor of the EC Treaty was clearly within their self-interest. They, and the Netherlands in particular, signaled to the CJEU that they would accept and follow its judgments whatever they might be. In the event that France or Germany did not accept its rulings,[87] they would be the ones regarded as the violators of the treaty, whereas the CJEU would be deemed its guardian.[88]

Finally, there was a fourth premise: that the CJEU, with the cooperation of the NCs–at least the NCs of the three smaller members–was sufficiently independent of the state executives and the EC institutions to protect the rights of the citizens. The court's interpretation was protected from subsequent modifications of the treaty, given the likely opposition from at least one of the three smaller member states.[89] Moreover, as Joseph Weiler argued, at least some of the member states had an interest in a strong court that could "mak[e] bargains stick."[90] In addition, the judgment was likely to be implemented by the Dutch

---

[82] Rasmussen, *supra* note 78, at 334 (citing Ivan Verougstraate's unpublished paper from 1981).

[83] *Id.* at 333.   [84] *Id.*

[85] Minister for Economic Affairs v. Fromagerie Franco-Suisse "Le Ski" [1972] C.M.L.R. 330.

[86] Cited in Rasmussen, *supra* note 78, at 334.

[87] On the resistance of the French, German and Italian courts to the reference to the CJEU, see Karen J. Alter, ESTABLISHING THE SUPREMACY OF EUROPEAN LAW (2001) Chapters 3 and 4; Rasmussen, *supra* note 78, at 307–25.

[88] As Geoffrey Garrett, R. Daniel Kelemen, and Heiner Schulz, noted, "the Court cannot afford to make decisions that litigant governments refuse to comply with or, worse, that provoke collective responses from the EU governments to circumscribe the Court's authority" (Geoffrey Garrett, R. Daniel Kelemen, & Heiner Schulz, *The European Court of Justice, National Governments, and Legal Integration in the European Union*, 52 INT'L ORG. 149, 174 (1998).

[89] George Tsebelis & Geoffrey Garrett, *The Institutional Foundations of Intergovernmentalism and Supranationalism in the European Union*, 55 INT'L ORG. 357, 359 (2001); Karen J. Alter, ESTABLISHING THE SUPREMACY OF EUROPEAN LAW 195 (2001).

[90] Joseph HH Weiler, *A Quiet Revolution: The European Court of Justice and Its Interlocutors*, 26 COMP. POL. STUD. 510, 527 (1994).

court.[91] The judges therefore knew that the Dutch court would carry out their judgment regardless of the position of the Dutch government. This is a key consideration for a court concerned about compliance with its judgments.[92]

The judges also felt personally safe. At the time, the "longstanding tradition" promised the CJEU judges reappointment to another six-year term if they so wished.[93] Furthermore, the appointment process involves "complicated political negotiations at the national level"[94] and the anonymous decisions made it "hard to pin activism on any particular national appointee."[95]

The jurisprudence of the EU suggests that although judicial intervention often preempts public deliberation, it can also encourage it; although it may preempt the vote, it can also ensure it. This was particularly true in Europe. As Weiler has argued in his seminal piece on the transformation of Europe,[96] the *Van Gend* "revolution," which closed the exit option for member states, increased their efforts to voice their preferences at the Community decision-making bodies. In addition to taking decision-making at the IO level more seriously, the costs imposed by judicial intervention were far outweighed by their benefits, when compared with the counterfactual of domination by the executives of the most powerful state parties. Democratic failures at both the national and international levels were addressed through greater interaction and coordination between national and international tribunals. Such coordination has proved itself capable of promoting democracy at both the domestic and the international levels by helping to ensure that the interests of a greater proportion of relevant stakeholders are taken into account by decision-makers and that the resulting outcomes are more appropriately informed and balanced.

As discussed in Chapter 5, NCs have been instrumental in strengthening domestic democratic mechanisms and developing legal tools that address the ongoing challenges posed by asymmetric information in

---

[91] *See supra* note 80.

[92] *See* Clifford James Carrubba & Matthew Joseph Gabel, *Courts, Compliance, and the Quest for Legitimacy in International Law*, 14 THEORETICAL INQUIRIES L. 505, 526 (2013) ("The court [...] rules against the government only if the likelihood of being obeyed is high enough.")

[93] Rasmussen, *supra* note 78, at 357. This changed in 1980 after France urged the other members of the European Council to "do something about the European Court and its illegal decisions." (*Id.* at 354).

[94] Alter, *supra* note 89, at 200.   [95] *Id.*

[96] Joseph H.H. Weiler, *The Transformation of Europe*, 100 YALE L. J. 2403, 2427 (1991).

democracies. Since, as suggested above, the policy-making processes at the global level are considerably more opaque than those at the domestic level in most democratic societies, the move to supranational decision-making has increased the need for courts to embrace an additional remedial balancing role. Nevertheless, to date, NCs have generally hesitated to challenge their respective executives out of fear that acting alone against the government or against the IO in which their state is a party might harm their economy or their state's foreign relations. Most likely, they have also feared potential government noncompliance with the judgment.

Fortunately, the Rome Treaty[97] provided the NCs with an invaluable tool to overcome this collective action problem: the recourse to the CJEU to interpret the Treaty. Such interpretation would bind all actors and require other NCs to follow suit. The Benelux NCs had another guarantee for ensuring at least partial adherence to the outcome: The domestic law in these jurisdictions ensured that the CJEU's interpretation would trump domestic law, and therefore all Benelux NCs would conform to the CJEU ruling.[98]

For the Benelux countries, a strong European court and strict adherence to the EC treaty not only promised to open the much larger markets of the big three, but also offered protection against potentially predatory policies adopted by a qualified majority. The CJEU had the largest proportional representation of the small countries of all major EEC institutions and thus was relatively the most favorable European institution for them.[99] In anticipation of the introduction of the qualified majority vote, a strong CJEU gave them assurances along the lines of those that a strong constitutional court grants minorities. Thus, even if the referred cases were not directly related to economic or regulatory disparities between different member states, the basic policy of supporting an evolving constitutional order through a strong court was the smaller states' underlying long-term preference. And indeed, the Benelux NCs referred significantly more questions to the CJEU (relative to the size of their population) than did the courts of the bigger states.[100]

---

[97] *Supra* note 78.   [98] *See supra* notes 81–88 and accompanying text.

[99] The CJEU was composed of seven members, of which three were from the small states (the Commission was composed of nine members, not more than two from any one state).

[100] Alter, *supra* note 89, at 34–35, provides the data: Belgian and Dutch courts brought much more references per-person than the rest of the European states. Between 1970 and 1979, Belgian and Dutch courts referred 4 cases per 500,000 persons per year (CPPY), while

Indeed, the courts of the big three–France, Germany, and Italy–regarded the CJEU with suspicion.[101] The latter–the French courts in particular–were significantly less enthusiastic about making references to the CJEU and made clear that they would not automatically embrace CJEU rulings. The German and Italian courts declared their competence to review the CJEU jurisprudence against their national constitutions.

As the story of the *Van Gend* judgment suggests,[102] NCs also provide support for ITs because it decreases the political pressure on ITs if they deviate from the preferences of executives of powerful states. If NCs are expected to rule against them eventually in any event, executives may be more inclined to tolerate an IT's ruling. Finally and most important, as mentioned above,[103] judicial cooperation holds the promise of overcoming the predatory policies of powerful states and economic actors who exploit divisions among relatively weak states in order to extort concessions. Unable to overcome their political barriers, wary of being exploited, and unsure whether they are involved in a repeated game, weak states find themselves competing against their peers to satisfy the demands of the powerful external actor, to the discontent of many of their domestic constituencies.

To conclude, at least at this juncture in the evolution of the global regulatory regime, IO-driven policies pose more severe counter-majoritarian concerns than judicial review by NCs. The *Van Gend* case offers a clear example for the claim that, judicial review by NCs is more likely to enhance domestic democracy than curtail it.

Celebrating *Van Gend* may tend to obscure the fact that the direct outcome of the judgment meant that state parties became more constrained vis-à-vis Community bodies, as their laws became subjected to Community policies, while there was no immediate assurance that the Community institutions were accountable to the member states and their citizens. Obviously, the *Van Gend* judgment was not about the

German courts brought 2.2 CPPY and France, Italy, the United Kingdom, and Denmark less than 1; Between 1980 and 1989, Belgian and Dutch courts brought 7.1 CPPY each, while Germany 2.8, France 2.6, Italy 1, and the United Kingdom less than 1. Between 1990 and 1998 Belgian and Dutch courts referred around 6 CPPY each, Germany 3, France 2, Italy 3, and the United Kingdom 1. Of course, in the total account of the number of references, the bigger member states brought a higher number of references, with Germany having the highest number. But still, it is significant that during 1980–89 Germany, with 82 million people, sent 246 references to the CJEU, and the Netherlands, with a population of 16 million, brought 224 references.

[101] *See supra* note 87.   [102] *Supra* notes 81–88 and accompanying text.
[103] *See supra* notes 21–22, 32 and accompanying text.

compliance of the European bodies with their treaty obligations, but if *Van Gend* tightens the grip of these regional bodies on the member states, it nonetheless augments the democratic deficit within the members.

It is a general observation that ITs, like the CJEU in this case and in others, are generally more aggressive when reviewing member states for compliance with the IO policies than when they look inside and review the IO itself. As discussed in Chapter 4, ITs are acutely aware of the fundamental distinction between, on the one hand, reviewing a member state for noncompliance with an IO policy or conducting an internal review of low-level bureaucrats of the IO (a function that they tend to perform) and, on the other hand, reviewing an IO's policy or its policy-making process (which they prefer to avoid). However, the relief comes from the NCs: When the IT is timid in reviewing the IO, NCs can step in and provide the missing layer of protection against abuse of authority. It thus becomes apparent that the *Van Gend* judgment, while it has empowered lower courts in Europe by turning them into mini–constitutional courts,[104] has also drawn support from those NCs due to their implicit threat of refusal to accept European policies deemed incompatible with their domestic standards, and this has provided support for the more intrusive review by the CJEU of the European bodies.

It is obviously only speculative whether the CJEU envisioned this eventuality when rendering the *Van Gend* judgment. But this question is less important.[105] What is important is to note that the symbiosis between ITs and NCs, as exemplified in the EU context, provides the most effective judicial mechanism to check IO decision-making.

7.6   Conclusion: The Contributions of Judicial Review to Global Justice

Historically, NCs have been instrumental in strengthening domestic democratic mechanisms and developing legal tools to address the ongoing challenges posed by asymmetric information in democracies. Increasingly, this remedial judicial role has grown more important, because the policy-making processes at the global level are considerably more opaque than those at the domestic level in most

---

[104] Weiler, *A Quiet Revolution, supra* note 90.

[105] See Gary S. Becker, *THE ECONOMIC APPROACH TO HUMAN BEHAVIOR* 7 (1976) ("the economic approach does not assume that economic units are necessarily conscious of their efforts to maximize or can verbalize or otherwise describe . . . reasons for the systematic pattern of their behavior.").

democratic societies. The citizens of most states sense the deterioration of the value of democratic participation at the local level due to the increased role of international or regional policy-making and the increased influence of policies made by neighboring states.

This new environment is not one in which NCs can continue to give their state's chief executives carte blanche to fashion global regulatory policy as they see fit. To do so potentially impoverishes their states' domestic democratic and judicial processes and dramatically reduces the opportunity for citizens to thwart outcomes that may be detrimental to many of them. Fortunately, the growing interventionism on the part of courts in major democratic states has managed, at least to some extent, to impede the dilution of the democratic controls of government that can all too easily result from judicial deference to the government's dominance of international policy.

Accomplishing such judicial coordination in an era of global interdependency, rapid growth, and increased intergovernmental coordination will increasingly require that the judicial branches of governments forge cooperative coalitions across national boundaries. It is through these coalitions that they can coordinate their stances, as well as coordinate with international tribunals. In doing this NCs are not motivated by utopian globalism. Rather, like their counterparts in the executive branch, they are acting on behalf of domestic interests and concerns. But while doing so, these courts can promote democracy at both the domestic and the international levels by helping to ensure that the interests of a greater proportion of relevant stakeholders are taken into account by decision-makers and that the outcomes are more appropriately informed and balanced.

Such coordinated review on the part of courts–both national and international–is potentially one of the most effective avenues for promoting democratic accountability within states and also globally and should be welcomed by those interested in improving the legitimacy of those institutions.

Whether these goals are ultimately achieved depends on a number of factors, especially the future trajectory of the relationship between courts and international organizations. This relationship, like the broader struggle to govern while also containing government, is a dynamic one. Initially, it can be expected that international organizations will react to the prospect of judicial review by trying to preempt and otherwise limit it. The resulting give-and-take between these actors will shape their futures, as well as the evolution of accountability at both the domestic and the global levels.

~

Postscript

BY EYAL BENVENISTI

In this book, George Downs and I explored the challenges that the turn to international institutions poses to the ideals of democracy and the equitable allocation of benefits and burdens among states and communities. We sought to explain why these institutions, while part of the solution to global coordination and cooperation problems, also created a host of new problems. We identified courts–both national and international–as potentially offering institutional responses to resolve these new problems. Much at the insistence of these courts, what was initially a legal environment that allowed executives of a handful of powerful states almost unfettered freedom of action to operate through international organizations has incrementally shifted to a more disciplined environment of accountability. Our analysis has shown that, as traditionally has been the case in domestic settings, much of the law is being built incrementally from the bottom up, in particular, by judges in national courts. Through such actors and due to a growing "culture of accountability," norms, standards, and expectations that have crystallized in democratic domestic legal systems are migrating to the global sphere and beginning to frame perceptions about the legitimacy of global bodies. While this process of migration creates pressure for convergence, there remains considerable variation among norms and institutions. But we also explored initial countervailing responses to such demands. We were not naïve about the countervailing efforts to shield power from accountability and inclusion. And the story will continue to unfold.

George and I collaborated intensively over the course of a dozen years. We came from different disciplines but were curious about each other's work, and together curious about the changing political and legal global landscape. We set out to try to make sense of the ways in which international organizations function and to parse out the implications for individual rights and equality. When the host of a colloquium introduced us some years ago, he described us as Lewis and Clark exploring the evolving sphere of global governance.

In retrospect, I think that what inspired George to embark on this expedition was more than curiosity. He sought to explore how human rights and equality can be secured even in an anarchic world of self-interested rational actors whose primary motivation is power. And he was especially fascinated with the story of the emergence of human rights, in particular, from the early days of the movement for the abolition of the slave trade.

Together we sought clues that would identify institutions that could uphold the achievements of the human rights revolution of the late twentieth century in the face of the shift of power to international organizations. Our first articles focused on a number of concerns both specific and general: the growing influence of pharmaceutical companies whose rights, protected by international treaties, limited access to lifesaving drugs in the developing world and, more broadly, on the mechanisms that enabled powerful state actors to shape international law and institutions with little resistance.

But soon enough we found our heroes–judges of national and regional courts whose decisions restrained at least somewhat the excesses of power of foreign and global actors. The pattern that we identified–of judges cooperating with one another to curb, even if unwittingly, state executives and international bureaucrats–was initially criticized as holding out a false promise: The cases we relied upon were regarded as "rare" and "outliers." But we were confident in our findings because we understood the rationale behind them, namely, the motivation of judicial institutions to preserve their own power in the face of global challenges. Our expedition ended on a positive note, which pleased even so careful and critical a scholar as George.

BIBLIOGRAPHY

Abraham, C.M., *Environmental Jurisprudence in India* (1999)

Acemoglu, Daron & James A. Robinson, *Why Nations Fail* (2012)

Ackerman, Bruce A., *Beyond Carolene Products*, 98 Harv. L. Rev. 713 (1985)

    The Decline and Fall of the American Republic (2010)

Adalsteinsson, Ragnar, *The Current Situation of Human Right in Iceland*, 61/62 Nordic J. Int'l L. 167 (1992–93)

Aleinkoff, T. Alexander, *International Law, Sovereignty, and American Constitutionalism: Reflections on the Customary International Law Debate*, Am. J. Int'l L. 91 (2004)

Alford, Roger P., *Misusing International Sources to Interpret the Constitution*, 98 Am. J. Int'l L. 57 (2004)

Alivizatos, Nicos C., *Judges as Veto Players*, in Parliaments and Majority Rule in Western Europe 566 (Herbert Doering ed., 1995)

Alter, Karen J., *Establishing the Supremacy of European Law* (2001)

    The New Terrain of International Law (2015)

Alvarez, José E., *Contemporary International Law: An "Empire of Law" or the "Law of Empire"?*, 24 Am. U. Int'l L. Rev. 811 (2009)

    International Organizations as Law-Makers (2005)

Amerasinghe, C.F., *The World Bank Administrative Tribunal*, 31 Int'l & Comp. L.Q. 748 (1982)

Andersen, Michael J., *International Environmental Law in Indian Courts*, 7 Rev. Eur. Community & Int'l Envtl. L. 11 (1998).

Arezki, Rabah, Klaus Deininger, & Harris Selod, *What Drives the Global "Land Rush"?*, 29 World Bank Econ. Rev. 207 (2015)

Arrow, Kenneth J., *Social Choice and Individual Values* (1951)

Auer, Matthew R., *Geography, Domestic Politics and Environmental Diplomacy: A Case from the Baltic Sea Region*, 11 Geo. Int'l Envtl. L. Rev. 77 (1998)

Aust, Anthony, *Modern Treaty Law and Practice* (2000)

Avi-Yonah, Reuven S., *Globalization, Tax Competition and the Fiscal Crisis of the State*, 113 Harv. L. Rev. 1573 (2000)

    International Tax as International Law: An Analysis of the International Tax Regime (2007)

Bailer, Stefanie, *The European Commission and Its Legislative Activity – Not as Integrationist and Autonomous as Believed*, Center for Cooperative and International Studies Working Paper No. 24 (2006).

Barak-Erez, Daphne, *The International Law of Human Rights and Constitutional Law: A Case Study of an Expanding Dialogue*, 2 INT'L. J. CONST. L. 611 (2004)

Barnard, David, *In the High Court of South Africa, Case No. 4138/98: The Global Politics of Access to Low-Cost AIDS Drugs in Poor Countries*, 12 J. KENNEDY INST. ETHICS 159 (2002)

Bartolomei, Hector de la Cruz et al., THE INTERNATIONAL LABOR ORGANIZATION (1996)

Bates, Robert H., OPEN-ECONOMY POLITICS (1997)

Baum, Lawrence, JUDGES AND THEIR AUDIENCES: A PERSPECTIVE ON JUDICIAL BEHAVIOR (2006)

Baxi, Upendra, *"A Known but an Indifferent Judge": Situating Ronald Dworkin in Contemporary Indian Jurisprudence*, 1 I-CON 557 (2003)

Becker, Gary S., *A Theory of Competition among Pressure Groups for Political Influence*, 98 Q. J. ECON. 371 (1983)

THE ECONOMIC APPROACH TO HUMAN BEHAVIOR (1976)

Beitz, Charles, THE IDEA OF HUMAN RIGHTS (2009)

Bekker, Peter H.F., THE LEGAL POSITION OF INTERGOVERNMENTAL ORGANIZATIONS (1994)

Benedick, Richard Elliot, OZONE DIPLOMACY (1998)

Benhabib, Seyla, THE RIGHTS OF OTHERS: ALIENS, RESIDENTS AND CITIZENS (2004)

Benvenisti, Eyal & George W. Downs, *Court Cooperation, Executive Accountability and Global Governance*, 41 N.Y.U. J. INT'L. LAW & POL. 931 (2009)

Prospects for the Increased Independence of International Tribunals in 12 GERMAN L.J. 1057 (2011) (rep. in LAWMAKING BY INTERNATIONAL TRIBUNALS (Armin von Bogdandy & Ingo Venzke eds., 2012))

Democratizing Courts: How National and International Courts Promote Democracy in an Era of Global Governance, 46 N.Y.U J. INT'L L. & POL. 741 (2014)

Distributive Politics and International Institutions: The Case of Drugs, 36 CASE W. RES. J. INT'L L. 21 (2004)

Empire's New Clothes: Political Economy and the Fragmentation of International Law, 60 STAN. L. REV. 595 (2007)

National Courts and Transnational Private Regulation, in ENFORCEMENT OF TRANSNATIONAL REGULATION: ENSURING COMPLIANCE IN A GLOBAL WORLD 131 (Fabrizio Cafaggi ed., 2012)

Benvenisti, Eyal, *"Coalitions of the Willing" and the Evolution of Informal International Law*, in *"COALITIONS OF THE WILLING"–AVANTGARDE OR THREAT?* 1 (C. Calliess, G. Nolte, & T. Stoll eds., 2008)

Coalitions of the Willing, INFORMAL INTERNATIONAL LAWMAKING (Joost Pauwelyn, Ramses Wessel, & Jan Wouters eds., 2012)

Democracy Captured: The Mega-Regional Agreements and the Future of Global Public Law, 23 CONSTELLATIONS 58 (2016)

Exit and Voice in the Age of Globalization, 98 MICH. L. REV. 167 (1999)

Inter-Judicial Cooperation to Secure Independent Review of Counter-Terrorism Measures, in DEMOCRACY, SEPARATIONS OF POWERS AND THE FIGHTS AGAINST TERRORISM 251 (Andrea Bianchi & Alexis Keller eds., 2008)

Judges and Foreign Affairs: A Comment on the Institut de Droit International's Resolution on "The Activities of National Courts and the International Relations of Their State," 5 EUR. J. INT'L L. 423 (1994)

Judicial Misgivings Regarding the Application of International Norms: An Analysis of Attitudes of National Courts, 4 EUR. J. INT'L L. 159 (1993)

Judicial Review and Democratic Failures: Minimizing Asymmetric Information through Adjudication 32 IYUNEI MISHPAT (Tel-Aviv U. Law Rev.), 277 (2010) (Isr.) (Hebrew)

Party Primaries as Collective Action with Constitutional Ramifications: Israel as a Case Study, 3 THEORETICAL INQUIRIES L. 175 (2002)

Reclaiming Democracy: The Strategic Uses of Foreign and International Law by National Courts, 102 AM. J. INT'L L. 241 (2008)

Sovereigns as Trustees of Humanity: On the Accountability of States to Foreign Stakeholders, 107 AM. J. INT'L L. 295 (2013)

THE LAW OF GLOBAL GOVERNANCE (2014)

Berman, Ayelet, *The Role of Domestic Administrative Law in the Accountability of IN-LAW: The Case of the ICH*, in INFORMAL INTERNATIONAL LAWMAKING 468 (Joost Pauwelyn, Ramses A. Wessel, & Jan Wouters eds., 2012).

Bermann, George A., *Constitutional Implications of U.S. Participation in Regional Integration*, 46 AM. J. COMP. L., 463 (1998)

Bernhardt, Rudolf, *Evolutive Treaty Interpretation, Especially of the European Convention on Human Rights*, 42 GERM. Y.B. INT'L L. 11 (1999)

Bernstein, Lisa, *Merchant Law in a Merchant Court: Rethinking the Code's Search for Immanent Business Norms*, 144 U. PA. L. REV. 1765 (1996)

Opting Out of the Legal System: Extralegal Contractual Relations in the Diamond Industry, 21 J. LEGAL STUD. 115 (1992)

Besley, Timothy & Robin Burgess, *Can Labor Regulation Hinder Economic Performance? Evidence from India*, 119 Q. J. ECON. 91 (2004)

Bianchi, Andrea, Case Report: Ferrini v. Federal Republic of Germany, 99 AM. J. INT'L L. 242 (2005)

Bickel, Alexander, THE LEAST DANGEROUS BRANCH (1962)

Binder, Christina, *The Prohibition of Amnesties by The Inter-American Court of Human Rights*, 12 GERMAN L.J. 1203 (2011)

Binmore, Ken, GAME THEORY AND THE SOCIAL CONTRACT II: JUST PLAYING (1998)

Bloch, Alice, Treasa Galvin, & Liza Schuster (eds.), [Special issue] 13(1) J. REFUGEE STUD. (2000)

Bodansky, Daniel & Jutta Brunnée, *The Role of National Courts in the Field of International Environmental Law*, 7 Rev. Eur. Community Int'l Envtl. L. 11 (1998)

Bogdan, Michael, *Application of Public International Law by Swedish Courts*, 63 Nordic J. Int'l L. 3 (1994)

Bohman, James, Democracy Across Borders: From Dêmos to Dêmoi (2007)

Boix, Carles, Political Parties, Growth and Equality (1998)

Bradley, Curtis A., *International Delegations, the Structural Constitution, and Non-Self-Execution*, 55 Stan. L. Rev. 1557 (2003)

   The Charming Betsy Canon and Separation of Powers: Rethinking the Interpretive Role of International Law, 86 Geo. L.J. 479 (1998)

   The Treaty Power and American Federalism, 97 Mich. L. Rev. 390 (1998)

Bradley, Curtis A. & Jack L. Goldsmith, *Customary International Law as Federal Common Law: A Critique of the Modern Position*, 110 Harv. L. Rev. 815 (1997)

   The Current Illegitimacy of International Human Rights Litigation, 66 Fordham L. Rev. 319 (1997)

Brilmayer, Lea, *International Law in American Courts: A Modest Proposal*, 100 Yale L.J. 2277 (1991)

Brooks, Kim & Richard Krever, *The Troubling Role of Tax Treaties*, 51 Tax Design Issues Worldwide, Series on International Taxation 159 (Geerten M.M. Michielse & Victor Thuronyi eds., 2015)

Bruch, Carl et al., *Constitutional Environmental Law: Giving Force to Fundamental Principles in Africa*, 26 Colum. J. Envtl. L. 131 (2001)

Brummer, Chris, Soft Law and the Global Financial System: Rule Making in the 21st Century (2012)

Brutsch, Christian & Mihaela Papa, *Deconstructing the BRICS: Bargaining Coalition, Imagined Community, or Geopolitical Fad?* 6 Chinese J. Int'l Pol. 299 (2013)

Buchanan, Allen, Justice, Legitimacy, and Self-Determination: Moral Foundation for International Law (2004)

Bueno de Mesquita, Bruce & George W. Downs, *Development and Democracy*, Foreign Aff., Sept.–Oct. (2005)

Bueno de Mesquita, Bruce et al., The Logic of Political Survival (2003)

Burke-White, William W., *International Legal Pluralism*, 25 Mich. J. Int'l L. 963 (2004)

Byers, Michael, *Conceptualising the Relationship between Jus Cogens and Erga Omnes Rules*, 66 Nordic J. Int'l L. 211 (1997)

   Policing the High Seas: The Proliferation Security Initiative, 98 Am. J. Int'l. L. 526 (2004)

Campos, Jose E. & Hilton L. Root, The Key to the Asian Miracle: Making Shared Growth Credible (1996)

Carrubba, Clifford James, *A Model of the Endogenous Development of Judicial Institutions in Federal and International Systems*, 71 J. POL. 55 (2009)

Carrubba, Clifford James & Matthew Joseph Gabel, *Courts, Compliance, and the Quest for Legitimacy in International Law*, 14 THEORETICAL INQUIRIES L. 505 (2013)

Cassese, Sabino, THE GLOBAL POLITY: GLOBAL DIMENSIONS OF DEMOCRACY AND THE RULE OF LAW (2012)

Chander, Anupam, *Globalization and Distrust*, 114 YALE L.J. 1193 (2005)

Charney, Jonathan I., *The Implications of Expanding International Dispute Settlement Systems: The 1982 Convention on the Law of the Sea*, 90 AM. J. INT'L L. 69 (1996)

Chia-Hui Lee, G., PRIVATE FOOD STANDARDS AND THEIR IMPACTS ON DEVELOPING COUNTRIES, European Commission – DG Trade Unit G2 Paper (2006)

Churchill, R.R. & A.V. Lowe, THE LAW OF THE SEA (3rd edn., 1999)

Clark, Tom S., THE LIMITS OF JUDICIAL INDEPENDENCE (2011)

Clavin, Patricia & Wilhelm Jens, *Transnationalism and the League of Nations: Understanding the Work of Its Economic and Financial Organisation*, 14 CONTEMP. EUR. HIST. 465 (2005)

Cogen, Marc, *Human Rights, Prohibition of Political Activities and the Lending Policies of the World Bank and International monetary Fund, in* THE RIGHT TO DEVELOPMENT IN INTERNATIONAL LAW 387 (Chowdhury et al. eds., 1992)

Cohen, Jean, *Constitutionalism beyond the State: Myth or Necessity? (A Pluralist Approach)*, 2 HUMANITY: AN INT'L J. HUM. RTS., HUMANITARIANISM, DEVELOPMENT 127 (2011)

Compa, Lance A. & Stephen F. Diamond eds., HUMAN RIGHTS, LABOR RIGHTS, AND INTERNATIONAL TRADE (1996)

Conforti, Benedetto & Francesco Francioni, ENFORCING INTERNATIONAL HUMAN RIGHTS IN DOMESTIC COURTS (1997)

Cooter, Robert D., THE STRATEGIC CONSTITUTION (2000)

Coquillette, Daniel R., *Legal Ideology and Incorporation II: Sir Thomas Ridley, Charles Molloy, and the Literary Battle for the Law Merchant, 1607–1676*, 61 B.U. L. REV. 315 (1981)

COX, Gary W., MAKING VOTES COUNT: STRATEGIC COORDINATION IN THE WORLD'S ELECTORAL SYSTEMS (1997)

Crawford, James, CHANCE, ORDER, CHANGE: THE COURSE OF INTERNATIONAL LAW, GENERAL COURSE ON PUBLIC INTERNATIONAL LAW (2014)

Croley, Steven P. & John H. Jackson, *WTO Dispute Procedures, Standard of Review and Deference to National Governments*, 90 AM. J. INT'L L. 193 (1996)

D'Aspremont, Jean & Catherine Brölmann, *Challenging International Criminal Tribunals before Domestic Courts, in* CHALLENGING ACTS OF INTERNATIONAL ORGANIZATIONS BEFORE NATIONAL COURTS 111 (August Reinisch ed., 2010)

Dagan, Tsilly, *Community Obligations in International Taxation in* COMMUNITY INTERESTS IN INTERNATIONAL LAW (Eyal Benvenisti & Georg Nolte eds., forthcoming)

The Tax Treaties Myth, 32(4) N.Y.U. J. INT'L L. & POL. 939 (2000)

Dai, Xinyuan, *Who Defines the Rules of the Game in East Asia? The Trans-Pacific Partnership and the Strategic Use of International Institutions*, 15 INT'L RELATIONS OF THE ASIA-PACIFIC 1 (2014)

Danielsen, Dan, *How Corporations Govern: Taking Corporate Power Seriously in Transnational Regulation and Governance*, 46 HARV. INT'L L.J. 411 (2005)

Davis, Gerald F., Marina V.N. Whitman, & Mayer Nathan Zald, THE RESPONSIBILITY PARADOX: MULTINATIONAL FIRMS AND GLOBAL CORPORATE SOCIAL RESPONSIBILITY (Ross Sch. of Bus. Working Paper Series, Working Paper No. 1031, Apr. 2006).

De Brabandere, Eric, *Belgian Courts and the Immunity of International Organizations*, 10 INT'L ORG. L. REV. 464 (2014)

De la Rochère, J.D., *France, in* THE EFFECT OF TREATIES IN DOMESTIC LAW (Francis G. Jacobs & Shelley Roberts eds., 1987)

De Schutter, Olivier, *How Not to Think of Land-Grabbing: Three Critiques of Large-Scale Investments in Farmland*, 38 J. PEASANT STUDIES 249 (2011)

De Sena, Pasquale & Francesca De Vittor, *State Immunity and Human Rights: The Italian Supreme Court Decision on the* Ferrini *Case*, 16 EUR. J. INT'L L. 89 (2005)

De Wet, Erika & André Nollkaemper, *Review of Security Council Decisions by National Courts*, 45 GERMAN Y.B. INT'L L. 166 (2002)

De Witte, Bruno, *Direct Effect, Supremacy, and the Nature of Legal Order, in* THE EVOLUTION OF EU LAW 177 (Paul Craig & Gráinne de Búrca eds., 1999)

Del Vecchio, Giorgio, *Grotius and the Foundation of International Law*, 37 N.Y.U. L. REV. 260 (1962)

Deshman, Abigail C., *Horizontal Review between International Organizations: Why, How, and Who Cares about Corporate Regulatory Capture*, 22 EUR. J. INT'L L. 1089 (2011)

Dothan, Shai, REPUTATION AND JUDICIAL TACTICS: A THEORY OF NATIONAL AND INTERNATIONAL COURTS (2015)

Downs, George W. & David M. Rocke, OPTIMAL IMPERFECTION? (1995)

Downs, George W. & Michael A. Jones, *Reputation, Compliance and International Law*, 31 J. LEGAL STUD. 595 (2002)

Drahos, Peter, *Global Law Reform and Rent-Seeking: The Case of Intellectual Property*, 7 AUSTRALIAN J. CORP. L. 1 (1996)

Dulitzky, Ariel E., *An Inter-American Constitutional Court? The Invention of the Conventionality Control by the Inter-American Court of Human Rights*, 50 TEXAS INT'L L.J. 46 (2015)

Dunoff, Jeffrey L., *The Misguided Debate over NGO Participation at the WTO*, 1 J. INT'L ECON. L. 433 (1998)

Elkins, Zachary, Andrew T. Guzman, & Beth Simmons, *Competing for Capital: The Diffusion of Bilateral Investment Treaties, 1960–2000*, U. ILL. L. REV. 265 (2008)

Ely, John Hart, DEMOCRACY AND DISTRUST: A THEORY OF JUDICIAL REVIEW (1980)

Epstein, Richard A., *Exit Rights under Federalism*, 55 LAW & CONTEMP. PROBS. 147 (1992)

Evans, Peter B., Harold K. Jacobson, & Robert D. Putnam eds., DOUBLE-EDGED DIPLOMACY: INTERNATIONAL BARGAINING AND DOMESTIC POLITICS (University of California Press, 1993)

Falk, Richard A., THE ROLE OF DOMESTIC COURTS IN THE INTERNATIONAL ORDER (1964)

Ferejohn, John, *Judicializing Politics, Politicizing Law*, 65 LAW & CONTEMP. PROBS. 41 (2002)

Feunteun, Tristan, *Cartels and the Right to Food: An Analysis of States' Duties and Options*, 18 J. INT'L ECON. L. 341 (2015)

Fitzmaurice, Malgosia, *The Finnish-Swedish Frontier Rivers Commission*, 5 HAGUE Y.B. INT'L L. 33 (1992)

Fletcher, Eric G.M., *John Selden (Author of* Mare clausum*) and His Contribution to International Law*, 19 TRANSACTION GROTIUS SOC'Y 1 (1934)

Flynn, Sean M., Brook Baker, Margot Kaminski, & Jimmy Koo, *The U.S. Proposal for an Intellectual Property Chapter in the Trans-Pacific Partnership Agreement*, 28 AM. U. INT'L L. REV. 105 (2012)

Fox, Eleanor, *Antitrust without Borders: From Roots to Codes to Networks*, in COOPERATION, COMITY AND COMPETITION POLICY (Andrew T. Guzman ed., 2010)

Fox, HAZEL, THE LAW OF STATE IMMUNITY (2nd edn., 2008)

Franck, Thomas M., *The Courts, the State Department and National Policy: A Criterion for Judicial Abdication*, 44 MINN. L. REV. 1101 (1960)

Fraser, Nancy, *Reframing Justice in a Globalizing World*, 36 NEW LEFT REV. 69 (2005)

  SCALES OF JUSTICE: REIMAGING POLITICAL SPACE IN A GLOBALIZING WORLD (2009)

French, D., *Treaty Interpretation and the Incorporation of Extraneous Legal Rules*, 55 INT'L & COMP. L.Q. 281 (2006)

Friedman, Barry, *The Birth of an Academic Obsession: The History of the Countermajoritarian Difficulty, Part Five*, 112 YALE L.J. 153 (2002)

Frowein, Jochen A., *Federal Republic of Germany*, in THE EFFECT OF TREATIES IN DOMESTIC LAW (Francis G. Jacobs & Shelley Roberts eds., 1987)

Frowein, Jochen A. & Michael J. Hahn, *The Participation of Parliament in the Treaty Process in the Federal Republic of Germany*, 67 CHI.-KENT L. REV. 361 (1992)

Gadinis, Stavros, *Three Pathways to Global Standards: Private, Regulator, and Ministry Networks*, 109 AM. J. INT'L L. 1 (2015)

Gagné, Gilbert & Jean-Frédéric Morin, *The Evolving American Policy on Investment Protection: Evidence from Recent FTAs and the 2004 Model BIT*, 9 J. INT'L ECON. L. 357 (2006)

Gaja, Giorgio, *Italy, in* THE EFFECT OF TREATIES IN DOMESTIC LAW (Francis G. Jacobs & Shelley Roberts eds., 1987)

Galambos, Judit, *Political Aspects of an Environmental Conflict: The Case of the Gabcikovo-Nagymaros Dam System, in* PERSPECTIVES ON ENVIRONMENTAL CONFLICT AND INTERNATIONAL POLITICS 72 (Jyrki Kknen ed., 1992)

Garoupa, Nuno & Tom Ginsburg, *Judicial Audiences and Reputation: Perspectives from Comparative Law*, 47 COLUM. J. TRANSNAT'L L. 51 (2008–2009)

Garrett, Geoffre, R. Daniel Kelemen, & Heiner Schulz, *The European Court of Justice, National Governments, and Legal Integration in the European Union*, 52 INT'L ORG. 149 (1998)

Gavouneli, Maria & Ilias Bantekas, *Case Report: Prefecture of Voiotia v. Federal Republic of Germany*, 95 AM. J. INT'L L. 198 (2001)

Gellner, Ernest, NATIONS AND NATIONALISM (1983)

Ginsborg, Lisa & Martin Scheinin, *Judicial Powers, Due Process and Evidence in the Security Council 1267 Terrorist Sanctions Regime: The Kadi II Conundrum* (Eur. U. Inst., EUI Working Paper RSCAS 2011/44, 2011)

Ginsburg, Tom, *International Judicial Lawmaking* (2005) http://papers.ssrn.com/sol3/Delivery.cfm/SSRN_ID693861_code603.pdf?abstractid=693861&mirid=3

JUDICIAL REVIEW IN NEW DEMOCRACIES: CONSTITUTIONAL COURTS IN ASIAN CASES (2003)

Political Constraints on International Courts, in THE OXFORD HANDBOOK OF INTERNATIONAL ADJUDICATION 483 (Cesare PR Romano, Karen J. Alter, & Yuval Shany eds., 2014)

Glendon, Mary Ann, A WORLD MADE NEW (2001)

Goetz, Charles J. & Robert E. Scott, *Principles of Relational Contracts*, 67 VA. L. REV. 1089 (1981)

Goldstein, Judith L. et al. eds., LEGALIZATION AND WORLD POLITICS (Massachusetts Institute of Technology Press, 2001)

Goodin, Robert E., *Enfranchising All Affected Interests, and Its Alternatives*, 35 PHIL. & PUB. AFF. 40 (2007)

Goodwin-Gill, Guy S. & Jane McAdam, THE REFUGEE IN INTERNATIONAL LAW (3rd edn., 2007)

Grant, Ruth W. & Robert O. Keohane, *Accountability and Abuses of Power in World Politics*, 99 AM. POL. SCI. REV. 29 (2005)

Gray, John, FALSE DAWN: THE DELUSIONS OF GLOBAL CAPITALISM (1998)

Grotius, Hugo, THE FREEDOM OF THE SEAS (James Brown Scott ed., Ralph van Deman Magoffin trans., Oxford University Press, 1916) (1633)

Gulmann, Claus, *Denmark, in* THE EFFECT OF TREATIES IN DOMESTIC LAW (Francis G. Jacobs & Shelley Roberts eds., 1987)

Hackworth, Green Haywood, DIGEST OF INTERNATIONAL LAW (1943)

Halberstam, Daniel, Constitutionalism and Pluralism in Marbury and Van Gend, in THE PAST AND THE FUTURE OF EU LAW: REVISITING THE CLASSICS ON THE 50TH ANNIVERSARY OF THE ROME TREATY (M.P. Maduro & L. Azoulai eds., 2008)

Hathaway, James C., A Forum for the Transnational Development of Refugee Law: The IARLJ's Advanced Refugee Law Workshop, 15 INT'L J. REFUGEE L. 418 (2003)

    Harmonizing for Whom? The Devaluation of Refugee Protection in the Era of European Economic Integration, 26 CORNELL INT'L L.J. 719 (1993)

Hayward, M. Ann, International Law and the Interpretation of the Canadian Charter of Rights and Freedoms: Uses and Justifications, 23 U. W. ONT. L. REV. 9 (1985)

Heffter, August Wilhelm, DAS EUROPAISCHE VOLKERRECHT DER GEGENWART 7 (3rd edn., Berlin, E.H. Schroeder, 1855)

Helfer, Laurence R., Regime Shifting: The TRIPs Agreement and New Dynamics of International Intellectual Property Lawmaking, 29 YALE J. INT'L L. 1 (2004)

Helfer, Laurence R. & Anne-Marie Slaughter, Why States Create International Tribunals: A Response to Professors Posner and Yoo, 93 CAL. L. REV. 1 (2005)

Helfer, Laurence R. & Erik Voeten, International Courts as Agents of Legal Change: Evidence from LGBT Rights in Europe, 68 INT' ORG. 77 (2014)

Helfer, Laurence R. & Karen J. Alter, Nature or Nurture? Judicial Lawmaking in the European Court of Justice and the Andean Tribunal of Justice, 64 INT'L ORG. 563 (2010)

Henderson, David, THE MAI AFFAIR: A STORY AND ITS LESSONS (1999)

Henkin, Louis, CONSTITUTIONALISM, DEMOCRACY, AND FOREIGN AFFAIRS (1990)

    FOREIGN AFFAIRS AND THE UNITED STATES CONSTITUTION (2nd edn., 1996)

    International Law as Law in the United States, 82 MICH. L. REV. 1555 (1984)

Higgins, Rosalyn, United Kingdom, in THE EFFECT OF TREATIES IN DOMESTIC LAW (Francis G. Jacobs & Shelley Roberts eds., 1987)

Hilf, Meinhard, The Role of National Courts in International Trade Relations, 18 MICH. J. INT'L L. 321 (1997)

Hipold, Peter, UN Sanctions before the ECJ: The Kadi Case, in CHALLENGING ACTS OF INTERNATIONAL ORGANIZATIONAL BEFORE NATIONAL COURTS 18 (August Reinisch ed., 2010)

Hirschl, Ran, TOWARDS JURISTOCRACY: THE ORIGINS AND CONSEQUENCES OF THE NEW CONSTITUTIONALISM (2004)

Hirschman, Albert O., EXIT, VOICE AND LOYALTY (1970)

Ho, Laura et al., (Dis)assembling Rights of Women Workers along the Global Assembly Line: Human Rights and the Garment Industry, 31 HARV. C.R.-C.L. L. REV. 383 (1996)

Hobsbawm, Eric J., NATIONS AND NATIONALISM SINCE 1780 (2nd edn., 1992)

Holdsworth, William, A HISTORY OF ENGLISH LAW (3rd edn., 1945)

Hopewell, Kristen, *Different Paths to Power: The Rise of Brazil, India and China at the World Trade Organization*, 22 Rev. Int'l Pol. Econ. 311 (2015)

Howse, Robert, *Adjudicative Legitimacy and Treaty Interpretation in International Trade Law, in* the EU, the WTO and the NAFTA: Towards a Common Law of International Trade? 35 (Joseph H.H. Weiler ed., 2000)

Huber, Berthold, *The Application of Human Rights Standards by German Courts to Asylum-Seekers, Refugees and other Migrants*, 3 Eur. J. Migration & L. 171 (2001)

Huber, Katalin Tünde & Alejandro Rodiles, *An Ombudsperson in the United Nations Security Council: A Paradigm Shift?* 10 Anuario Mexicano de Derecho Internacional (2012)

Ikenberry, G. John, After Victory (2001)

Jackson, John H., *United States, in* The Effect of Treaties in Domestic Law (Francis G. Jacobs & Shelley Roberts eds., 1987)

World Trade and the Law of GATT (1969)

Jackson, Vicki, *Constitutional Comparisons: Convergence, Resistance, Engagement*, 119 Harv. L. Rev. 109 (2005)

Jacobs, Francis G. & Shelley Roberts eds., The Effect of Treaties in Domestic Law (Sweet & Maxwell, 1987)

Jervis, Robert, The Remaking of a Unipolar World, *Wash. Q.* Summer 2006

Johnson, Lise & Oleksandr Volkov, *Investor-State Contracts, Home-State "Commitments" and the Myth of Stability in International Law*, 24(3) Am. Rev. Int'l Arb. 361 (2013)

Johnstone, Ian, *Legislation and Adjudication in the UN Security Council: Bringing Down the Deliberative Deficit*, 102 Am. J. Int'l L. 275 (2008)

Kaminski, Margot E., An Overview and the Evolution of the Anti-Counterfeiting Trade Agreement, PIJIP Research Paper Series, paper no. 17 (2011)

The Capture of International Intellectual Property Law through the U.S. Trade Regime, 87 S.Cal. L. Rev. 977 (2014)

Kapczynski, Amy, *Engineered in India – Patent Law 2.0*, 369 N. Engl. J. Med. 497 (2013)

The Trans-Pacific Partnership–Is It Bad for Your Health? N. Engl. J. Med. 201 (2015)

Katz Cogan, Jacob, *Competition and Control in International Adjudication*, 48 Virginia J. Int'l L. 412 (2008)

Keck, Margaret E. & Kathryn Sikkinik, Activists beyond Borders (1998)

Kennedy, David, *Primitive Legal Scholarship*, 27 Harv. Int'l L.J. 1 (1986)

Kennedy, Paul, The Parliament of Man (2006)

Keohane, Robert O., Stephen Macedo, & Andrew Moravcsik, *Democracy-Enhancing Multilateralism*, 63 Int'l Org., 1 (2009).

Keohane, Robert O. et al., *Legalized Dispute Resolution: Interstate and Transnational*, 54 Int'l Org., 457 (2000)

Kingsbury, Benedict & Kevin Davis, OBLIGATIONS OVERLOAD: ADJUSTING THE OBLIGATIONS OF FRAGILE OR FAILED STATES (Nov. 22, 2010) (Preliminary Draft)

Kingsbury, Benedict, Nico Krisch, & Richard B. Stewart, The Emergence of Global Administrative Law, 68 L. & CONTEMP. PROBS. 15 (2005)

Kirby, Michael, International Law–The Impact on National Constitutions, 99 ASIL PROC. 1, 2 (Seventh Annual Grotius Lecture, 2005)

Kiss, Alexandre, 2–3 REVUE JURIDIQUE DE L'ENVIRONNEMENT, 307–09 (1986)

Klabbers, Jan, AN INTRODUCTION TO INTERNATIONAL ORGANIZATIONS LAW (3rd edn., 2015)

Knop, Karen, Here and There: International Law in Domestic Courts 32 NYU J. INT'L L. & POL. 501 (2000)

Koh, Harold H., The Fast Track and United States Trade Policy, 18 BROOK. J. INT'L L. 143 (1992)

 Commentary: Is International Law Really State Law?, 111 HARV. L. REV. 1824 (1998)

 International Law as Part of Our Law, 98 AM. J. INT'L L. 43 (2004)

 The "Haiti Paradigm" in United States Human Rights Policy, 103 YALE L.J. 2391 (1994)

 Transnational Public Law Litigation, 100 YALE L.J. 2347 (1991)

Kokkot, Juliane, Report on Germany, in THE EUROPEAN COURT AND NATIONAL COURTS – DOCTRINE AND JURISPRUDENCE 77 (Anne-Marie Slaughter, Alec Stone Sweet, & J.H.H. Weiler eds., 1998)

Kosař, David & Lucas Lixinski, Domestic Judicial Design by International Human Rights Courts, 109 AM. J. INT'L L. 713 (2016)

Koskenniemi, Martti, FRAGMENTATION OF INTERNATIONAL LAW: DIFFICULTIES ARISING FROM THE DIVERSIFICATION AND EXPANSION OF INTERNATIONAL LAW, Report of the Study Group of the International Law Commission (2006)

 The Fate of Public International Law: Between Technique and Politics, 70 MOD. L. REV. 1 (2007)

 What Is International Law For?, in INT'L L. 89 (Malcolm D. Evans ed., 2003)

Koskenniemi, Martti & Päivi Leino, Fragmentation of International Law? Postmodern Anxieties, 15 LEIDEN J. INT'L L. 553 (2002)

Krisch, Nico, International Law in Times of Hegemony: Unequal Power and the Shaping of the International Legal Order, 16 EUR. J. INT'L L. 369 (2005)

 The Decay of Consent: International Law in an Age of Global Public Goods, 108 AM. J. INT'L L. 1 (2014)

 The Pluralism of Global Administrative Law, 17 EUR. J. INT'L L. 247 (2006)

Kumm, Matthias, Democratic Constitutionalism Encounters International Law. Terms of Engagement, in THE MIGRATION OF CONSTITUTIONAL IDEAS 256 (Sujit Choudhry ed., 2007)

L'Heureux-Dubé, Claire, The Importance of Dialogue: Globalization and the International Impact of the Rhenquist Court, 34 TULSA L.J. 15 (1998)

Lampe, Markus, *Explaining Nineteenth-Century Bilateralism: Economic and Political Determinants of the Cobden–Chevalier Network*, 64 ECON. HIST. REV. 644 (2011)

Landes, William M. & Richard A. Posner, *The Independent Judiciary in an Interest-Group Perspective*, 18 J. L. & ECON. 875 (1975)

Lauterpacht, Hersch, THE DEVELOPMENT OF INTERNATIONAL LAW BY THE INTERNATIONAL COURT OF JUSTICE (1958)

The Grotian Tradition in International Law, 23 BRIT. Y.B. INT'L L. 1 (1946)

Łazowski, Adam, *Poland. Constitutional Tribunal on Conformity of the Accession Treaty with the Polish Constitution. Decision of 11 May 2005*, 3 EUR. CONST. L. REV. 148 (2007)

Lehavi, Amnon, *Land Law in the Age of Globalization and Land Grabbing*, in RESEARCH HANDBOOK ON COMPARATIVE PROPERTY LAW 25 (Michele Graziadei & Lionel Smith eds., 2015)

Leitner, Kara & Simon Lester, *WTO Dispute Settlement 1995–2015 – A Statistical Analysis*, 19 J. INT'L ECON. L. 289 (2016)

Lohmann, Susanne, *An Information Rationale for the Power of Special Interests*, 92 AM. POL. SCI. REV. 809 (1998)

Lord Steyn, *2000–2005: Laying the Foundations of Human Rights Law in the United Kingdom*, 4 EUR. HUM. RTS. L. REV. 349 (2005)

Lord Templeman, *Treaty-Making and the British Parliament*, 67 CHI.-KENT L. REV. 459 (1991)

Lowenfeld, Andreas F., *Investment Agreements and International Law*, 42 COLUM. J. TRANSNAT'L L. 123 (2003)

Luff, Patrick A., *Captured Legislatures and Public-Interested Courts*, 2013 UTAH L. REV. 519 (2012)

Lupu, Yonatan & Eric Voeten, PRECEDENT ON INTERNATIONAL COURTS: A NETWORK ANALYSIS OF CASE CITATIONS BY THE EUROPEAN COURT OF HUMAN RIGHTS (2010)

Lustig, Doreen & Eyal Benvenisti, *The Multinational Corporation as "the Good Despot": The Democratic Costs of Privatization in Global Settings*, 15 THEORETICAL INQUIRIES L. 125 (2014)

Lustig, Doreen, *International Corporate Regulation in the 20th Century: A History of Failure?* (forthcoming, 2017)

Macey, Jonathan R., *Promoting Public-Regarding Legislation through Statutory Interpretation*, 86 COLUM. L. REV. 223 (1986)

MacKenzie, Ruth & Philippe Sands, *International Courts and Tribunals and the Independence of the International Judge*, 44 HARV. INT'L L.J. 271 (2003)

Maclachlan, C., *The Principle of Systemic Integration and Article 31(3)(c) of the Vienna Convention*, 54 INT'L & COMP. L.Q. 279 (2005)

Macneil, Ian R., *Economic Analysis of Contractual Relations: Its Shortfalls and the Need for a "Rich Classificatory Apparatus,"* 75 NW. U. L. REV. 1018 (1981)

The Many Futures of Contract, 47 S. CAL. L. REV. 691 (1974)

THE NEW SOCIAL CONTRACT (1980)

Marks, Axel et al., PRIVATE STANDARDS AND GLOBAL GOVERNANCE: ECONOMIC, LEGAL AND POLITICAL PERSPECTIVES (2012)

Marston Danner, Allison, *When Courts Make Law: How the International Criminal Tribunals Recast the Laws of War*, 59 VAND. L. REV. 1 (2006)

Mashaw, Jerry, *Public Law and Public Choice: Critique and Rapprochement*, in RESEARCH HANDBOOK ON PUBLIC CHOICE AND PUBLIC LAW (Daniel A. Farber & Anne J. O'Connell eds., 2010)

Maupin, Julie A., *Public and Private in International Investment Law: An Integrated Systems Approach*, 54(2) VIRGINIA J. INT'L L. 367 (2014)

Mazower, Mark, GOVERNING THE WORLD: THE HISTORY OF AN IDEA (2012)

Mazumder, Soumyajit, *Can I Stay a BIT Longer? The Effect of Bilateral Investment Treaties on Political Survival*, 10(3) REV. INT'L ORG. 1 (2015)

Mcadam, Jane, COMPLEMENTARY PROTECTION IN INTERNATIONAL REFUGEE LAW (2007)

McNollgast, *Conditions for Judicial Independence*, 15 J. CONTEMP. LEGAL ISSUES 105 (2006)

    Politics and the Courts: A Positive Theory of Judicial Doctrine and the Rule of Law, 68 S. CAL. L. REV. 1631 (1995)

McWhinney, Edward, *Law, Politics and "Regionalism" in the Nomination and Election of World Court Judges*, 13 SYRACUSE J. INT'L L. COM. 1 (1986)

Melo Araujo, Billy A., *Regulating Services through Trade Agreements – A Comparative Analysis of Regulatory Disciplines Included in EU and US Free Trade Agreements*, 6 TRADE L. & DEV. 393 (2014)

Meron, Theodor, HUMAN RIGHTS AND HUMANITARIAN NORMS AS CUSTOMARY LAW (1989)
    Revival of Customary Humanitarian Law, 99 AM. J. INT'L L. 817 (2005)

Meron, Theodor & Betty Elder, *The New Administrative Tribunal of the World Bank*, 14 N.Y.U. J. INT'L L. & POL. 1 (1981)

Mersel, Yigal, *Judicial Review of Counter-Terrorism Measures: The Israeli Model for the Role of the Judiciary during the Terror Era*, 38 N.Y.U. J. INT'L L. & POL. 67 (2005)

Messerlin, Patrick, *The Much Needed EU Pivoting to East Asia*, 10 ASIA PACIFIC J. EU STUD. 9 (2012)

Miller, David, NATIONAL RESPONSIBILITY AND GLOBAL JUSTICE (2008)

Milner, Helen V., INTERESTS, INSTITUTIONS, AND INFORMATION (1997)

Morettini, Simona, *Community Principles Affecting the Exercise of Discretionary Power by National Authorities in the Service Sector*, in GLOBAL AND EUROPEAN CONSTRAINTS UPON NATIONAL RIGHT TO REGULATE: THE SERVICES SECTOR 106 (Stefano Battini & Giulio Vesperini eds., 2008)

Nagel, Thomas, *The Problem of Global Justice*, 33 PHIL. & PUB. AFF. 113 (2005)

Nair, Gupakumar G., Andreya Fernandes, & Karthika Nair, *Landmark Pharma Patent Jurisprudence in India*, 19 J. INTEL. PROP. RTS. 79 (2014)

Naske, Nina & Georg Nolte, Case Report: "Aerial Security Law," in 101 AM. J. INT'L L. 466 (2007)

Neuman, Gerald L., *Buffer Zones against Refugees: Dublin, Schengen, and the German Asylum Amendment*, 33 VA. J. INT'L L. 503 (1993)

    Sense and Nonsense about Customary International Law: A Response to Professors Bradley and Goldsmith, 66 FORDHAM L. REV. 371 (1997)

    The Uses of International Law in Constitutional Interpretation, 98 AM. J. INT'L L. 82 (2004)

Niskanen, William A., *US Trade Policy, in* 3 REGULATION 34 (1988), *reprinted in* WILLIAM A. NISKANEN, POLICY ANALYSIS AND PUBLIC CHOICE 183 (1998)

Nye, Joseph S., Jr., THE PARADOX OF AMERICAN POWER (2002)

Oellers-Frahm, Karin & Andreas Zimmermann, *France's and Germany's Constitutional Changes and Their Impact on Migration Law: Policy and Practice*, 38 GERMAN Y.B. INT'L L. 249 (1995)

Olson, Mancur, THE LOGIC OF COLLECTIVE ACTION (1965)

    THE RISE AND DECLINE OF NATIONS (1982)

Onzivu, William, *International Environmental Law, the Public's Health, and Domestic Environmental Governance in Developing Countries*, 21 AM. U. INT'L L. REV. 597 (2006)

Oudendijk, J.K., STATUS AND EXTENT OF ADJACENT WATERS (1970)

Palan, Ronen, *Tax Havens and the Commercialization of State Sovereignty*, 56 INT'L ORG. 151 (2002)

Paul, Joel R., *The Geopolitical Constitution: Executive Expediency and Executive Agreements*, 86 CAL. L. REV. 671 (1998)

Pauwelyn, Joost, *The Rule of Law without the Rule of Lawyers? Why Investment Arbitrators Are from Mars, Trade Adjudicators from Venus*, 109 AM. J. INT'L L. 761 (2015)

    The UNESCO Convention on Cultural Diversity, and the WTO Diversity in International Law-Making, AM. SOC'Y INT'L L. INSIGHT (Nov. 15, 2005)

Pauwelyn, Joost, Ramses A. Wessel, & Jan Wouters, *When Structures Become Shackles: Stagnation and Dynamics in International Lawmaking*, 25 EUR. J. INT'L L. 733 (2014)

Pauwelyn, Joost, Ramses Wessel, & Jan Wouters eds., INFORMAL INTERNATIONAL LAWMAKING (Oxford University Press, 2012)

Pearce, Fred, GREEN WARRIORS (1991)

Petras, James, *The Western Welfare State: Its Rise and Demise and the Soviet Bloc*, GLOBAL RESEARCH (Jul. 4, 2012)

Phuong, Catherine, *Persecution by Non-state Agents: Comparative Judicial Interpretations of the 1951 Refugee Convention*, 4 EUR. J. MIGRATION & L. 521 (2002)

Picciotto, Sol, *The WTO's Appellate Body: Legal Formalism as a Legitimation of Global Governance*, 18 GOVERNANCE 477 (2005)

Pogge, Thomas, WORLD POVERTY AND HUMAN RIGHTS: COSMOPOLITAN RESPONSIBILITIES AND REFORMS (2nd edn., 2008)

Polakiewicz, J. & V. Jacob-Foltzer, *The European Human Rights Convention in Domestic Law*, 12 HUM. RTS. L.J. 65 (Part I), 125 (Part II) (1991)

Posner, Eric A., *The Decline of the International Court of Justice* 23 (U. Chicago L. & Econ., Olin Working Paper No. 233, 2004)

Posner, Eric & Miguel de Figueiredo, IS THE INTERNATIONAL COURT OF JUSTICE BIASED? (U. Chicago L. & Econ., Olin Working Paper No. 234)

Posner, Richard A., *The Supreme Court 2004 Term - Forward: A Political Court*, 119 HARV. L. REV. 32 (2005)

Prows, Peter, TOUGH LOVE: THE DRAMATIC BIRTH AND LOOMING DEMISE OF UNCLOS PROPERTY LAW (N.Y.U. L. Sch. Pub. L. & Legal Theory Research Paper Series, Paper No. 06–19, 2006)

Putnam, Robert D., *Diplomacy and Domestic Politics: The Logic of Two-Level Games*, 42 INT'L ORG. 427 (1988)

Ramseyer, Mark J., *The Puzzling (In)dependence of Courts: A Comparative Approach*, 23 J. LEGAL STUD. 721 (1994)

Ranganathan, Surabhi, STRATEGICALLY CREATED TREATY CONFLICTS AND THE POLITICS OF INTERNATIONAL LAW (2014)

Ranjan, Shikhar, *Legal Controls on the Transboundary Movements of Hazardous Wastes into India - An Evaluation*, 41 INDIAN J. INT'L L. 44 (2001)

Rasmussen, Hjalte, ON LAW AND POLICY IN THE EUROPEAN COURT OF JUSTICE (1986)

Raustiala, Kal, *The Architecture of International Cooperation: Transgovernmental Networks and the Future of International Law*, 43 VA. J. INT'L L. 1 (2002)

 The Domestic Politics of Global Biodiversity Protection in the United Kingdom and the United States, in THE INTERNATIONALIZATION OF ENVIRONMENTAL PROTECTION 42 (Elizabeth Economy & Miranda A. Schreurs eds., 1997)

Rehnquist, William, ALL THE LAWS BUT ONE: CIVIL LIBERTIES IN WARTIME (1998)

Reinisch, August, INTERNATIONAL ORGANIZATIONS BEFORE NATIONAL COURTS (2000)

 The Immunity of International Organizations and the Jurisdiction of Their Administrative Tribunals, 7 CHINESE J. INT'L L. 285 (2008)

 The International Relations of National Courts: A Discourse on International Law Norms on Jurisdictional and Enforcement Immunity, in THE LAW OF INTERNATIONAL RELATIONS - LIBER AMICORUM HANSPETER NEUHOLD 289 (August Reinisch & Ursula Kriebaum eds., 2007)

Reisman, W. Michael, *An International Farce: The Sad Case of the PLO Mission*, 14 YALE J. INT'L L. 412 (1989)

 THE QUEST FOR WORLD ORDER AND HUMAN DIGNITY IN THE TWENTY-FIRST CENTURY CONSTITUTIVE PROCESS AND INDIVIDUAL COMMITMENT (2013)

Resnik, Judith, *Law's Migration: American Exceptionalism, Silent Dialogues, and Federalism's Multiple Ports of Entry*, 115 YALE L.J. 1564 (2006)

Reynolds, Scott, *European Council Directive 2001/55/EC: Toward a Common European Asylum System*, 8 COLUM. J. EUR. L. 359 (2002)

Riesenfeld, Stefan A. & Frederick M. Abbott, *Foreword: Symposium on Parliamentary Participation in the Making and Operation of Treaties*, 67 CHI.-KENT L. REV. 293 (1991)

The Scope of U.S. Senate Control over the Conclusion and Operation of Treaties, 67 CHI.-KENT L. REV. 571 (1991)

Risse-Kappen, Thomas, *Structures of Governance and Transnational Relations: What We Have Learned?*, in BRINGING TRANSNATIONAL RELATIONS BACK IN 280 (Thomas Risse-Kappen ed., 1995)

Roach, Kent, *Must We Trade Rights for Security? The Choice between Smart, Harsh, or Proportionate Security Strategies in Canada and Britain*, 27 CARDOZO L. REV. 2151 (2006)

Sources and Trends in Post 9/11 Anti-Terrorism Laws (U. Toronto Legal Stud. Res. Paper 899291, Apr. 2006)

Roelofsen, C.G., *Grotius and International Law: An Introduction to Some Themes in the Field of Grotian Studies*, in GROTIUS READER 3 (L.E. van Holk & C.G. Roelofsen eds., 1983)

Grotius and the International Politics of the Seventeenth Century, in HUGO GROTIUS AND INTERNATIONAL RELATIONS 95 (Hedley Bull et al. eds., 1990)

Rokkan, Stein et al., CITIZENS, ELECTIONS, PARTIES: APPROACHES TO THE COMPARATIVE STUDY OF THE PROCESSES OF DEVELOPMENT (1970)

Rosenbaum, Michael D., *Domestic Bureaucracies and the International Trade Regime: The Law and Economics of Administrative Law and Administratively-Imposed Trade Barriers*, 42 TEX. INT'L L.J. 241 (2006)

Sadurska, Romana & C.M. Chinkin, *The Collapse of the International Tin Council: A Case of State Responsibility?*, 30 VA. J. INT'L L. 845 (1990)

Sadurski, Wojciech, *"Solange, chapter 3": Constitutional Courts in Central Europe–Democracy–European Union*, 14 EUR. L.J. 1 (2008)

Salacuse, Jeswald W. & Nicholas P. Sullivan, *Do BITs Really Work?: An Evaluation of Bilateral Investment Treaties and Their Grand Bargain*, 46 HARV. INT'L L.J. 67 (2005)

Salve, Harish, *Justice between Generations: Environment and Social Justice*, in SUPREME BUT NOT INFALLIBLE: ESSAYS IN HONOUR OF THE SUPREME COURT OF INDIA 360 (B.N. Kirpal et al. eds., 2000)

Samson, Klaus, *The Standard-Setting and Supervisory System of the International Labour Organisation*, in AN INTRODUCTION TO THE INTERNATIONAL PROTECTION OF HUMAN RIGHTS 149 (Raija Hanski & Markku Suksi eds., 1997)

Sandler, Todd, GLOBAL CHALLENGES (1997)

Schermers, Henry G., *Netherlands*, in THE EFFECT OF TREATIES IN DOMESTIC LAW (Francis G. Jacobs & Shelley Roberts eds., 1987)

Schermers, Henry G. & Niels M. Blokker, INTERNATIONAL INSTITUTIONAL LAW (3rd rev. edn., 1995)

Schmid-Drüner, Marion, *Germany's New Immigration Law: A Paradigm Shift?* 8
  Eur. J. Migration & L. 191 (2006)
Schmitthoff, Clive M., *International Business Law: A New Law Merchant, in*
  Clive M. Schmitthoff's Select Essays on International Trade Law 20 (Chia-
  Jui Cheng ed., 1988)
Schneiderman, David, *Investing in Democracy? Political Process and International*
  Investment Law, 60 U. Toronto L.J. 909 (2010)
Schuster, Liza, *A Comparative Analysis of the Asylum Policy of Seven European*
  Governments, 13 J. Refugee Stud. 118 (2000)
Schwabach, Aaron, *Comment, The Sandoz Spill: The Failure of International Law to*
  Protect the Rhine from Pollution, 16 Ecology L.Q. 443 (1989)
Schwartz, Alan, *Relational Contracts in the Courts: An Analysis of Incomplete*
  Agreements and Judicial Strategies, 21 J. Legal Stud. 271 (1992)
Seidman, Louis Michael, Our Unsettled Constitution (2001)
Selden, John & Mare Clausum, Of the Dominion, Or, Ownership of the Sea
  (Marchamont Nedham trans., London, William Du-Gard, 1652) (1635)
Shah, Sheetal B., *Illuminating the Possible in the Developing World: Guaranteeing*
  the Human Right to Health in India, 32 Vand. J. Transnat'l L. 435 (1999)
Shany, Yuval, Regulating Jurisdictional Relations between National and
  International Courts (2007)
Sheehan, Reginald S., William Mishler, & Donald R. Songer, *Ideology, Status, and*
  the Differential Success of Parties before the Supreme Court, 86 Am. Pol. Sci.
  Rev. 464 (1992)
Shugart, Matthew S. & John M. Carey, Presidents and Assemblies (1992)
Simma, Bruno, *Universality of International Law from the Perspective of a*
  Practitioner, 20 Eur. J. Int'l L. 265 (2008)
Simmons, Beth, Mobilizing Human Rights: International Law in Domestic Politics
  (2009)
Simpson, A.W. Brian, In the Highest Degree Odious: Detention without Trial in
  Wartime Britain (1994)
Singer, Michael, *Jurisdictional Immunity of International Organizations: Human*
  Rights and Functional Necessity Concerns, 36 Va. J. Int'l L. 53 (1996)
Slaughter, Anne-Marie, A New World Order (2004)
  A Typology of Transjudicial Communication, 29 U. Rich. L. Rev. 99 (1994)
Sripati, Vijayashri, *Toward Fifty Years of Constitutionalism and Fundamental*
  Rights in India: Looking Back to See Ahead (1950–2000), 14 Am. U. Int'l
  L. Rev. 413 (1998)
Steinberg, Richard H., *In the Shadow of Law or Power? Consensus-Based Bargaining*
  and Outcomes in the GATT/WTO, 56 Int'l Org. 339 (2002)
  Judicial Lawmaking at the WTO: Discursive, Constitutional, and Political
  Constraints, 98 Am. J. Int'l L. 247 (2004)

Steinhardt, Ralph, *Human Rights Litigation and the "One Voice" Orthodoxy in Foreign Affairs*, in World Justice? U.S. Courts and International Human Rights 23 (Mark Gibney ed., 1991)

Stephenson, Mark C., *"When the Devil Turns . . . ": The Political Foundations of Independent Judicial Review*, 32 J. Legal Stud. 59 (2003)

Stephenson, Matthew, *Court of Public Opinion: Government Accountability and Judicial Independence*, 20 J. Law, Econ. & Org. 379 (2004)

Stewart, Richard B., *Madison's Nightmare*, 57 U. Chi. L. Rev. 335 (1990)
   Remedying Disregard in Global Regulatory Governance: Accountability, Participation, and Responsiveness, 108 Am. J. Int'l L. 211 (2014)

Stigler, George J., *The Theory of Economic Regulation*, 2 Bell J. Econ. & Mgmt. Sci. 3 (1971)

Stiglitz, Joseph E. & Martin Guzman, *The Rule of Law for Sovereign Debt*, Project Syndicate (Jun. 15, 2015)

Stone Sweet, Alec, *The Politics of Constitutional Review in France and Europe*, 5 Int'l J. Const. L. 69 (2007)

Storey, Hugo, *The Advanced Refugee Law Workshop Experience: An IARLJ Perspective*, 15 Int'l J. Refugee L. 422 (2003)

Stumberg, Robert, *Sovereignty by Subtraction: The Multilateral Agreement on Investment*, 31 Cornell Int'l L.J. 491 (1998)

Sykes, Alan O., *Domestic Regulation, Sovereignty, and Scientific Evidence Requirements: A Pessimistic View*, 3 Chi. J. Int'l L. 353 (2002)

The Federalist No. 10 (James Madison)

The Federalist No. 51 (James Madison)

The Federalist No. 78 (Alexander Hamilton)

Trachtman, Joel P., *The Domain of WTO Dispute Resolution*, 40 Harv. Int'l L.J. 333 (1999)

Tribe, Lawrence H., American Constitutional Law (3rd edn., 2000)

Trimble, Phillip R., *A Revisionist View of Customary International Law*, 33 UCLA L. Rev. 665 (1986)

Tsebelis, George & Geoffrey Garrett, *The Institutional Foundations of Intergovernmentalism and Supranationalism in the European Union*, 55 Int'l Org. 357 (2001)

Tushnet, Mark, Weak Courts, Strong Rights: Judicial Review and Social Welfare Rights in Comparative Constitutional Law (2009)

Tzanakopoulos, Antonios, *Domestic Court Reactions to UN Security Council Sanctions*, in Challenging Acts of International Organizations before National Courts 54 (August Reinisch ed., 2010)

Urbinati, Nadia & Mark E. Warren, *The Concept of Representation in Contemporary Democratic Theory*, 11 Ann. Rev. Pol. Sci. 387 (2008)

Vagts, Detlev F., *The Exclusive Treaty Power Revisited*, 89 Am. J. Int'l L. 40 (1995)

Van den Bossche, Peter, FROM AFTERTHOUGHT TO CENTERPIECE: THE WTO APPELLATE BODY AND ITS RISE TO PROMINENCE IN THE WORLD TRADING SYSTEM (Maastricht Fac. Law, Working Paper No. 2005/1, 2005)

Van der Molen, Gezina H.J., ALBERICO GENTILI AND THE DEVELOPMENT OF INTERNATIONAL LAW (1937)

Van Dunn, Jan M., *Liability in Tort for the Detrimental Use of Fresh Water Resources under Dutch Law in Domestic and International Cases, in* THE SCARCITY OF WATER 196 (Edward H.P. Brans et al. eds., 1997)

Vogel, David, *Private Global Business Regulation*, 11 ANN. REV. POL. SCI. 261 (2008)

Von Bernstorff, Jochen, *The Global "Land-Grab", Sovereignty and Human Rights*, 2(9) EUROPEAN SOC'Y OF INT'L L. REFLECTIONS (2013)

Von Bogdandy, Armin, *Law and Politics in the WTO–Strategies to Cope with a Deficient Relationship, in* 5 MAX PLANCK Y.B. OF U.N. L. 609 (J.A. Frowein & R. Wolfrum eds., 2001)

Von Bogdandy, Armin & Ingo Venzke, IN WHOSE NAME? A PUBLIC LAW THEORY OF INTERNATIONAL ADJUDICATION (2014)

    In Whose Name? An Investigation of International Courts' Public Authority and International Tribunals Democratic Justification, 23 EUR. J. INT'L L. 7 (2012)

Vreeland, Hamilton & Hugo Grotius, THE FATHER OF THE MODERN SCIENCE OF INTERNATIONAL LAW (1917)

Waibel, Michael, SOVEREIGN DEFAULTS BEFORE INTERNATIONAL COURTS AND TRIBUNALS (2011)

Waldron, Jeremy, *Foreign Laws and the Modern Ius Gentium*, 119 HARV. L. REV. 129 (2005)

Walter, C., Vöneky, S., Röben, V., & Schorkopf, F. eds., TERRORISM AS A CHALLENGE FOR NATIONAL AND INTERNATIONAL LAW: SECURITY VERSUS LIBERTY? (Springer, 2004)

Waters, Melissa A., *Creeping Monism: The Judicial Trend toward Interpretive Incorporation of Human Rights Treaties*, 107 COLUM. L. REV. 628 (2007)

Watson, Russel et al., *The Blot on the Rhine*, NEWSWEEK, Nov. 24, 1986

Weiler, Joseph H.H., *The Rule of Lawyers and the Ethos of Diplomats: Reflections on the Internal and External Legitimacy of WTO Dispute Settlement* 11 (Harv. Jean Monnet Working Paper No. 9/00, 2000)

    A Quiet Revolution: The European Court of Justice and Its Interlocutors, 26 COMP. POL. STUD. 510 (1994)

    The Geology of International Law – Governance, Democracy and Legitimacy, 64 ZEITSCHRIFT FÜR AUSLÄNDISCHES ÖFFENTLICHES RECHT UND VÖLKERRECHT, 547 (2004)

    The Transformation of Europe, 100 YALE L.J. 2403 (1991)

Weingast, Barry R., *The Constitutional Dilemma of Economic Liberty*, J. ECON. PERSP. (Summer 2005)

Wertenbaker, William, *The Law of the Sea-I, The New Yorker*, Aug. 1, 1983

    The Law of the Sea-II, The New Yorker, Aug. 8, 1983

Wiener, Antje & Philip Liste, *Lost without Translation? Cross-Referencing and a New Global Community of Courts,* 21 INDIANA J. GLOB. LEG. STUD. 263 (2014)

Young, Ernst A., *Foreign Law and the Denominator Problem,* 119 HARV. L. REV. 148 (2005)

Zalewski, Christopher S. & Paul F. McQuade, *A Stalemate on Biosafety Pact,* THE NAT'L L.J., May 24, 1999

Zappalà, Salvatore, *Do Heads of State in Office Enjoy Immunity from Jurisdiction for International Crimes? The* Ghaddafi *Case before the French Cour de Cassation,* 12 EUR. J. INT'L L. 595 (2002)

ZEITSCHRIFT FÜR AUSLÄNDISCHES ÖFFENTLICHES RECHT UND VÖLKERRECHT 547 (2004)

Zurn, Christopher F., DELIBERATIVE DEMOCRACY AND THE INSTITUTIONS OF JUDICIAL REVIEW (2007)

INDEX

For EU product safety concerns, contact us at Calle de José Abascal, 56–1°,
28003 Madrid, Spain or eugpsr@cambridge.org.

www.ingramcontent.com/pod-product-compliance
Ingram Content Group UK Ltd.
Pitfield, Milton Keynes, MK11 3LW, UK
UKHW020330140625
459647UK00018B/2092